W9-BGN-655

Jesus

IN RED

365
Meditations
on the
Words of Jesus

Ray Comfort

BroadStreet
P U B L I S H I N G

BroadStreet Publishing® Group, LLC
Savage, Minnesota, USA
BroadStreetPublishing.com

Jesus IN RED: *365* Meditations on the Words of Jesus

978-1-4245-5884-1 (faux leather)
978-1-4245-5885-8 (e-book)

Unless indicated otherwise, all Scripture quotations are from the New King James Version. Copyright © 1982 by Thomas Nelson, Inc. Used by permission. All rights reserved. Scripture quotations marked AMP are taken from the Amplified Bible. Scripture quotations marked KJV are taken from the King James Version of the Bible.

Italics in Scripture quotations are added by the author for the sake of emphasis.

Stock or custom editions of BroadStreet Publishing titles may be purchased in bulk for educational, business, ministry, fundraising, or sales promotional use. For information, please email info@broadstreetpublishing.com.

Cover and interior by Garborg Design at GarborgDesign.com

Printed in China

19 20 21 22 23 5 4 3 2 1

Behind the Red Letters

Jesus in Red is a strange name for a devotional, but there's a good reason for this title. The color red alarms us and grabs our attention. God saw fit to give every nation red blood, and when we see human blood, it intuitively sets off alarm bells.

We've taken the divine cue and made our stop signs red. Authorities want to tell approaching drivers that the sign is more than important. They are saying, "Take notice here, or you could be killed!" Red fire engines, red emergency exits, and red fire extinguishers communicate that same vital message.

The words of Jesus in this devotional are in red. They speak of our eternity—how we must be born again, how the day will come when all who are in their graves will hear His voice, and how His words are spirit and life.

But having the words of Jesus in red is nothing new. What is unique about this devotional is that each day's devotion looks *only* at His words. For example, John 4:32 says, "But He said to them, 'I have food to eat of which you do not know.'" Instead of the full verse, I simply state, "I have food to eat of which you do not know."

In this devotional, His words are isolated in red and without quotation marks, so you can focus on what He said without restriction or distraction. While it would be unwise to take the words of any normal human being out of context, Jesus is no normal human being. The focus is only momentary. And as you will see, I encourage reading them in context as part of the devotional exercise.

I am an unashamed dog-lover. When I meet small dogs, I almost always go low. I bend down. This isn't just because smaller dogs feel less threatened when we go down to their level, but because I know that my own dog loves me getting down on the floor and going eye to eye with him. I get up close and personal and whisper key words: "We rode the bike today and saw a cat, didn't we? We also saw a dog, but we didn't see any squirrels." As I say those key words, I can see his eyes processing the information. He is remembering our time together. It is an intimate time, and we both love it.

In Christ, God came low so that we could go eye to eye with Him. The Gospels contain Jesus' key words so we can process them and glean more about God and his ways and how he sees us.

In Scripture, we see why God came low: "But we see Jesus, who was made a little lower than the angels, for the suffering of death crowned with glory and honor, that He, by the grace of God, might taste death for everyone" (Hebrews 2:9).

He came low to suffer and die, and in doing so, He not only opened wide the door of everlasting life, but He also proved His great love for vile sinners like us, so His precious words take on an even greater meaning.

When officers were sent to arrest Him, they came back empty-handed saying, "No man ever spoke like this Man!" (John 7:46). No human being in history ever said anything remotely similar to the things Jesus said. His words are absolutely alarming, and if anything in this short life should get our undivided attention, it's the words of Jesus of Nazareth.

As you read this devotional, I suggest that you not only read Jesus' words deliberately, but that you also carefully consider how you can take these words into your everyday life. Read them straight out of the Bible along with the verses before and after, so you can better understand why He said the powerful words that He did.

Do you try to feed your stomach daily? Of course not. You just do it because it comes naturally every day of your life. If you are having friends over during dinnertime, would you feed them your food? Or would you have them watch you eat it? You would invite them to eat with you! God Himself gives humanity a universal invitation to dine with Him through the gospel:

> "Ho! Everyone who thirsts,
> Come to the waters;
> And you who have no money,
> Come, buy and eat.
> Yes, come, buy wine and milk
> Without money and without price."
> (Isaiah 55:1)

We are commanded to go into all the world and preach the gospel to every creature. As you read this book throughout the year, my prayer is that with each day you grow hungrier for God's Word. And as your hunger and desire to get into His Word increases, I pray you will anticipate spreading the good news to those around you. We can look the other way, stay busy, keep our heads down, and just check our devotionals off the to-do lists. But as you read, study, meditate, and etch the words Jesus spoke onto your heart, I pray you won't be able to hold back from saving the unsaved. Like a firefighter runs into a burning building, it is my prayer that you will want to run after all the lost and save them from the darkness of hell.

May this small devotional be a big step in prioritizing God's Word in your everyday life. And may the isolation of Jesus' words further open the eyes of your understanding and create a desire in your heart to share them like you never have before.

January

A Good Jewish Boy

*Why did you seek Me? Did you not know
that I must be about My Father's business?*
LUKE 2:49

These are the first recorded words of Jesus, and they show us that like any good Jewish son, He wanted to be involved in His Father's business. But this wasn't carpentry. This was the business of building the kingdom of God.

What if every twelve-year-old lived for the Father's will? Many at that age are potential prodigals who are more interested in discovering the pleasures of the world.

We should all be about our Father's business, and His business is to reach the world with the glorious gospel of Jesus Christ.

May you and I be like Jesus and say that today we *must* be about our Father's business and seek and save that which is lost. His will is that sinners believe in His Son.

SOUL SEARCH

What can I do to remind myself to live today for heaven's pleasure rather than for my own?

Father, may I be about your business today.

The Cool, Inviting Door

It is written, "Man shall not live by bread alone,
but by every word of God."
LUKE 4:4

Jesus was tempted by the devil in the area of His appetite. That's consoling because that is a constant battle for most of us. The devil whispers to us from the refrigerator, urging us to open the cool door and indulge. He wants us to forget about self-control and feed our faces without fear.

We must remember that God seeks only our good when He tells us to restrain the beast by pulling in the reigns of appetite. As Jesus did here, we wrestle not against flesh and blood but against principalities and powers and spiritual wickedness in high places. We must never forget that Satan came to kill, steal, and destroy, and overeating to a point of obesity is destructive. And so when we are tempted to overindulge, we need to imitate Jesus and close the door. Tight.

SOUL SEARCH

What measures am I going to take to make sure that I am in control of the reigns of my appetite today?

Father, never let it be said of me that my god is my belly.

A Shocking Thought

Get behind Me, Satan! For it is written,
"You shall worship the LORD your God,
and Him only you shall serve."

LUKE 4:8

It's shocking to think that Jesus was tempted to be a Satan worshiper. But He was tempted, and with that came a promise of power— from the Father of Lies. Just bow the knee. Even though Jesus was tempted, He stayed free from all sin. He resisted temptation.

We are tempted to bow the knee to Satan every time sin calls our name. Satan's will for us is that we indulge in the flesh, whether it is through lust, greed, gossip, bitterness, hatred, self-ishness, gluttony, pride, jealousy, and a host of other sins.

Once again Jesus used the Word of God to resist the Evil One. The Word is our authority, and it says that God is the only one that should be worshiped.

SOUL SEARCH

In what areas am I weak and open to temptation? And what am I doing to be ready to resist the devil?

Father, help me to be like Jesus today and never give my primary adoration to anyone or anything but you.

Tempted to Jump

It has been said, "You shall not tempt the LORD your God."
LUKE 4:12

Satan tempted Jesus the third time by challenging him to jump from the pinnacle of the Temple. He even cited verses from the book of Psalms to sweeten up the temptation.

How tragic it is when someone obeys the whispers of the one who Jesus warned came to kill and destroy. In a moment, the heartbreaking act of suicide can occur when perhaps the problem could have been solved.

Notice the choice of words Jesus used. He said, "The Lord, your God." Our Creator is everyone's God because He made us all. But He is not our Lord until we yield to His Lordship, as unbelieving Thomas did when he fell to his knees and cried, "My Lord and my God" (John 20:28).

Whatever the case, if thoughts of self-destruction plague you, deal with them the way Jesus did. Remember that God created you for a purpose; yield to His Lordship, and then resist the enemy of your soul with the Word of God. God promises that the enemy will flee from you.

SOUL SEARCH

Do I remember a particular time when I yielded all to God? How did that change my life?

Father, help me to always be vigilant in the fight against spiritual wickedness.

How Could We Not Follow?

What do you seek?
JOHN 1:38

When we hear Jesus speak, how can we help but follow Him? No man ever spoke like this Man, and once we understand who He is, we ask with Peter, "Lord, to whom shall we go? You have the words of eternal life" (John 6:68). No one else ever dared say the things that Jesus said. He was the preexistent God manifest in human form. He was the only way to God. He could forgive sins and raise the dead. When once we were enamored by the ugliness of sin, now we are drawn to the beauty of the Savior.

John introduced Jesus in the hearing of two of his disciples: "Behold, the Lamb of God" (John 1:29). He was the promised One, the Messiah who had come to suffer for the sin of the world. We look back and see His suffering, and such demonstrated love makes us love Him and seek Him even more.

SOUL SEARCH

How can I best keep my love for the Savior as my "first love"?

Father, keep the cross ever before me, for that's where I see the demonstration of your love.

A Divine Invitation

Come and see.
JOHN 1:39

Jesus gave them an open invitation—come and see. What an honor to see where Jesus stayed. Little did they know that by coming to the Savior, they would eventually see much more than where He lived. They would see Jesus walking on water, raising the dead, healing the sick, giving sight to the blind, and at the climax, dying in agony on the cross.

But that was just the beginning—the first step in reconciling humanity to God. Because they belonged to Jesus, they would be made pure in heart by His blood and eventually see God.

This is all we need to say to the skeptic: "Come and see. Blind world, come and see."

SOUL SEARCH

How can I come and see Jesus daily? What can I do today to make that a reality?

Father, keep me coming and seeing the Savior.

The Use of the Trumpet

*Behold an Israelite indeed,
in whom is no guile!*
JOHN 1:47 (KJV)

Jesus knew Nathaniel. He said of him that he was an Israelite, but he was more than just an Israelite. Jesus used the trumpet of "behold" to announce him. He was an Israelite indeed, not just in word. As a Jew, Nathaniel was brought up eating, drinking, and sleeping the Law of Moses. He understood the true nature of sin, and like Paul—who was brought up at the feet of Gamaliel (the great teacher of the Law), he knew that sin was "exceedingly sinful" (Romans 7:13).

But Jesus went further by saying that Nathaniel was without guile and without deceit—the ultimate character reference. He didn't twist the Law as the Pharisees did, causing it to lose its power to reveal sin. Their traditions had become their doctrine, thus cancelling out the purpose and effectiveness of the Law. Nathaniel did not fit this pattern. The Law was a schoolmaster to bring him to Christ (Galatians 3:24).

SOUL SEARCH

Is my heart without deceit? Are my motives always pure before God?

Father, search my deceitful heart today, and show me if I'm walking in guile.

Every Individual Hair

Before Philip called you,
when you were under the fig tree, I saw you.
JOHN 1:48

Nathaniel was amazed that Jesus knew so much about him. It is a life-changing revelation when we find out that God knows us as individuals and that His knowledge is intimate. Consider what Psalm 139 says:

> O LORD, You have searched me and known me.
> You know my sitting down and my rising up;
> You understand my thought afar off.
> You comprehend my path and my lying down,
> And are acquainted with all my ways.
> For there is not a word on my tongue,
> But behold, O LORD, You know it altogether.
> (vv. 2–4)

For the unsaved, the thought that God sees their every move is disconcerting. But for those of us who have peace with God through Jesus, such thoughts are comforting and wonderful, in the truest sense of the word.

SOUL SEARCH

Pray the psalmist's words earnestly. How will they affect my day?

Father, thank you for comforting me with your words today. You know me well. Help me to be mindful that you know all of my ways and to live in that reality.

The Greatest Revelation

Because I said to you,
"I saw you under the fig tree,"
do you believe?

JOHN 1:50

The greatest revelation any human being can have is to understand the identity of Jesus of Nazareth. He is the Son of God. He is the Creator manifest in the flesh (1 Timothy 3:16). He is the life source in human form who came to destroy the power of death by dying humanity.

When Peter knew who Jesus was, his response was, "You are the Christ, the Son of the Living God" (Matthew 16:16). Jesus then told him that he was blessed because the Father Himself had revealed this to him. This is the revelation upon which the church is built. Peter is not the rock, as some erroneously believe. Jesus said, "And on this rock I will build My church" (v. 18).

When we repent and trust in Jesus as Savior and Lord, our sins are forgiven, our feet are established upon the rock—and we come out of darkness into light, out of death into life.

SOUL SEARCH

Am I living my life in accordance with the truth of the Scriptures? Will I make all of today's thoughts and decisions in that light?

Father, help me build every aspect of my life on the Rock.

Under the Tree

You will see greater things than these.

JOHN 1:50

Nathaniel believed that Jesus was the Son of God because Jesus saw him under the fig tree. We don't know what he was thinking under that tree. Only God and Nathaniel know that detail. Perhaps he was crying out for the promised Messiah. Perhaps he was praying desperately to know the truth about Jesus' identity. Perhaps he was heavy laden under the weight of his own sins.

Whatever his intimate thoughts, whatever he was doing, he was known by God, and that incredible truth caused Nathaniel to acknowledge the deity of Jesus of Nazareth.

Each of us should have a similar testimony. God knows us personally, He knows us by name, knows our deepest thoughts and fears. Our testimony can be that when we cried out to the Lord, He heard our cry, and He delivered us from all of our fears.

SOUL SEARCH

Do I remember the moment I understood God's omniscience? How did it change my life?

Father, you are awesome beyond words.

The Only Ladder

Most assuredly, I say to you,
hereafter you shall see heaven open,
and the angels of God ascending
and descending upon the Son of Man.

JOHN 1:51

When a weary Jacob laid his head on a stone and slept, he saw angels ascending and descending into the heavens on a ladder (Genesis 28:10–17). Jesus told Nathaniel that he was going to see angels ascending and descending upon Him. In other words, Jesus is the pathway to heaven.

The exclusivity of Christianity is probably as offensive to this world as the doctrine of eternal judgment. The gospel states that there is only one way to the Father (John 14:6). Objectionable though it may be to an unbeliever, it's the truth. "Neither is there salvation in any other: for there is no other name under heaven given among men, whereby we must be saved" (Acts 4:12). We need a Savior who satisfies the demands of eternal justice and the demands of God's Law. Jesus, through His suffering and death, took the punishment for those crimes. He alone has the power on earth to forgive sin.

SOUL SEARCH

Am I trusting alone in the grace of God today? Is there any self-righteousness in me?

Father, Your grace is truly amazing. Help me to meditate on that today.

The Symbol of Life

*Woman, what does your concern have to do with Me?
My hour has not yet come.*

JOHN 2:4

Wine is symbolic of blood, and blood is symbolic of life. Mary was simply concerned that the wine had run out. She wasn't talking about her Son's life being taken from Him as He shed His blood for the sin of the world. Jesus was about His Father's business and seemed to be talking in riddles.

He always had the cross before Him. How could He not? It was the reason for His life here on earth. He was born to die—to enter into the winepress, the horrific baptism of suffering, and He could never take His rest until that was accomplished (Luke 12:50).

He was thinking of another marriage—the marriage supper of the Lamb, where He would come for His spotless virgin bride, the church: "Let us be glad and rejoice and give Him glory, for the marriage of the Lamb has come, and His wife has made herself ready" (Revelation 19:7).

SOUL SEARCH

Do I often meditate on the agony of the cross as I should? What can I do to keep the cross ever before me (Galatians 6:14)?

Father, open the eyes of my understanding and help me to be ever grateful for Calvary.

Do Whatever He Says

Fill the waterpots with water.
JOHN 2:7

There are those who exalt Mary above her womanhood and ignore the necessity of the new birth. Jesus said that every person must be born again to enter heaven, and Mary said to do what Jesus said (John 3:1–5). Those who have never trusted in Jesus alone and been born again should therefore obey both Mary and Jesus and be born again.

While salvation is by grace alone through the medium of faith, the door of salvation hinges upon obedience (Hebrews 5:8). When Jesus told the servants to fill the waterpots, they obeyed and filled them to the brim. An obedient heart is evidence that we have passed from death to life. If we love Him, we will keep His Commandments and fully delight to do God's will. May our loving obedience to God fill our cup of salvation to overflowing, spilling over into the world.

SOUL SEARCH

Do I do everything for God with my whole heart? What can I do to keep from dragging my feet when it comes to evangelism, fellowship, reading the Word, giving, or prayer?

Father, may I always delight to do your will.

The Holy Whip

Take these things away!
Do not make My Father's house
a house of merchandise!
JOHN 2:16

Many within the church don't think of prosperity preachers (who talk of nothing but gaining wealth) as those who make the church into a house of merchandise. But they do. They preach godliness as a means of gain. Speaking of evil men, this verse says, "Useless wranglings of men of corrupt minds and destitute of the truth, who suppose that godliness is a means of gain. From such withdraw yourself" (1 Timothy 6:5).

I'm sure that when Jesus took a whip to the buyers and the sellers who had invaded the Temple, the fear of God entered their hearts. The whip added power to His words. Proponents of prosperity teaching need to understand the fear of God. Perhaps then they would realize that this doctrine, focused on selfishness and greed, would one day be judged for the sin that it is. Repentance is in order. Truth must be preached so that this lost world will flee from the wrath of God and come to the Savior.

SOUL SEARCH

Am I attracted to self-centered messages that have no concern for the unsaved? Do I see Christianity merely as a means of monetary gain?

Father, help me to be free from selfishness, and to keep my eyes on the true riches.

Study and Search

*Destroy this temple,
and in three days I will raise it up.*

JOHN 2:19

The religious leaders used this statement to condemn Jesus at His mock trial (Matthew 26:57–68). They took it to mean that He would destroy their beloved temple. He was, of course, speaking of the temple of His body, and His prophetic words were fulfilled when they crucified Him and three days later He rose again. Later on, He said, "No one takes it from Me, but I lay it down of Myself. I have power to lay it down, and I have power to take it again. This command I have received from My Father" (John 10:18).

The religious leaders weren't seeking truth. They were seeking evidence to condemn Jesus and justify themselves, as do the proud and self-righteous of today. Bible verses are often taken out of context and ridiculed rather than read in context in an effort to seek truth. Unfortunately, men love darkness rather than light. They cower from the light of truth because their deeds are evil, and the light of God's Word exposes them.

SOUL SEARCH

Do I take the time to study God's Word and daily search the Scriptures in an effort to find truth, or do I merely read the Word out of a sense of duty? I resolve today to seek truth.

Father, help me to be as the Bereans who searched the Scriptures daily to see if these things were so (Acts 17:11).

The New Birth

Most assuredly, I say to you,
unless one is born again,
he cannot see the kingdom of God.
JOHN 3:3

Natural men think naturally. They can't help but do so. They are blind to spiritual truth, and until they are born again, they *cannot* see the kingdom of God. Spiritual blindness needs to be treated as gently as we would treat someone who is physically blind. Unbelievers cannot see, and so we must show them patience and seek to give them light.

In the Sermon on the Mount, Jesus explained the true meaning of the Law by expanding the meaning of the Ten Commandments to their fullest extent (Matthew 5–7). When a sinner sees himself in the light of the Law, the need for mercy comes clear and paves the way to an understanding of the cross. Nicodemus was a humble and godly Jew who was instructed in the Law, and so when Jesus presented Himself as the suffering Savior, Nicodemus was able to understand the gospel. The Law was a schoolmaster that brought him to Christ (Galatians 3:24).

SOUL SEARCH

Do I imitate Jesus when it comes to sharing the Good News, or am I influenced by the unbiblical methods of modern evangelism? How can I mirror Jesus in my witnessing?

Father, teach me how to reach the lost.

Natural Birth

Most assuredly, I say to you, unless one is born of water and the Spirit, he cannot enter the kingdom of God. That which is born of the flesh is flesh, and that which is born of the Spirit is spirit. Do not marvel that I said to you, "You must be born again."

JOHN 3:5–7

Some say that Jesus is referring to water baptism when He spoke of being born of water, but it is clear that He is speaking of natural birth. We know this because Jesus immediately qualifies the statement by speaking about being born of the flesh. A babe in the womb is cushioned in water until the moment of birth.

Water baptism is an outward expression of an inward change. Those who believe it is necessary for salvation are forgetting that when the Holy Spirit was given to the Gentiles, the Bible says that they received the gift of salvation before they were baptized in water (Acts 10:44–48). Salvation is by grace alone through faith alone, and nothing we do can merit it. Ephesians 2:8–9 says, "For by grace you have been saved through faith, and that not of yourselves; it is the gift of God, not of works, lest anyone should boast."

SOUL SEARCH

May I never forget the amazing grace shown to me even before I was born, and may my passion be to share that truth with the lost.

Father, it was your grace that taught my heart to fear, and grace my fears relieved. May I always remember that truth.

The Invisible Wind

The wind blows where it wishes, and you hear the sound of it,
but cannot tell where it comes from and where it goes.
So is everyone who is born of the Spirit.

JOHN 3:8

The wind is a mystery. It's not only invisible but it's strange in that it can blow a gale in one place, and a few miles away, it can be calm and peaceful. What makes the gale stop and the tranquility begin?

The Spirit of God is like the wind. He is invisible and blows winds of revival in one place, but not in another.

I was once sharing the gospel with two young men. One listened intently to every word I said. The other sat across the room showing no obvious interest at all. But he was the one who later came to the Savior. While we can never predict or be sure of the salvation of any sinner, we can be sure of one thing. If we faithfully sow the Word of God, God is faithful to watch over it. It never returns void—our labor is never in vain (1 Corinthians 15:58).

SOUL SEARCH

What can I do to keep from becoming discouraged, negative, and fearful when it comes to evangelism?

Father, please help me to be like Jesus and to joyfully obey his command of going into all the world and preaching the gospel to every creature.

The Great Teacher

Are you the teacher of Israel, and do not know these things? Most assuredly, I say to you, We speak what We know and testify what We have seen, and you do not receive Our witness. If I have told you earthly things and you do not believe, how will you believe if I tell you heavenly things?

JOHN 3:10-12

Nicodemus was a great teacher in Israel. He was knowledgeable in the Law of God, and yet Jesus asked why he didn't know about the necessity of the new birth. Surely he was familiar with the great promise of salvation: "I will give you a new heart and put a new spirit within you; I will take the heart of stone out of your flesh and give you a heart of flesh. I will put My Spirit within you and cause you to walk in My statutes, and you will keep My judgments and do them" (Ezekiel 36:26–27).

This was the new covenant—the miracle of the new birth. If we believe what Jesus told us about earthly things, the door to the knowledge of heavenly things will open. Faith is the key that opens the door.

SOUL SEARCH

Am I familiar with all the promises of God? What promise am I standing on today?

Father, I will live forever because you are faithful to your promises. May I never insult you with an "evil heart of unbelief" (Hebrews 3:12).

Carry Some Salt

No one has ascended to heaven but He who came down from heaven, that is, the Son of Man who is in heaven.

JOHN 3:13

To carry a grain of salt means to have a healthy skepticism. It's always good to carry a sack of salt when people say that they've been to heaven and met God. Jesus said that no one has ascended to heaven, and the Word says that no man has seen God at any time (John 1:18). People have seen manifestations of God through burning bushes and angels, but no one can see Him in essence and live (Exodus 33:20).

The reason no one can see God is because He's a fire of burning holiness. If sinful creatures stood in His presence, His wrath would consume them. The Bible describes Him as a consuming fire (Hebrews 12:29). Only the pure in heart will see God, and that's what we are in Christ—perfectly righteous and able to stand in the presence of a holy God.

SOUL SEARCH

Is my image of God biblical? Can I say with the psalmist, "My flesh trembles for fear of You, and I am afraid of Your judgments" (Psalm 119:120)?

Father, please give me a revelation of your holiness, that I might fear you.

The Biting Serpents

*And as Moses lifted up the serpent in the wilderness,
even so must the Son of Man be lifted up.*

JOHN 3:14

The whole tragedy of the human race, with its death and destruction, pain, and suffering began when a serpent beguiled Eve.

Numbers 21:4–9 tells the story of another serpent. The children of Israel bitterly complained against God and Moses for their wilderness woes. In response, God sent poisonous snakes, and many died. When the people cried out to God for deliverance, God told Moses to put a replica of a snake on a pole. When those who had been bitten looked at it, they were healed. The Law of Moses is like those biting snakes because it brings nothing but the curse of death. But when repentant sinners look to Jesus, who became a curse for us on the cross, they are delivered from death. That is why we must take sinners through the moral Law. Its purpose is to bring death to their futile efforts to be saved (Romans 7:10) and make them look to Jesus as their only way to life. The Law is a schoolmaster to bring people to Christ so they may be justified by faith.

SOUL SEARCH

What emotions do I have when I think of Jesus becoming a curse for me? Am I truly horrified, grateful, contrite, and left in awe?

Father, there are no words to express my feelings when it comes to the cross. Help me be an instrument to lovingly share your love with others.

Cereal and Milk

*That whoever believes in Him
should not perish but have eternal life.*
JOHN 3:15

Childlike faith is a stumbling block to the proud. They refuse to trust in Jesus because faith in Him implies weakness in them. It means they have to let go of their intellectual reason and trust in an invisible God, which is offensive to a proud person.

Think about this: We trust people and things daily. When we drive a car, we trust that the wheels are well secured, the gas tank isn't leaking, the steering wheel works, the tires won't blow, the traffic lights are functioning, the driver on the other side of the yellow line will stay on his side, and that he is not texting, drinking, high on drugs, or suicidal. When we sit down and pour milk on our cereal, we trust a chair. We are confident that the food we are about to eat is germ free and bug free!

So many of the things we trust can let us down. But faith in Jesus will never disappoint us.

SOUL SEARCH

Do I trust the Lord in every area of my life? What can I do to remind myself to first look to Him with every decision to get His smile or frown?

Father, remind me to seek you in everything, even in the small things.

Diagnosis First

*For God so loved the world
that He gave His only begotten Son,
that whoever believes in Him
should not perish but have everlasting life.*

JOHN 3:16

Thanks to zealous Christians at sporting events, John 3:16 has become the most famous Bible verse. It is held up on signs as the essence of the gospel message.

Years ago a well-known preacher, Paris Reidhead, stated, "Don't preach John 3:16 because America has become 'gospel-hardened.'" This was because for many years, modern evangelism had presented an unbiblical message of the gospel. People had failed to follow the pattern in Scripture given by Jesus, Paul, and the apostles, which is to always preach Moses before we preach Jesus. The Law must come before grace. There must be diagnosis of the disease before the cure is given. The Law gives the diagnosis of sin, and the gospel is the cure. Without the Law of Moses to bring the knowledge of sin, John 3:16 is foolishness to the world (1 Corinthians 1:18). It is to give a cure to a man who doesn't know he has a disease.

SOUL SEARCH

Have I presented the cure of the gospel without explaining the disease of sin? Why is this an attractive alternative?

Father, please give me the wisdom to present the gospel biblically.

Somebody Loves Me

For God did not send His Son into the world to condemn the world, but that the world through Him might be saved.

JOHN 3:17

Ask people how they know God loves them and they will probably point to prosperity. When something goes right, they say things like, "Somebody up there loves me." Their thought is that every blessing comes because they merit divine favor. Yet, if God's love is evidenced by prosperity, billionaires are far more loved by God than the desperately poor.

The Christian looks to the cross as evidence of God's love. "This is love: not that we loved God, but that he loved us and sent his Son as an atoning sacrifice for our sins" (1 John 4:10 NIV). God's love is never earned by what God sees in us. It is extended to guilty sinners because He is the essence of love. I don't make the sun shine on me; its rays have nothing to do with what I do. The sun shines on me because that's what the sun does. So it is with the love of God, because "God is love" (v. 8).

SOUL SEARCH

Have I ever deceived myself into believing that my virtues commend me to God or that my good works are pleasing to Him without faith in the Savior? Can I think of any areas in my life where my good works have replaced my faith?

Father, thank you for the mercy of the cross.

Condemned Already

He who believes in Him is not condemned; but he who does not believe is condemned already, because he has not believed in the name of the only begotten Son of God.

JOHN 3:18

Every now and then, someone will say that we shouldn't take a sinner through the Ten Commandments because it makes them feel condemned—Jesus didn't come to condemn, but to forgive.

However, the reason sinners need forgiveness is because they are "condemned already." The Bible says all liars will have their part in the lake of fire (Revelation 21:8) and that no adulterer, fornicator, or thief will inherit God's kingdom (1 Corinthians 6:9–10). God's Word says that if we have looked with lust, we've already committed adultery (Matthew 5:27–28). Sinners are children of wrath, and every time they sin, they are storing up wrath that will be revealed on the day of judgment. Once they understand their danger, they will flee to the Savior, believe in Him, and find mercy.

SOUL SEARCH

Would I rather tell someone that God loves them or talk to them about sin? Why?

Father, help me to think more about sinners' fates than my own fear of rejection.

The Real Reason

And this is the condemnation, that the light has come into the world, and men loved darkness rather than light, because their deeds were evil. For everyone practicing evil hates the light and does not come to the light, lest his deeds should be exposed.

JOHN 3:19–20

Here is the reason sinners stay away from the gospel: They don't want to find God for the same reason a criminal doesn't want to bump into a police officer. It's not that they can't find Him. The prodigal son went to a far country to spend his money on prostitutes (Luke 15:30). The obvious reason he went to a far country was to get away from his father—because he knew that his father would frown upon what he wanted to do.

Atheism is a far country. It's as far away from God as a sinner thinks he can get. Yet nothing has changed since the beginning of creation when Adam sinned against God and hid from his Creator. That's what guilty sinners do. They love the darkness and stay away from the light because the light exposes their evil deeds.

May God's Law expose them so that they will find mercy before the day of judgment.

SOUL SEARCH

Do I ever feel guilt when I let the light of God's Word shine? If so, why?

Father, please search me right now. Shine the light on me and expose anything that I shouldn't or should be doing.

The Freeway Chase

But he who does the truth comes to the light, that his deeds may be clearly seen, that they have been done in God.
JOHN 3:21

If you have ever seen a freeway chase, you will know that the police don't give up easily. The law hounds guilty criminals. And God's Law will never give up until guilty sinners are brought to justice. What a fearful thing it would be to be arrested by death and stand guilty before the judgment bar of a holy God who knows every secret sin of the heart.

In a freeway chase it's hard to understand why criminals keep running. They are not going to get away since a helicopter is following them. Logic says they should stop running, surrender, and fling themselves upon the mercy of the judge. It is also a mystery as to why sinners keep running from God. They are not going to get away. God will judge every work as well as every secret thing whether it is good or evil.

Our plea to sinners is to stop running, surrender all, and fling themselves upon the mercy of the Judge. The Bible says that God is rich in mercy to all that call upon Him (Psalm 86:5).

SOUL SEARCH

Do I have the love and courage to pray that today God will orchestrate an encounter with someone who needs to hear the gospel?

Father, please give me a divine encounter today and the courage to share the truth.

Being Wise

Give Me a drink.
JOHN 4:7

How amazing that God manifest in the flesh, the Creator of all things, would need to ask a woman to get Him a drink. However, His need to speak to her was more important than His need for water at that moment.

This is an example of the divine way to share the gospel. The Bible says that the natural man does not receive the things of the Spirit of God; they are foolishness to him (1 Corinthians 2:14). Therefore, the way to communicate spiritual things with a stranger is to first speak to him or her in the natural realm. It may be as simple as a morning greeting or "How are you doing?" A point of contact has been made. Then I usually give the person one of our Ten Commandment coins and say, "It's a coin with the Ten Commandments on it. Do you think there's an afterlife?" When people respond to that question, the door to a spiritual conversation opens. Conversation has just shifted from the natural to the spiritual in seconds because of the Master's example.

SOUL SEARCH

Do I practice what I preach? Do I care enough for the lost to make myself ready for a conversation as the Bible commands? Think of several conversation openers and questions to pose.

Father, your Word says that if I win souls, I'm wise. Give me the wisdom and the courage I need to engage people in conversation.

Thirsting Horses

*If you knew the gift of God, and who it is who says to you,
"Give Me a drink," you would have asked Him,
and He would have given you living water.*

JOHN 4:10

If this dying world knew the gift God had for them, they would ask for it. The problem is that the Bible says there is none who seek after God (Romans 3:11). So how do we help the ungodly become interested in the gospel?

It's been said that although you can lead a horse to water, you can't make him drink—but you can salt his oats. The way to salt the oats of the lost is to do something that will make them thirsty for righteousness. We can do this with the moral Law. Like Jesus did in the Sermon on the Mount, we can apply the Law of God to the heart. People need to understand that without righteousness on the day of judgment, the sinner will be damned forever. This is a terrifying thought. The Law strips the ungodly of false hope. It shows him that his good works will not suffice on that Day. Once he sees his sins, he begins to question, "What should I do to be made right?" He begins to thirst for righteousness.

SOUL SEARCH

What made you thirst for righteousness? Was it because you saw your sin as being exceedingly sinful? Incorporate that element of your salvation experience into your testimony.

*Father, give me the light of understanding as to my moral state
without the Savior's blood.*

Lasting Happiness

Whoever drinks of this water will thirst again, but whoever drinks of the water that I shall give him will never thirst. But the water that I shall give him will become in him a fountain of water springing up into everlasting life.

JOHN 4:13–14

Contemporary evangelism often interprets the satisfaction that we have in Christ as "true and lasting happiness." But the water that quenches a sinner's thirst is really satisfying a thirst for righteousness. Without it, we will be damned.

When we come to the foot of the cross, we should be crying, "God be merciful to me, a sinner" (Luke 18:13). We need to be cleansed of our sins. It is at the cross we are justified—made right in the sight of a holy God.

Without righteousness we will be at odds with the Law and justly perish on the day of wrath. Happiness on that day will be irrelevant. Many evil people are happy in their sins, enjoying the pleasures of sin for a season. But they are not righteous in Christ. The wrath of the moral Law abides upon us until we come to Jesus Christ where its demands are satisfied. Our case is dismissed and the death sentence removed.

SOUL SEARCH

Today I determine to walk with the attitude, "But for the grace of God, there go I," and let empathy guide me to a lost soul.

Father, make this day count for eternity.

He Sees All

*Go, call your husband, and come here. You have well said,
"I have no husband," for you have had five husbands,
and the one whom you now have is not your husband;
in that you spoke truly.*

JOHN 4:16–18

One of the greatest revelations any of us can ever have is that God has numbered every hair on our sinful heads and every thought in our human hearts. As Christians this is a wonderful consolation. But for the ungodly, the omniscience of God should make them tremble because every time they sin, they are storing up His wrath (Romans 2:4–6). The psalmist describes divine omniscience:

> O LORD, You have searched me and known me.
> You know my sitting down and my rising up;
> You understand my thought afar off.
> You comprehend my path and my lying down,
> And are acquainted with all my ways.
> For there is not a word on my tongue,
> But behold, O LORD, You know it altogether.
> (Psalm 139:1–4)

SOUL SEARCH

Today I will live every moment aware of your presence.

Father, set a guard on my tongue. Let the virtue of discretion guide me.

February

The Power of Believing

Woman, believe Me, the hour is coming when you will neither on this mountain, nor in Jerusalem, worship the Father. You worship what you do not know; we know what we worship, for salvation is of the Jews. But the hour is coming, and now is, when the true worshipers will worship the Father in spirit and truth; for the Father is seeking such to worship Him.

JOHN 4:21-23

When the apostle Paul stood up and preached on Mars Hill, he told his hearers that they were worshiping a Creator they did not know. They lacked understanding. Then he said, "The One whom you worship without knowing, Him I proclaim to you" (Acts 17:23).

While we often refer to the gospel as a message, we are in reality preaching a person. We are preaching Christ and Him crucified. We are magnifying the Savior so that people will flee to Him for mercy, and when they do, their status changes—from His enemy to His friend.

Jesus asked the woman to believe Him. While skeptics often look down on believers with disdain, we know that believing something has life-changing ramifications. If you believed that you were drinking poison, you would stop. Beliefs govern our actions, and believing the gospel changes our eternal destiny.

SOUL SEARCH

Today I am going to be with people who ignorantly believe in God. They lack knowledge. Do I have courage to share the truth in love like Paul did?

Father, today let me see sinners through your eyes.

The Life Source

*God is Spirit, and those who worship Him
must worship in spirit and truth.*

JOHN 4:24

God is the source of all life. He is Spirit. He is immortal, and He is invisible. When we receive Jesus Christ through the power of the Holy Spirit, we don't receive a religion. We receive the invisible source of life. We are sealed with the life of the Holy Spirit, and that life of God in us conquers death as light conquers darkness.

There are no words that can describe the treasure that we have in earthen vessels. There is nothing in the universe more precious than life, and that's what we have in the Savior. When He said that He was the way, the truth, and the life, He meant it literally (John 14:6). The apostle John said that they had found the very source of life and actually touched and handled it (1 John 1:1). May we have a revelation of the precious nature of what we have in Jesus and never fail to be zealous to share it with a dying world.

SOUL SEARCH

Today I will meditate on what I have in Christ.

Father, nothing on this earth compares to you. May I ever worship you in spirit and in truth.

Greatest Treasure

I who speak to you am He.
JOHN 4:26

Millions of God's people had been born, lived, and died without seeing the promised Messiah. The Old Testament pointed toward the day when God would be manifest in the flesh. The angels heralded His coming with song to Bethlehem. The greatest event ever known to humanity was when our glorious Creator invaded this earth to defeat our greatest enemy.

Jesus came to destroy the power of death for you and me. If only the world knew who He was and what He did for dying sinners, they would embrace Him gladly. They would fall on their knees and thank Him for the cross and for conquering death. Oh, how we lack the right words to describe this good news.

The apostle Paul called the gospel the "unspeakable gift" (2 Corinthians 9:15 KJV). Our problem is that the laborers are few. You are needed today to tell the world this unspeakably good news—to lift up your voice like a trumpet—to shout from the housetops the glorious gospel of everlasting life.

SOUL SEARCH

May I get victory today over paralyzing fear, and may my anxious fears subside. Take a few moments to declare your victory over anxiety in Jesus' name!

Father, though I'm weak, you are mighty; hold me with your powerful hand.

Divine Priority

I have food to eat of which you do not know.
JOHN 4:32

Jesus cared about the unsaved. Isn't that the understatement of all time? He so loved them that He suffered unspeakable agony on the cross so that they could have everlasting life. It was that same love that caused Him to speak to the woman at the well. Concern for the lost should be as natural to a Christian as breathing. We have the love of Christ within us (2 Corinthians 5:14).

We know it is not God's will that any should perish, and so every human being needs to hear the gospel. If you were in a lifeboat and all around you people were drowning, would you involve yourself in polishing the wood on the boat? Of course not! You would be consumed by doing all you could to save lives.

Human beings are dying before our eyes, and we must be about the business of evangelism. Nothing should ever distract us from this sobering task.

SOUL SEARCH

Am I busy polishing wood instead of saving lives? Do an inventory of your activities. How can you incorporate the gospel into the things you are doing?

Father, may your priority always be my priority.

Our Food

My food is to do the will of Him who sent Me, and to finish His work. Do you not say, "There are still four months and then comes the harvest"? Behold, I say to you, lift up your eyes and look at the fields, for they are already white for harvest!

JOHN 4:34–35

Is there something that you love to do so much that you forget to eat? I get close to that when I'm editing a movie. The process is so creative and intellectually absorbing that time seems to fly at lightning speed.

I also know that when I'm really hungry, I can think of nothing but food. As Christians we should not be able to think of anything else but feeding on the Word of God with an all-consuming appetite to do His will.

Jesus told His disciples that even though it wasn't harvest time, they were to lift up their eyes and look at the fields—they were ready to be harvested.

When people complain that few are coming to Christ, remember that salvation is of the Lord. He is the One who saves sinners, and He said that the harvest is ready.

SOUL SEARCH

Do I lift up my eyes and look at the fields and believe that they are ripe for harvest? I determine to do that today.

Father, I will keep my eyes on you this day and rest in your wonderful promises.

God Grew the Tree

And he who reaps receives wages, and gathers fruit for eternal life, that both he who sows and he who reaps may rejoice together. For in this the saying is true: "One sows and another reaps." I sent you to reap that for which you have not labored; others have labored, and you have entered into their labors.

JOHN 4:36–38

When we pray with someone to come to faith, we must realize that we are co-laborers with both God and others who have planted before us. When we pick a fruit, we know that God grew the tree, even though somebody else planted and watered it.

Science often speaks of standing on the shoulders of those who have gone before us. In other words, no single person can take all the credit for scientific discoveries because others have labored before them and paved the way. And so we must always remember that there are John the Baptists who have endured the heat of the desert sun as they have planted, watered, and tended the seed of the gospel. At times we have the privilege of harvesting the fruit and seeing the fulfillment of their labor.

SOUL SEARCH

Am I going to plant the precious seed of the gospel today, or am I secretly avoiding such thoughts because of my fears and lack of faith in God?

Father, separate me from my fears by deepening your love in my heart.

The Inference of Faith

Unless you people see signs and wonders,
you will by no means believe.

JOHN 4:48

The world can easily identify with doubtful Thomas. He wanted to see because he believed that seeing would enable him to believe. However, to believe and not see is to exercise trust, and when we completely trust someone, we pay them a great compliment. If I believe in you and what you say, it means that I consider you worthy of my trust. Jesus said that if we believe in Him we are blessed because we honor Him when we consider Him worthy of our trust.

Belief is a matter of the human will. It's a choice. Jesus said, "You will by no means believe." The psalmist said, "The wicked in his proud countenance does not seek God; God is in none of his thoughts" (Psalm 10:4). In their pride, many refuse to trust in Jesus—to their own peril—because salvation comes to us by grace through childlike faith (Ephesians 2:8–9).

SOUL SEARCH

Are there times when I lose faith in God? Do I ever consider how insulting that is? Is there any human being in whom I have lost faith? Why?

Father, help me to trust you in the good times and in the seemingly bad.

Unprecedented Savior

Go your way; your son lives.

JOHN 4:50

Jesus had power over death. His creative words brought about life in the genesis of creation, and here, when He told death to leave, it bowed the knee and left. Jesus said, "Your son lives," and it was so.

How foolish it is to think that He was merely a great teacher or spiritual leader. He spoke to a storm, and it obeyed Him. At His command, atoms that He created held hands and upheld His body—He walked on water. This was a feat that no other feet have done in history (except for Peter's for a short time).

Jesus spoke to a tree, and it withered at His words. He called Lazarus from the grave, and the Grim Reaper lowered his sickle and released him.

But the greatest of miracles was the love He displayed at the cross. What could possibly keep us from falling at His beautiful feet, worshiping, loving, and adoring Him? Why would we hesitate to obey His command to go into all the world and preach His glorious gospel to every creature?

SOUL SEARCH

Is Jesus the focal point of my affections? Can I spend some time today in worship and prayer to help me focus on glorifying God?

Father, I need you this day. You are my life.

Pretty Ugly

The Spirit of the Lord is upon Me, because He has anointed me to preach the gospel to the poor . . .
LUKE 4:18

When Jesus said He came for the poor, He didn't mean only the monetarily or physically poor. He also came for the rich, like Zacchaeus (Luke 19:1–10).

Most importantly, Jesus came for the poor in spirit—those who realize that they are morally destitute before a holy God—as Zacchaeus did.

God uses the Law of Moses as the agent to convince us of our poverty. The Law reveals God's holiness, His perfect righteousness, and His supreme standard of morality. The Ten Commandments strip away any false piety. They act as a perfectly clean mirror that reflects our true spiritual state. To a sensitive conscience, the image can be pretty ugly. We are by nature liars, thieves, blasphemers, and adulterers.

The Commandments give us a standard by which we can judge ourselves and see our desperate need of His mercy. In doing so, we are blessed because as we acknowledge our poverty, we become rich.

SOUL SEARCH

Did I realize my absolute spiritual poverty before I came to the cross? Set some time aside to study the Ten Commandments (see Matthew 5).

Father, I see that without a Savior, I would be hopelessly lost in sin. Thank you for rescuing me from my spiritual poverty.

The Virtue of Contrition

He has sent Me to heal the brokenhearted.

LUKE 4:18

This verse isn't necessarily referring to being brokenhearted over life's tragic circumstances. Many a mother is brokenhearted over the loss of a child. There's nothing "blessed" about such a tragedy. Jesus is rather speaking of the blessing of being brokenhearted over our sinful condition, that is, of having a sorrow for our sins that will lead us to repentance (2 Corinthians 7:10).

When addressing sinners, James says, "Let your laughter be turned to mourning and your joy to gloom" (James 4:9). This is a godly sorrow that works repentance—and repentance leads us to the everlasting life, which is only in the person of Jesus Christ. That's the healing for those who are brokenhearted over sin.

It is the moral Law that shows us the serious nature of our sin; it helps us to understand the cost of our redemption. And it is seeing the cross in its terrible reality that breaks our hearts and brings tears to our once dry eyes.

SOUL SEARCH

Have I ever shed a tear at the cost of the cross? If not, why?

Father, help me to be horrified at the expense of our redemption and broken by your love.

Dark Prison

The Spirit of the Lord is upon me . . .
to proclaim liberty to the captives.

LUKE 4:18

When Jesus spoke of liberty to the captives, He wasn't speaking about criminals who were in prison and would be released when they heard the gospel. Rather, He was speaking of those who are held captive by Satan to do his will. The Bible says, "And a servant of the Lord must not quarrel but be gentle to all, able to teach, patient, in humility correcting those who are in opposition, if God perhaps will grant them repentance, so that they may know the truth, and that they may come to their senses and escape the snare of the devil, having been taken captive by him to do his will" (2 Timothy 2:24–26).

Like Peter when he was in jail, we are also prisoners—held captive by the chains of sin and death. But when Light shone in Peter's dark prison, his chains fell off and the doors were opened (Acts 12:5–10).

Those who escape from the prison of sin are the ones who are blessed through the gospel. When we come to the Savior, our chains fall off. We are set free from the power of sin and death.

SOUL SEARCH

Do I care about bringing that same deliverance to this world bound for hell? Am I planning to share the gospel today? If not, why not?

Father, please use me to reach the lost. Release me from the chains of fear and pride.

Another Blindness

And recovery of sight to the blind,
to set at liberty those that are oppressed.

LUKE 4:18

When Jesus spoke of the blind receiving their sight, He wasn't just speaking of the physically blind receiving their physical sight when they heard the gospel. Many a blind man had his eyes opened by the Savior. But there is another kind of blindness that afflicts all the offspring of Adam.

This verse is speaking of those who are spiritually blind—whose understanding is darkened by the god of this world because of their unbelief.

The moment we come to Christ, the eyes of our understanding are opened and we suddenly see into the spiritual realm. The gospel is no longer foolishness to us, but the power of God unto salvation. We pass from the kingdom of darkness into the glorious light, and with ex-slave trader John Newton, we can say, "I once was blind, but now I see." When Jesus opens our spiritually blind eyes, nothing looks the same.

SOUL SEARCH

Have I truly been born again? Have the eyes of my understanding been enlightened?

Father, may I see your influence in everything I look at today.

His Gentle Hand

The Spirit of the Lord is upon me . . .
to set at liberty those who are oppressed.
LUKE 4:18

When Jesus spoke of setting at liberty those who are bruised, He was speaking of God's gentle handling of those bruised by this world. In speaking prophetically of His message, the following verse says, "A bruised reed he will not break" (Isaiah 42:3 NIV). In other words, He didn't come with a message of condemnation and wrath, rather with a gentle message of love and forgiveness.

We see this so clearly illustrated with the woman caught in the act of adultery in John 8:1–11. She was waiting to be stoned. The Law, with its justifiable wrath, called for her death, but Jesus responded with tender mercy. Instead of taking up stones, He gently took her by the hand and lifted her up. She came to Him laboring and heavy laden under the weight of the Law, and in Him she found rest: "The LORD upholds all who fall, and raises up all who are bowed down" (Psalm 145:14).

The condemned woman was able to be blessed because Jesus was on His way to the cross to redeem condemned sinners from the curse of the Law.

SOUL SEARCH

Do I appreciate the tenderness of the gospel? In what ways can I show Jesus' mercy to others today?

Father, thank you for your gentleness and everlasting mercy.

Resting from Work

To preach the acceptable year of the Lord.
LUKE 4:19 (KJV)

Isaiah 61:2 says that the purpose of the coming Messiah's ministry would be, "To proclaim the acceptable year of the LORD, and the day of vengeance of our God; to comfort all that mourn."

The great religions of the world are vainly striving to find acceptance with God. They are working for their salvation. However, we have good news for them. All the work has already been done. The cross is a finished work.

Ephesians 1:6 says, "to the praise of the glory of His grace, by which He made us accepted in the Beloved." Jesus purchased peace with God through His suffering and death on the cross.

We are now acceptable to the Father because Jesus took upon Himself the vengeance of God for our sins. The Spirit of the Lord was upon Him because God had anointed Him to preach the gospel, and the acceptance of God means that we can live forever!

May the Spirit of the same Lord be upon us to preach the same wonderful gospel—to take this wonderful good news to the lost and dying.

SOUL SEARCH

Do I tremble at the holiness of God and the contrasting sinfulness of mankind? Am I motivated by that revelation?

Father, may I forever say with the apostle Paul, "Thanks be to God for the unspeakable gift!"

The Light of the Word

Today this Scripture fulfilled in your hearing.

LUKE 4:21

If there ever was a presumptuous remark, this was it. Jesus applied the Holy Scriptures to Himself! He was only a simple man whose father was known by most at the synagogue in Nazareth, probably as a common carpenter. And yet, Jesus claimed to be the promised One, the Messiah—the blessed One of God.

However, if people had believed the sacred writings, they would have known that Jesus was indeed fulfilling prophecy by His virgin birth and by His impeccably sinless life. Instead, they were repelled by His gracious words and tried to kill Him for what they perceived to be blasphemy. He came to His own, and His own received Him not (John 1:11–13 KJV). What a terrible tragedy. How could they have been so blind?

It is imperative that we study and believe the Word as well as know the times in which we live. The Bible is a lamp to our feet and a light to our path (Psalm 119:105). Without that light, we will stumble as did the religious leaders.

SOUL SEARCH

Do I strive to be like Apollos—mighty in knowledge of the Scriptures (Acts 18:24)? How can I make room in my daily schedule to allow time for Bible study?

Father, help me to be disciplined to daily soak my soul in your Word.

The Special Coat

You will surely say this proverb to me, "Physician, heal yourself! Whatever we have heard done in Capernaum, do also here in your country" . . . Assuredly, I say to you, no prophet is accepted in his own country.

LUKE 4:23-24

Our immediate families are probably our biggest critics. They know us up close and personal and have seen our flaws and weaknesses. Jesus, however, was without sin up close and personal, so any criticism of Him was completely unfounded. He was morally perfect in thought, word, and in deed. Everything He did pleased the Father.

In Genesis 37, we see how those who knew Joseph best hated him because of their father's favoritism. His brothers were green with envy over his coat of many colors.

Those who know Jesus as revealed in the Word of God know that the Father loved the Son, clothed Him in a coat of perfect righteousness, and one day would exalt Him to the right hand of God.

SOUL SEARCH

Am I ever guilty of jealousy? How do I react when others are praised?

Father, help me always to rejoice in the exultation of others.

The Weather Department

But I tell you truly, many widows were in Israel in the days of Elijah, when the heaven was shut up three years and six months, and there was a great famine throughout all the land.

Luke 4:25

Nature is the window through which we see the handiwork of God. Every drop of rain has been formed by His hand. Even when there is an overabundance, we ought to be thankful for it because water brings life to all living things on the earth.

In an increasingly godless world, the great biblical truth that God is the giver and withholder of rain is ignored. Science attempts to explain the fluctuation in weather patterns as somehow determined by man's actions. But it is God alone who causes the rain to fall on the just and the unjust.

When there is a season of drought and the heavens withhold the rain, it happens only with God's permission. Not one drop ever falls without His consent. Such thoughts are foreign to the ungodly, but should never be far from our minds.

SOUL SEARCH

Am I cognizant of God's presence in every aspect of life? At day's end, take a moment to thank God for the beauty and variety of nature.

Father, may I always see your genius and the graciousness of your hand in all of nature.

Remembering the Widow

But to none of them was Elijah sent except to Zarephath, in the region of Sidon, to a woman who was a widow.

LUKE 4:26

God loves the afflicted and distressed. He sent the prophet Elijah all the way over to Sidon to speak with a single widow. Jesus exemplified the same care for the downtrodden and neglected. He was accused of being the friend of sinners and outcasts, of tax collectors and lepers. The poor heard him gladly. He touched the unclean lepers and forgave those who were caught in acts of sin.

Here the Bible makes special mention of a widow, and so do other passages. Our hearts must go out to them in their grief; they need our care.

May God help us to empathize with the widow in her heartache as she attempts to move forward after the loss of her beloved husband. And may we always be ready to comfort and assist them in their affliction.

SOUL SEARCH

Am I guilty of neglecting widows? Reach out to someone you know who is a widow. Make a phone call; drop a card in the mail to let her know she is not forgotten.

Father, help me to be an empathetic believer, ready to help those in pain.

Senseless Washing

*And many lepers were in Israel
in the time of Elisha the prophet,
and none of them was cleansed
except Naaman the Syrian.*

LUKE 4:27

We see the gospel so clearly illustrated through the wonderful story of Naaman. He was successful and proud but was afflicted with the horrific disease of leprosy. His only hope of cleansing would come through faith, humility, and obedience. He was told to wash in a river and he would be cleansed of his disease. That made no sense. He wasn't dirty; he had incurable leprosy! But when he humbled himself and bathed in the Jordan River, he was completely cleansed of his disease (2 Kings 5:1–14).

Before we were cleansed by the river of mercy, we were helpless, afflicted by the terminal disease of sin. When we humbled ourselves and obeyed the gospel, we were saved by grace through faith. God washed away the grime and granted us everlasting life.

SOUL SEARCH

Do I still secretly long for the old pleasures of sin? If so, identify those areas, confess and forsake them before the Lord. Do not let the devil have an opportunity.

Father, help me to fear you, and in doing so, to stay away from the leprous filth of sin.

The New Kingdom

Be quiet, and come out of him!
LUKE 4:35

Being a Christian means submitting to God and resisting the devil until he flees from us (James 4:7). We tell the enemy to hold his peace. We left his kingdom of darkness when we were translated into the kingdom of light, and we are no longer children of wrath but children of God. We neither give place to the devil nor give ear to his whispering.

Sin is no longer our master. We once ran to do the enemy's will even though our wages were paid by death (Romans 6:23).

Our old master came to kill, steal, and destroy, and we see him doing that daily in this sin-serving world—through drug addiction, suicide, alcoholism, murder, and a thousand and one other atrocities in this life.

We resist the source of evil, stand firm in the faith, and say with Jesus, "Get behind Me, Satan" (Matthew 16:23).

SOUL SEARCH

Do I ever listen to the discouraging lies of the enemy? Ask God for the ability to discern between God's voice, the enemy's lies, and your own self-talk.

Father, may I only have an ear for your voice.

The Purpose of the Incarnation

*I must preach the kingdom of God to the other cities also,
because for this purpose I have been sent.*

LUKE 4:43

Jesus had a clear agenda from the Father. "For this purpose the
Son of God was manifest, that He might destroy the works of the
devil" (1 John 3:8). God was manifested in the flesh to destroy
the power of death so that all who trust alone in Him could say,
"O Death, where is your sting?" (1 Corinthians 15:55).

We have the same agenda. We must preach the gospel to
those who are helpless and hopeless as they sit in the shadow of
death.

May God help us to number our days so that we might
fulfill the mission God has put before us. We must be about the
business of seeking and saving the lost. This is urgent because the
time will come when the door of grace will be closed, and those
who continue to serve sin will be damned in a terrible place
called hell.

Such a thought should shake us to the depths of our souls. We
must preach the kingdom of God.

SOUL SEARCH

Do I have the same agenda as the Savior? Do my coworkers
even know that I'm a Christian? What are some ways I can let my
light shine today?

*Father, help me to die to myself and live to reach sinners for the
kingdom.*

No Other Name

Unless you people see signs and wonders,
you will by no means believe.

JOHN 4:48

Prosperity tends to foster complacency. However, when trials come—when we have serious financial needs or when the cold hand of death approaches a loved one—we tend to pray in desperation. The safest place to be is on our knees during difficulties, but that is also the safest place to be when all is well.

During times of trial, we tend to reorder life's priorities. Nothing else mattered to the desperate nobleman whose son was near death. He rushed to see Jesus and implored Him to heal his son before it was too late.

We go to a dentist when we have toothache, a plumber when there's a leak, a doctor when we are sick, but we can only go to Jesus when we want to overcome death. There's no one else who can help. Death couldn't hold the Son of God and neither can it hold those whom He holds. There is salvation in no other. There's no other way, no other truth, and there is no other life outside of Jesus Christ.

SOUL SEARCH

Could I adequately explain the exclusivity of Christianity to a skeptic? If not, search for some helpful material today to begin your study.

Father, help me to study how to answer difficult questions so that I'm always ready to give an answer to those who ask (1 Peter 3:15).

Launch Out and Let Down

*Launch out into the deep
and let down your nets for a catch.*
LUKE 5:4

The disciples had washed their nets after toiling all night without catching one fish. Yet Jesus told them to launch out into the deep and cast their nets again. Peter, although skeptical, obediently let down the nets again by faith.

We are called to be fishers of men, but Jesus knows that it is an impossible task without Him (John 15:5). Now is not the time to procrastinate. We are in a race against time because people are dying daily without Christ. But we cannot toil in the darkness without the Lord; it will be a fruitless waste of precious time and effort.

We are to be co-laborers with God (1 Corinthians 3:9). And so we must always pray as we go—imploring Him to go with us—and then preach the Word according to the pattern God has given us.

SOUL SEARCH

Have there been times when I've tried to do things in my own strength? What lessons did I learn?

Father, never let me waste my time by not including you in my labors.

From Now On

> *Do not be afraid.*
> *From now on you will catch men.*
> LUKE 5:10

When speaking of evangelism, the first words that Jesus said were, "Fear not." He was probably referring to the overwhelming reverence Peter felt at the magnitude of the miracle he had just witnessed. When we think of who Jesus really is, how can we help but tremble? The incarnation is breathtaking on so many levels. Jesus even had control over a shoal of fish in the ocean!

When it comes to evangelism, most of us are paralyzed by fear. We are afraid of being rejected; we are afraid of not knowing what to say. However, if we care about humanity and where they will spend eternity, and if we believe in a very real hell, we will say with the disciples, "We cannot but speak that which we have seen and heard" (Acts 4:20). May evangelism become our priority. Let's begin to catch men now!

SOUL SEARCH

Am I more concerned for my own well-being than I am that guilty sinners will end up in hell? Do I need to repent of my lack of concern?

Father, help me to be a fisher of men from now on.

Full of Leprosy

I am willing; be cleansed.
LUKE 5:13

We know from God's Word that sin is like leprosy. In speaking of our attitude toward the sinner and his sins, the Bible says, "And some have compassion, making a difference. And others save with fear, pulling them out of the fire; hating even the garment spotted by the flesh" (Jude 1:23). The spots are a reference to the spots of leprosy. In Luke 5, we are told that this man was *full* of leprosy just as we are full of sin, unclean in the eyes of a holy God. But because of the cross, God can extend His hand and say, "Be clean," and our sin is immediately removed as far as the east is from the west (Psalm 103:12). Sin departs from us and we depart from sin.

The promise of salvation is universal. Whosoever will may come. God is not willing that any perish. So when any sinner calls upon the name of the Lord, he can be confident that God really wants to cleanse him. Jesus said, "All that the Father gives Me will come to Me, and the one who comes to Me I will by no means cast out" (John 6:37).

SOUL SEARCH

Do I envy sinners because they can enjoy the pleasures of sin? Is there any wickedness remaining in my heart?

Father, help me to hate all sin, not just because of what it does, but because of what it is.

A Testimony to Them

But go and show yourself to the priest,
and make an offering for your cleansing,
as a testimony to them, just as Moses commanded.

Luke 5:14

Obedience and dependence on His Word is proof that we have been saved by the grace of God. God says it should forever be settled for those who love Him.

Those who name the name of Christ but do not depart from iniquity have no assurance that they have passed through the new birth, God gives us a new heart with a new set of desires. One indication that we have experienced salvation is that we walk in His statutes. We love the things that God loves and hate the things that God hates (James 4:4).

Jesus said that those who keep His commandments are those who love Him: "And he who has My commandments and keeps them, it is he who loves Me. And he who loves Me will be loved by My Father, and I will love him and manifest Myself to him" (John 14:21). It should be evident to the world that we have been cleansed of sin. Our behavior is our testimony.

SOUL SEARCH

Is my heart quick to obey the Word of God? Is my testimony evident to the world? Take a moment to assess your words and actions.

Father, help me to be a testimony of your cleansing.

Both Were Impossible

Man, your sins are forgiven you.
LUKE 5:20

When Jesus said that He had power on earth to forgive sins, the Pharisees believed that He had blasphemed, a sin punishable by death.

The answer Jesus gave to them was interesting. He asked which was easier—to miraculously heal a man of a terrible disease or to miraculously forgive sins? Both were impossible for man, but not for God. If Jesus could heal the paralyzed man miraculously, then without a doubt He had the power to forgive his every sin. So the healing of the man, both physically and spiritually, was evidence that Jesus was from God, the promised Messiah.

If God can transform us overnight through the gospel, giving us a new heart with new desires through the new birth, it is evident that with Him nothing is impossible.

Jesus said, "Your sins are forgiven you." When we come to the Savior our sins are immediately and miraculously forgiven.

SOUL SEARCH

Do I negate the power of God in my life by considering some things to be impossible? And do I rejoice that my sins have been forgiven? Declare to your own soul today that nothing is impossible with God.

Father, thank you that my sins are past tense. They are gone. Forgotten by you.

The Great Letdown

Man, your sins are forgiven you.
LUKE 5:20

The men in this story showed their love for their diseased and hopeless friend by hauling him onto the roof and lowering him through an opening so Jesus could touch him. His friends lowered him down.

The Bible tells us that Jesus saw their faith. Their trust in Him was evident by their actions. Faith without works is dead (James 2:14).

We also see in this passage that although this man was diseased, Jesus dealt with his sin first. "Man, your sins are forgiven you," he said. Jesus encourages us to bring all our problems to his throne of grace. However, we should primarily come to Him not to be healed, not to be blessed, and not to receive anything but the forgiveness of our sins. It is because of our sin that we should seek first the kingdom of God and His righteousness, and all other necessary things will be added.

His righteousness and our lack of it should be the primary concern.

SOUL SEARCH

Am I guilty of asking God to do things for me rather than seeking His righteousness?

Father, let my love not be confined only to those who love me.

March

Boundless Faith

Why are you reasoning in your hearts?
LUKE 5:22

Jesus perceived that His hearers were reasoning in their hearts. Something didn't add up for His disciples.

Man is a reasoning creature. God created us with the ability to reason about life and understand spiritual truths, which separates us from the animals. We ask questions: Why are we here? What is the purpose of our existence? What was in the beginning? Are we alone in the universe? Is there life after death? Is there ultimate justice?

However, sometimes our reasoning can hinder our faith. It's not plausible to think that a man can walk on water, raise the dead, or feed five thousand people with five loaves and two fishes.

It was Charles Spurgeon who rightly said that where faith may swim, reason may only paddle. Reason has limits. Faith knows no bounds.

SOUL SEARCH

Does my effort to try and figure things out sometimes hinder my faith in God?

Father, help me to always trust you with all of my heart, and not to lean on my own understanding (Proverbs 3:5–6).

Collecting Money

Follow Me.
LUKE 5:27

Perhaps Matthew had heard of Jesus or maybe wondered at the rumors floating around about the many miracles He had done. But the words that captured him on this day from the lips of the Savior were "Follow Me." There was no explanation, and there were no conditions. It was simply a call to follow. This is the call of every Christian. We are to follow the Good Shepherd because He has promised to lead us into the green pastures of everlasting life. The compelling voice of the Son of God drew Matthew irresistibly. He left everything to follow the Savior.

Life is in Jesus. How can we be content to spend our lives pursuing material things? Unfortunately, that's what so many in the world prefer to do. They are rich in this world and destitute before God.

Millions have heard His voice and have left the pursuit of riches. Trusting Christ with both their present and their future, not one will be disappointed.

SOUL SEARCH

Am I ever tempted to let the pursuit of personal gain monopolize my time and focus?

Father, help me to follow you closely today.

Only the Sick

Those who are well have no need of a physician,
but those who are sick.
I have not come to call the righteous,
but sinners, to repentance.

LUKE 5:31–32

Healthy people don't need a doctor. Only the sick do. A sinful man, suffering from the terminal disease of sin ought to be crying out to God for help. He alone is the Great Physician who holds the cure to death in His hand.

To call the message we preach "good news" is a gross understatement. The English language lacks adequate adjectives. The closest we can get is the biblical phrase, "the unspeakable gift." Everlasting life offered in the gospel is a free gift, but repentance is a prerequisite. We are called to repentance. Never drop that word from your appeal to this sinful world. There are some who wrongly believe that we can serve God and sin, but we must forsake sin at the cross of Christ.

Our evangelistic message is to convince people that they are terminally ill and desperately need a cure. Without it, they are heading for a very real hell. May God help us to be faithful to this task.

SOUL SEARCH

Am I deeply concerned today about this terminal and hell-bound world? Ask the Lord to give you His heart for the lost.

Father, please give me your concern for the unsaved.

Our Choice

But that you may know that the Son of Man has power on earth to forgive sins. I say to you, arise, take up your bed, and go to your house.

JOHN 5:24

While God stretches out His hand and offers each of us everlasting life (whosoever will may come), He doesn't disregard our will. If sinners don't want everlasting life, they don't have to take it. If they prefer hell to heaven, that's their choice. If they foolishly say that they would rather have everlasting suffering than pleasure forever more, they will get it. As preposterous as that sounds, people actually say they prefer hell to heaven.

The sick man in this story had been in that condition for a very long time. Why on earth would he want to stay that way? But Jesus asked him anyway. Jesus then told him to get up, pick up his bed and walk. He no longer needed a sick bed.

It's time for us to stop languishing on our beds of ease, set aside our complacency, and be about the business of sharing the good news of Christ. The secular life is unsatisfying to the true believer—it is futile, chasing the wind. We have a high calling, and this dying world is waiting.

SOUL SEARCH

Have I had the revelation that the pleasures of this world are futile? Can you identify any areas in your life where you are "chasing the wind?"

Father, open my eyes today to the contrast between the futility of this world and the reality of what I have in Christ.

God is Working

My Father has been working until now,
and I have been working.
JOHN 5:17

It seems a little strange that the omnipotent God would be *working*. However, He certainly does work. Consider the life of Joseph. God was working His purposes all throughout Joseph's life—when his jealous brothers sold him into slavery and when Potiphar's lusty wife had him thrown into prison as a sexual predator. God was working His internal purposes when the butler, the baker, and Pharaoh had their strange dreams. As a result, Joseph was exalted to the highest position in the land.

If you love God, never think that the things that happen to you have no purpose. Take a moment to commit this great consolation to memory: "And we know that all things work together for good to those who love God, to those who are the called according to His purpose" (Romans 8:28).

SOUL SEARCH

If I am utterly convinced that God is working all things out for my good, how will this knowledge affect my day?

Father, today I believe that you are working on my behalf because you love me.

Overwhelming Thoughts

*Most assuredly, I say to you, the Son can do nothing of
Himself, but what He sees the Father do; for whatever He does,
the Son also does in like manner. For the Father loves the Son,
and shows Him all things that He Himself does; and He will
show Him greater works than these, that you may marvel.*

JOHN 5:19-20

Although they are distinct Persons, the Father cannot be separated from the Son. God was in Christ reconciling the world back to Himself (2 Corinthians 5:19). When that tiny baby lay in the manger in Bethlehem, this was Almighty God manifest in the flesh. "The Word became flesh and dwelt among us" (John 1:14).

Jesus was the express image of the invisible God. This is the foundational teaching of Christianity and why it is ridiculous to compare Jesus to great men in history. There is no comparison. It is like comparing the noonday sun to a dead flashlight.

SOUL SEARCH

Do I give much thought to the fact that Jesus is really God in the flesh? Ask God for a revelation of the incarnation of Almighty God.

Father, open my eyes to the amazing incarnation. You prepared a human body for yourself! Such thoughts are truly overwhelming.

Those Dry Bones

For as the Father raises the dead and gives life to them, even so the Son gives life to whom He will. For the Father judges no one, but has committed all judgment to the Son, that all should honor the Son just as they honor the Father. He who does not honor the Son does not honor the Father who sent Him.

JOHN 5:21-23

God raised the dead a number of times in the Old Testament, including Ezekiel's massive army of dry bones (Ezekiel 37:1–14). Before we came to Christ, we were nothing but dry bones. We were dead in our trespasses and sins until we heard the Word of the Lord and came to Jesus. We weren't given a religion in Christ, rather forgiveness for our sins and life eternal.

Every sinner will stand before Jesus Christ as Lord and give an account of every idle word spoken, every deed done in darkness, every secret sexual sin, and every murderous act. Nothing and no one will escape the wrath of His Law except those who are sheltered in the shadow of the cross.

SOUL SEARCH

Have I become proficient in my knowledge of the Bible? Am I familiar with every story in the Scriptures? If not, how can I carve out a few extra minutes a day for that purpose?

Father, give me a hunger to learn from your Word and uncover the nuggets of truth.

The Preacher

Most assuredly, I say to you, he who hears My word and believes in Him who sent Me has everlasting life, and shall not come into judgment, but has passed from death into life.

JOHN 5:24

He who hears—but how shall they hear without a preacher (Romans 10:14)?

Is your heart burdened for the lost? If you are a new creature in Christ, you are a new preacher for Christ. Do you ever cry out in prayer for those who are still in their sins and in a moment of time could be snatched by death and damned in hell? These are not pleasant thoughts, but they are thoughts that every Christian should have.

God is trusting you to be His ambassador. He is calling you to share the truth of the gospel so those who hear His Word and believe in Him will have everlasting life. The moment we repent and trust alone in Jesus, we will pass from death to life.

May God open our eyes to the important and sobering task He has set before us.

SOUL SEARCH

Do I see myself as a preacher, or do I leave that to the professionals? Ask God to show you that being an ambassador for Christ is simply sharing what you know.

Father, please use my words today to bring the message of everlasting life to some dying sinner.

Legitimate Pleasures

Most assuredly, I say to you, the hour is coming, and now is, when the dead will hear the voice of the Son of God; and those who hear will live. For as the Father has life in Himself, so He has granted the Son to have life in Himself, and has given Him authority to execute judgment also, because He is the Son of Man.

JOHN 5:25–27

This passage begins with the words, "Most assuredly." There are few things in life that we can be really sure of, but this is one. The hour will come when every dead person will hear the voice of Jesus Christ. We have already heard it and have trusted in His mercy, but there are multitudes who will hear it and come under His judgment. Those who hear His voice now will live. Those who hear it then will be damned. There are no words to express the terror of such a day! How can we waste our precious time pursuing our own pleasures when we know what is coming to this world?

Many of our pleasures are legitimate and good. Chatting with friends and family around a swimming pool is a wonderful pleasure. But not while a child is drowning in the pool.

May God help us to order our priorities.

SOUL SEARCH

Is there a sense of urgency in my heart? Do I see today as a day to spend on myself or as a possible occasion to reach someone who is lost? Keep your eyes open today and look for a divine opportunity.

Father, deepen my love for you and for the lost.

Don't be Impressed

Do not marvel at this; for the hour is coming in which all who are in the graves will hear His voice and come forth—those who have done good, to the resurrection of life, and those who have done evil, to the resurrection of condemnation.

John 5:28-29

Do not marvel. Do not be impressed. Raising every human being from the dead is not a marvelous act for God. It will take nothing but a gentle whisper of His voice. Death must obey His every Word and bow the knee. This is the same Word that spoke the suns into existence and fashioned every intricate atom in the universe. Nothing is impossible for Him, so don't marvel at this.

Those who have done good will have their works follow them into eternity. They will be rewarded by God. And those who have done evil will have their evil works follow them, which will be evidence of their guilt. Every murderer who thought he got away with it will stand before his Creator and face perfect justice. We cannot but both rejoice and tremble at such sobering thoughts. We rejoice that justice will be done and tremble for those on whom eternal justice will fall.

SOUL SEARCH

Have I thought about an atom and considered the intricacies of each one? It takes trillions of them to form a rock or a human hand. Now, think of their Maker.

Father, take the blinders off my mind.

Helpless without Him

*I can of Myself do nothing. As I hear, I judge;
and My judgment is righteous, because I do not seek
My own will but the will of the Father who sent Me.*
JOHN 5:30

If Jesus could do nothing without the Father's help, how much more do we need His help? Have you ever put all of your time and energies into something you thought was good and right, but forgot to consult the Lord? It may have turned out to be what some call diddley-squat. That's why we need to pray about everything—our marriages, our jobs, our daily tasks, and especially in our evangelistic endeavors. Prayer is the oxygen of the Christian life. We breathe prayer; we pray without ceasing. Prayer gives life to the dead, energizes us for the day, and resuscitates us after the evils of the day attack.

The billionaire who ignores his Creator is nothing, achieves nothing, and dies with nothing. Time will turn his empire to dust. But we know better. We know that what is done in Christ is eternal, and so we pray about both the small things and those issues we think are big. Without Him we can do nothing.

SOUL SEARCH

Today may I see the seed of the gospel as being something small that can become something massive, because God is part of it.

Father, may something eternal be achieved today because you are guiding me.

The Brilliant Light

If I bear witness of Myself, My witness is not true. There is another who bears witness of Me, and I know that the witness which He witnesses of Me is true.

JOHN 5:31-32

When Jesus spoke of Himself, God bore witness to the truth of His words—they were substantiated by His Father and filled with power.

When we share the truth of the gospel to this world, our words are also backed by the power of God. The gospel is a supernatural message that carries with it the innate ability to transform guilty sinners into new creatures in Christ.

We must never tire of our labor. When a nation is plagued with the sins of abortion, blasphemy, adultery, pornography, fornication, homosexuality, violence, corruption, and a thousand other evils, we know that the gospel is the only hope of salvation. In a world full of darkness and lies, the gospel is a shining sun of absolute truth. God's witness is true. It heals in this life and delivers from wrath in the next.

SOUL SEARCH

Could I present the biblical gospel in less than a minute? If not, I need to practice what I preach so I can share with people who will just give me a minute of their time.

Father, help me to be thoroughly familiar with your precious gospel.

The Lighthouse

You have sent to John, and he has borne witness to the truth.
Yet I do not receive testimony from man, but I say these things
that you may be saved. He was the burning and shining lamp,
and you were willing for a time to rejoice in his light.

JOHN 5:33–35

There was no one like John the Baptist. He was a burning light of humility and consecration. He was set apart from this world to be a lighthouse in the storm to illuminate the coming One. Jesus testified to his godly character, saying that there was no one born of women greater than he (Luke 7:28).

One of John's greatest virtues was that he walked in the fear of the Lord. He rebuked those who came to hear him speak. He stood up to the religious leaders. He rebuked Herod and ended up losing his life because of his stand for righteousness. In the desert of this world, may we be like John, seeking only the smile of God even if it means getting the frown of this evil world.

SOUL SEARCH

Do I have godly attributes? Am I set apart from this world but at the same time shining like a lighthouse for Jesus?

Father, let the light of your love shine through me today.

Living Hope

But I have a greater witness than John's; for the works which the Father has given Me to finish—the very works that I do— bear witness of Me, that the Father has sent Me.

JOHN 5:36

Although John was a burning and shining light, like the moon, his light was a mere reflection. Jesus of Nazareth was the brilliant noonday sun who performed miracles to prove to Israel He was the Messiah. He spoke to storms, raised the dead, healed the sick, opened the eyes of the blind, unplugged deaf ears, and multiplied loaves and fishes. John didn't do any of these things.

This same Jesus does miracles today. He gives sight to blind sinners, opens ears that are deaf to His Word, calms storms in our lives, and multiplies the Bread of Life to feed our hungry souls.

How can this world live without Jesus? How do people cope in life's frightening storms? How can they live knowing that death is a shadow that follows their every step? We must reach out to them. How can we not shout from the housetops that Jesus gives us a living hope for eternal life?

SOUL SEARCH

Today I will count my blessings. I will name them one by one, beginning with the cross.

Father, I am so often asking something from you. Today I give you the freewill offering of my praise.

The Fear of the Lord

And the Father Himself, who sent Me, has testified of Me.
You have neither heard His voice at any time,
nor seen His form.

JOHN 5:37

The religious leaders were whitewashed tombs. They were impressive on the outside, but their hearts were full of sin (Matthew 23:27). They lived for the praise of men and not for the praise of the God they supposedly represented. Jesus said that with all their rich tradition, long prayers, and professed piety, they had never heard from God. At any time.

This verse reveals their great error. They had never "seen His form." This isn't a reference to physical sight because no man has seen God at any time. He was clearly saying that their image of God was wrong. The god they served didn't require truth in the inward parts—he wasn't to be feared because he didn't exist. Idolatry is the root cause of most sin because even though it acknowledges God, it lacks the fear of the Lord. The fear of the Lord causes men to depart from evil, but those who don't fear Him keep evil in their hearts.

SOUL SEARCH

Is my image of God biblical? If I truly feared the Lord, what would change in my life?

Father, let me fear you as Jesus did. The Word says that He was heard because He feared (Hebrews 5:7).

Simple Faith

But you do not have His word abiding in you,
because whom He sent, Him you do not believe.

JOHN 5:38

When we are born again, Christ enters—the hope of glory. He is the Word that brought life into being in the beginning. He became human flesh, and through the Holy Spirit, the Word abides in us. He who has the Son has life, and we are sealed by Him for eternity.

The world discounts faith—they think it is for the weak. In one sense that's true, but through faith, the weak are made strong. It was faith that gave David the courage to defeat Goliath. It was faith that made Daniel strong in the face of hungry lions. Without faith, both of these men would have been weak and fearful.

Faith is like a parachute defying gravity. I am weak against its pull, but faith makes me strong and carries me through. It delivers me from my fears. Through simple faith in Jesus, I have deliverance from death!

SOUL SEARCH

What are some of my greatest weaknesses? How am I going to deal with them?

Father, I trust you to guard me from the enemy who walks about as a roaring lion.

The Missed Tree

You search the Scriptures, for in them you think you have eternal life; and these are they which testify of Me. But you are not willing to come to Me that you may have life.

JOHN 5:39–40

Searching the Scriptures without a humble and truth-seeking heart is like reading them in the pitch dark. Humility of heart captures the ear of God. It is to the humble that He says: "But on this one will I look: On him who is poor and of a contrite spirit, and who trembles at My word" (Isaiah 66:2).

The proud religious leaders trusted in their vain piety to save them. Yet with all religious trappings and empty head-knowledge, they missed the Messiah. They missed seeing Him who was pierced for us and was bruised for our iniquities (Isaiah 53:5).

Because they looked for a lion, they didn't see the Lamb. The tree of the cross was hidden by the forest of their religious works that puffed them up with pride. They wanted a conquering king, not a suffering servant, so they didn't see and believe the testimony of Holy Scripture. Instead of accusing Him of blasphemy and plotting His death, they would have bowed the knee in humility.

SOUL SEARCH

Do I search Scripture with an open mind, or do I carry my own opinions and presuppositions into the experience?

Father, never let me take for granted the light that comes from your Word. It's a lamp to my feet and a light to my path (Psalm 119:105).

Honoring the Truth

*I do not receive honor from men. But I know you, that
you do not have the love of God in you. I have come in My
Father's name, and you do not receive Me; if another comes
in his own name, him you will receive.*

JOHN 5:41–43

Jesus utters four very penetrating words: But I know you. Jesus
knew their darkest of sins. He knew of their hypocrisy and their
man-honoring motives.

The ungodly will embrace anything but the truth of God's
Word. They will quote the so-called gospels of Thomas and Judas
and other spiritual writings and will believe without question the
history books penned by fallible and even wicked men. Yet these
same men are religiously skeptical of every word of the Bible.

They fight tooth and nail at every turn, straining the tiny
gnat and swallowing a two-humped, fully laden camel (Matthew
23:24). They don't care about the honor that comes from heaven.
Their lives are not God-honoring, and by default, they serve the
devil.

Neither did they have God's love within them.

Those who love God and want to honor Him will always
embrace His Word.

SOUL SEARCH

Do I, without a doubt, believe the historical writings of men
yet doubt promises of God? Today I determine to change that.

*Father, this day I reaffirm and esteem the truth of every promise in
your Word.*

The Honor of Men

How can you believe, who receive honor from one another,
and do not seek the honor that comes from the only God?
JOHN 5:44

Seeking the honor that comes from fellow human beings isn't confined to the realm of the religious. Think of the sports world. While we would like to think that athletes love their sport, many play only for praise. They live for the roar of the crowd, the clapping of the hands, the patting of the back, the praise of men, or the attention of the media—mainly for the honor that comes from the world.

It's the same in the fashion world. If no one was around to observe how we dressed or what our hair looked like, we wouldn't spend the time trying to impress.

While it's no sin to want to look respectable or to enjoy a sporting hero, we should never let the praise of the world overtake our desire to seek the honor that comes from God.

SOUL SEARCH

Does fashion dictate what I wear? Does it consume my time and money, or do I have my own mind when it comes to my appearance? Evaluate your priorities in this area.

Father, turn my heart from worthless things.

Ten Cannons

Do not think that I shall accuse you to the Father; there is one who accuses you—Moses, in whom you trust. For if you believed Moses, you would believe Me; for he wrote about Me. But if you do not believe his writings, how will you believe My words?

JOHN 5:45–47

The gospel will only make sense when the moral Law precedes it. It is the Law of Moses that incriminates the sinner. The Commandments thunder accusations of lying, stealing, lust, hatred, blasphemy, murder, adultery, and a multitude of sins that offend our holy Creator.

The Law pointed ten loaded cannons at Israel, but the people weren't alarmed. They missed the whole purpose of the Law. Had they believed the words of Moses, they would have received the words of Jesus, repented of their sins, and trusted in the Savior. The Law makes us aware of our sin and leads us to the Savior.

Use the Law of Moses from the pages of Deuteronomy and let the ten cannons loose to do their work on an evil generation. Millions of lost people are deluded into thinking that all is well between heaven and earth.

SOUL SEARCH

How can I use the Law of Moses in my witnessing?

Father, make me like Jesus. Give me His love and uncompromising boldness to confront sinners with their sin.

Worldly Accusations

Can you make the friends of the bridegroom fast while the bridegroom is with them? But the days will come when the bridegroom will be taken away from them; then they will fast in those days.

Luke 5:34–35

The Pharisees were concerned that the followers of Jesus didn't fast. Their concern was telling. They blew a trumpet when they fasted to let everyone know how spiritual they were, but the disciples were blowing no trumpet.

The Bible asks the rhetorical question: "Who shall bring a charge against God's elect?" (Romans 8:33).

The answer is obvious: No one. Because of the freedom we have in Christ, no one can accuse us of anything or dictate our actions. Everything we do is between God and us. Look at our liberty: "Do you have faith? Have it to yourself before God. Happy is he who does not condemn himself in what he approves" (14:22).

Never let the words of an accusing world steal your joy. We have one Lord, and we are ultimately responsible only to Him.

SOUL SEARCH

Do I ever have an unhealthy judgmental attitude toward other Christians?

Father, help me today to have grace toward my brethren and toward the unsaved.

Common Sense

Have you not even read this, what David did when he was hungry, he and those who were with him: how he went into the house of God, took and ate the showbread, and also gave some to those with him, which is not lawful for any but the priests to eat?

Luke 6:3-4

There is such a thing as the spirit of the law. Some laws are harsh and unforgiving, and they don't take mitigating circumstances into account. And so, a judge will exercise his discretion and use the *spirit* of the law, often seen as simple common sense.

That's what Jesus was doing in the face of the religious hypocrites that pointed accusing fingers at His disciples. David was hungry, and God allowed him to feed himself.

The spirit of the Law overshadowed its letter.

The perfect Law rightly called for our death and damnation, but the kindness of the Lawgiver offered us the Bread of Life. Thank God for the spirit of the Law.

SOUL SEARCH

Do I fully appreciate the mercy of the cross? I will take some time today to praise God for the sacrifice He made for me.

Father, may I always remember that even though there were no mitigating circumstances, you made a way of escape from death.

Rise Up in the Midst

Rise up, and stand forth in the midst.
LUKE 6:8 (KJV)

This man had a withered hand, but Jesus didn't immediately address that need. Jesus told him to rise up and stand forth in the midst and then to stretch out his hand. Jesus was deliberately making it clear that He was healing the man on the Sabbath day.

Much of the Body of Christ has a withered hand when it comes to reaching the lost. Outreach is not a priority. Most of the contemporary church is caught up in the busyness of their business. A church that neglects evangelism isn't at all healthy. It is terribly diseased.

If we want to be healed of this affliction, we should stand forth in the midst of the ungodly and reach out to them with the gospel. It's not enough for us to sit in church and hope that they will somehow find their way there. We must go to them as we've been commanded, in the power of the Holy Spirit (Mark 16:15).

SOUL SEARCH

Do I delight to do God's will? How can I overcome my fear of reaching out?

Father, help me to delight in the irksome task of evangelism. Heal my withered hand.

Blessed Poor

Blessed are you poor,
For yours is the kingdom of God.
LUKE 6:20

While it's true that the physically poor heard Jesus gladly, what we see listed in the beatitudes are virtues of the godly. It is the poor in spirit who recognize that they need God's grace and mercy. Those who are righteous in their own eyes see no need to repent and trust the Savior.

Those who are poor in spirit are blessed because they desperately need forgiveness. They see that they are immoral and have a depraved heart before God. When we are at the end of our rope morally, God steps in with a new rope of hope.

It is the moral Law that strips us of the delusion of self-righteousness. That's why we need to apply the Ten Commandments to the conscience of the lost, as Jesus did (Mark 10:17–22). The Commandments will, by the grace of God, open the eyes of their understanding and show them their need for the Savior. And in their poverty, they will become rich and blessed.

SOUL SEARCH

Do I understand the poverty of my spiritual state without the Lord?

Father, thank you for the spiritual riches I have in Christ.

Spiritual Hunger

Blessed are you who hunger now,
For you shall be filled.
LUKE 6:21

There's nothing blessed about the terrible pains of hunger for physical food, but there is blessing when we hunger for righteousness. The moment we come to Jesus, by faith we are made righteous in the sight of God. The Law is satisfied with the cross, and the sinner is made whole. The accusing mouth of Moses is stopped by the sinless blood of Jesus. There is no more blessed state on earth than to be cleansed of all sin.

It is the moral Law that causes us to desire a right standing with God. It's when we understand that lust is adultery in God's eyes and hatred is murder that we see a need for the righteousness that comes through faith.

Charles Spurgeon said:

> But no man ever becomes hungry and thirsty after righteousness unless he has first passed through the three preliminary stages—has been convinced of his soul poverty, has been made to mourn for sin and has been rendered humble in the sight of God.[1]

SOUL SEARCH

In what ways has God's Law shown me that sin is exceedingly sinful?

Father, help me to always thirst after righteousness.

The State of Contrition

Blessed are you who weep now,
For you shall laugh.

LUKE 6:21

It happened in a matter of seconds, but I will never forget it. I approached two men in their early twenties and asked, "Would you like to do an interview for YouTube?" The man on my left was immediately angered and said, "Get out of here!" Then with increasing anger demanded, "Go away, get out of here!" I said, "May I give you a gift?" To which the other man said, "Sure." I handed him a card. "It's a Subway gift card . . . for dinner tonight. Here's one for your friend."

That's when I heard a strange sound—a groan coming from the angry man. With tears in his voice, he muttered, "I'm so sorry!" As I turned to leave, I replied, "That's okay."

In those few seconds, I caught a glimpse of the power of love to defuse anger and bring about contrition.

That's what happens when a sinner truly sees the love of God demonstrated at Calvary: "But God demonstrates His own love toward us, in that while we were still sinners, Christ died for us" (Romans 5:8). That's why we go through the arduous task of opening up the Commandments—to showcase the glorious cross.

SOUL SEARCH

What causes me to weep tears of contrition?

Father, in the light of the love of the cross, help me to have a broken spirit and a contrite heart.

Remember to Leap

Blessed are you, when men hate you, and when they exclude you, and revile you, and cast out your name as evil, for the Son of Man's sake. Rejoice in that day and leap for joy! For indeed your reward is great in heaven, for in like manner their fathers did to the prophets.

LUKE 6:22–23

If you are ever hated because you belong to Jesus, or if you have people exclude you from their company or look upon you as being evil, make sure you obey the Word and rejoice. It is natural to be depressed when this happens, but we are told to rejoice anyway.

Then Jesus said to do something else—"leap for joy" when we are persecuted for our faith. So go somewhere private and physically jump up and down! It will make you laugh, and at the same time it will prove to yourself that you are prepared to be obedient to what Jesus said, even though you may feel foolish. It will lift your spirits.

SOUL SEARCH

What is my response to persecution? Depression or joy?

Father, help me to rejoice and leap for joy when I'm persecuted because I belong to you.

The Desire to Be Rich

But woe to you who are rich,
For you have received your consolation.
Luke 6:24

Riches tend to make human beings live independently from God. However, while money may buy us comfort in this life, it stops dead at the fancy gravestone.

Jesus told the story of a man who was so rich and successful he decided to build bigger facilities in which he planned to keep all his goods. But because he was rich in this world and poor toward God, Jesus called him a fool (Luke 12:20).

"But those who desire to be rich fall into temptation and a snare, and into many foolish and harmful lusts which drown men in destruction and perdition"(1 Timothy 6:9).

The Bible warns that those who want to be rich pierce themselves through with many sorrows (1 Timothy 6:10). It's not always the rich that desire more money. Poor people can be consumed with covetousness and become discontent.

Our sole consolation should be in our godliness. Scripture tells us godliness with contentment is great gain (1 Timothy 6:6–10).

SOUL SEARCH

Am I content with God as my chief source of joy? Who else do I turn to in times of need?

Father, may you ever be my strong consolation.

Spiritual Hunger

Woe to you who are full,
For you shall hunger.
LUKE 6:25

Jesus is obviously not speaking of those who have eaten a great meal and are thanking God for it. He is likely speaking of those who recklessly indulge in the sinful pleasures of this world—like the rich man who feasted sumptuously and ignored the will of God (Luke 16:19).

In the story of Lazarus and the rich man, the rich man's sin wasn't that he was physically rich, but that he was not rich toward God. He was selfish and self-indulgent. He lavishly clothed and fed himself and had no concern for his neighbor, who was starving at his gate. What a picture of the rich, overfed contemporary church that has no concern for the unsaved.

May we never be like that toward the lost.

SOUL SEARCH

Am I concerned about those who sit in the shadow of death outside of the church? Who can I reach out to today who is starving for the truth?

Father, help me to love my neighbors as I love myself and to be deeply concerned about their salvation.

The Joy of Laughter

Woe to you who laugh now,
For you shall mourn and weep.
LUKE 6:25

How good it is to laugh! It's a refreshing tonic for the sometimes sad and weary soul. Clearly, Jesus wasn't condemning the joy of laughter. The Bible says that a merry heart does good like a medicine (Proverbs 17:22). But rather He was speaking to those who derive pleasure, joy, and laughter from the sinful pleasures of this world. Perhaps Jesus was also referring to those who cynically laugh at those who belong to God.

The Bible says that Moses chose to suffer affliction with the people of God rather than enjoy the pleasures of sin for a season (Hebrews 11:25).

Those who love the things that are offensive to God and enjoy the pleasures of sin will weep and mourn on the day of judgment, when God dispenses perfect and terrible justice, and His wrath falls.

May we take up our cross daily and deny ourselves such attractive pleasures, and instead look to Him as the source of joy.

SOUL SEARCH

Am I like Lot's wife (Genesis 19:26)? What do I secretly desire from the sinful world?

Father, help me today to see your invisible omnipresence.

The Smile of Man

Woe to you when all men speak well of you,
For so did their fathers to the false prophets.
LUKE 6:26

The Bible says that all who live godly in Christ Jesus will suffer persecution (2 Timothy 3:12). If we aren't being persecuted in some way, it's probably because we're not boldly living our faith in Christ Jesus. Something is wrong when criminals don't have a fear of the police. Rarely do those who violate the law speak well of its officers.

Neither should we expect the world to admire us if we stand for righteousness.

The preachers who seek the smile of men will have to deal with the frown of God. They don't fear Him, and so they preach messages that tickle ears, neglecting their sobering responsibility.

When we preach sin, righteousness, and judgment, we will often offend a sin-loving world, but we dare not water down the medicine—it will lose its curative properties.

We must faithfully preach the truth in love. God help us to be motivated by His fear rather than the fear of man.

SOUL SEARCH

Am I ever persecuted for my faith? If not, why not?

Father, help me to fear you and have the courage to speak out boldly.

April

Loving Enemies

But I say to you who hear:
Love your enemies,
do good to those who hate you.

LUKE 6:27

Jesus said, "I say to you who hear." Not everyone can hear this saying because it's not easy to love your enemies, nor does it come naturally. Instead, anger, fear, resentment, even hatred toward our enemies comes almost instinctively.

The simple fact is that we cannot love our enemies without a supernatural gift of love given to us by the Holy Spirit. This is the same love we see displayed on the cross when Jesus prayed on behalf of those who crucified Him, "Father, forgive them for they do not know what they do" (Luke 23:34).

Pray for those who hate you because you belong to Jesus. Buy them gifts. Give them no reason to hate you. Whenever someone shows offense toward the gospel and refuses even a conversation, I say, "May I give you a gift?" Then I hand them a five-dollar gift card. Almost without exception, I watch resentment immediately disappear. Carry some with you.

We are able to love our enemies because the love of Christ constrains us.

SOUL SEARCH

Am I a selfish or a loving person? What can I do to show my love?

Father, please fill me with your love today and give me the opportunity to share that love with the lost.

Evident Token

Bless those who curse you,
and pray for those who spitefully use you.
LUKE 6:28

Blessing people who curse us is not natural human behavior. It doesn't come easily.

To bless people means more than wishing God's smile upon them. It also might mean buying a gift for someone who spitefully uses us. Sometimes a small, thoughtful gift can mean much more to an unbeliever then an eloquent sermon. I once secretly sent a gift card from Sue and myself to a high profile atheist who publicly railed on me like no other. It so touched her heart that she spent ten emotional minutes talking about it on a video to her hundreds of thousands of subscribers (see "Crazy Bible" YouTube).

A gift is a visible token of genuine love, which happens to be the most powerful force in the universe. Love drove Jesus to the cross, and it's what will compel us to carry that cross and walk in His footsteps.

SOUL SEARCH

Do I pray for people who don't like me? Who can I pray for today?

Father, help me to exhibit the virtues of your divine nature.

Let God Handle It

*To him who strikes you on the one cheek, offer the other also.
And from him who takes away your cloak, do not withhold
your tunic either.*

LUKE 6:29

Some see these words of Jesus as promoting passivity or even
pacifism. But in reality, the Christian isn't to fight back because
he needs to allow God to do the fighting for him. The Bible says
that Jesus, when He was persecuted, didn't retaliate: "Who, when
He was reviled, did not revile in return; when He suffered, He
did not threaten, but committed Himself to Him who judges
righteously" (1 Peter 2:23).

If someone wrongs us, we don't take the law into our own
hands. Rather we commit ourselves to God in prayer, and He will
be our defense and administer justice if He sees fit to do so.

Instead, we need to show love to those who hate us and
kindness to those who steal from us in the hope that the person
will get right with God before the day of wrath. Complete trust in
God is imperative.

SOUL SEARCH

Do I take everything to God in prayer? What do I need to let
go of and let God handle?

Father, please help me to trust you with all that happens today.

Give to Everyone

Give to everyone who asks of you. And from him who takes away your goods do not ask them back.

LUKE 6:30

Here is the true test of our love for God and our fellow man: "Give to everyone who asks of you." There is just no way around this passage. Does this mean you have to give money every time someone asks you for some? No, Jesus didn't say what to give; neither did He say how much to give. But we are to give according to what is needed.

Jesus is speaking here of an attitude that we should have toward the unsaved. We should be kind and generous for the gospel's sake, but whatever we give, we need to make sure it points people to the gospel. A kind word about the Savior or a gospel tract needs to accompany the gift.

I almost feel sick if I give to someone who asks but don't give them a gospel tract or something that directs them to God. It's like patting a sinner on the back as he's on his way to hell.

SOUL SEARCH

Am I ready to give to everyone who asks of me? When was the last time I gave willingly and with joy?

Father, help me to have a loose hand on the things that I temporarily own.

The Rule of Thumb

And just as you want men to do to you,
you also do to them likewise.

LUKE 6:31

I often think how the Golden Rule is wonderful advice for drivers, especially on a freeway. There would be no road rage, fewer accidents, and far less stress if everybody treated others on the road as they would like to be treated.

The world thinks the Golden Rule is merely a good suggestion, but it is far more than that. It is the essence of the moral Law. He who loves his neighbor as himself treats his neighbor as he would like to be treated himself. He doesn't lie to him, steal from him, commit adultery with his wife, covet his goods, or hate him. "Love does no harm to a neighbor; therefore love is the fulfillment of the law" (Romans 13:10).

It was the Good Samaritan's rule of thumb. We know that because he treated the wounds of a stranger (Luke 10:25–37).

So this *good advice* in truth shows us how far we fall short of the perfect standard of God's Law, and reveals to us that we need the Savior.

SOUL SEARCH

Would God smile in approval at the way I drive?

Father, help me today to treat others as I would like to be treated.

Love . . . No Matter What

But if you love those who love you, what credit is that to you?
For even sinners love those who love them.

LUKE 6:32

Human nature is desperately selfish. When asked why we love someone, we will probably reply that it's because they love us. We find it easy to love when we are loved. But to love when we are hated is divine. It is supernatural.

We can see this displayed in the tragic and horrific death of Stephen. He accused the religious leaders of not keeping the moral Law, and they completely lost control. They dragged him out of the city and murdered him. As this loving and innocent man was being stoned to death, he cried, "Lord, lay not this sin to their charge" (Acts 7:60 KJV).

Few have ever had their love put to the test in such an extreme way. But all of us, with the help of God, can exhibit God's love to others in some way today.

SOUL SEARCH

Would I be considered by others to be a loving person? What is one way I can show love to someone today?

Father, please give me an opportunity today to exhibit godly love to another.

Personal Rights

And if you lend to those from whom you hope to receive back, what credit is that to you? For even sinners lend to sinners to receive as much back. But love your enemies, do good, and lend, hoping for nothing in return; and your reward will be great, and you will be sons of the Most High. For He is kind to the unthankful and evil.

LUKE 6:34-35

This world isn't our home, and neither are its ways our ways. When we came to the Savior, we gave up our rights by saying, "Not my will, but yours be done" (Luke 22:42 NASB). God's ways have now become our ways, which is demonstrated by how we treat our enemies.

Jesus declares that Christians should love their enemies, do them good, and lend to them hoping for nothing in return. Our personal rights don't enter into the picture. But as we obey the words of Jesus, we are both imitating and glorifying our heavenly Father while having the consolation that He will always take care of us.

SOUL SEARCH

Do I show love to those that hate me, hoping for nothing in return?

Father, help me to show my love in practical ways to those who may dislike me.

The Power of Mercy

Therefore be merciful, just as your Father also is merciful.
Luke 6:36

Notice the first word in this verse: "Therefore." In other words, because the previous verses speak of giving up personal rights and loving enemies, we should be merciful.

It is reasonably easy for us to show mercy if we remember that God has shown us mercy through the cross. If we have seen our own sinfulness, we have no right to point an accusing finger at any other human being with a "holier than thou" attitude. We are guilty ourselves.

We should also show mercy to others because in doing so, we protect ourselves from self-destructive resentment, bitterness, anger, and hatred. Mercy is a safeguard and is beneficial for all involved.

SOUL SEARCH

Am I ever condescending to those who are different from me in the way they look or talk?

Father, help me to show mercy to others as you do.

Judge Not

Judge not, and you shall not be judged.
Condemn not, and you shall not be condemned.
Forgive, and you will be forgiven.

LUKE 6:37

This is perhaps the most misquoted verse in the entire Bible. It is often used against Christians who talk about the sins of the world. In other words, if we make a moral judgment about someone's sins, God will judge us for it. This just isn't true.

In context, this verse is directed to Christians. It is saying that we're not to judge one another about what we should eat or what day we should keep sacred. These things are between the believer and God, as it says in Romans 14.

In John 7:24, Jesus said that when we judge we are to use "righteous judgment." In other words, we are free to make moral judgments about right and wrong. We can say that murder and rape are wrong as well as lying, stealing and so on.

Meanwhile, when we do talk about the sins of this world, we are to do it in a spirit of love and gentleness, warning every man that they may be made perfect in Christ Jesus.

SOUL SEARCH

Am I always loving and gentle when sharing the gospel?

Father, help me to "reprove and rebuke, with all long suffering and doctrine" (2 Timothy 4:2 KJV).

A Giving Heart

Give, and it will be given to you: good measure, pressed down, shaken together, and running over will be put into your bosom. For with the same measure that you use, it will be measured back to you.

LUKE 6:38

Most of us are tempted to love money. We tend to be selfish and would rather get than give. Money is not sinful in itself but can easily replace God in our lives if we rely on it as our primary source of all we need. God wants us to look to Him for peace, security, and joy.

The best way to manage our attitude toward money is to hold it with a loose hand, with a readiness to give when a need arises, or just to bless someone. Living with an open hand will keep us from loving money and make sure that God is our source of peace and joy and the supplier of our needs.

If we give with a generous heart, God promises to take care of us because He especially loves a cheerful giver (2 Corinthians 9:6–7).

SOUL SEARCH

Am I ever tempted to love money? When was the last time I gave generously to someone in need?

Father, help me to give as you give.

Learning of the Savior

A disciple is not above his teacher, but everyone who is perfectly trained will be like his teacher.
Luke 6:40

Not many students know more than their teachers. If they did, the teachers should be sitting at the students' feet. The teacher's job is to transfer his knowledge to his students, and when the students are completely trained, they will be like their teacher.

We should strive to love as He loved, forgive as He forgave, and to preach the gospel as He did to this dying world. May this blind world see Jesus in us.

Our goal in life should be Christlikeness. We know we are growing in Christ when we exhibit the virtues of the Savior in our own character. We sit at His feet and learn of Him by feeding on His Word: "Take My yoke upon you and learn from Me, for I am gentle and lowly in heart, and you will find rest for your souls" (Matthew 11:29).

SOUL SEARCH

Do I obey the command to learn of Jesus? How am I going to do that today?

Father, may the virtues of your divine nature be evident in my life.

The Plank

*And why do you look at the speck in your brother's eye,
but do not perceive the plank in your own eye?*
LUKE 6:41

Caricatures tend to make us laugh. Exaggerated ears, nose, chin, forehead, or eyes can be hilarious. This verse is a verbal caricature, and this time humor makes a point.

If we have something in our spiritual eye, it's not easy to see ourselves or others clearly. Consequently we tend to be harsh in our judgment of others and show an abundance of grace to ourselves.

Hypocrisy means to be self-deceiving. It blinds us to our own sins. We need to search our hearts regularly for the subtle sin of pride, which continually lifts us above others.

The moral Law is once again at work. It reveals our sins, humbles us, and stops the mouth of self-justification that is quick to judge others.

SOUL SEARCH

Am I full of grace and mercy when looking at other people's sins? Do I tend to justify my own failings while judging others?

Father, help me to always judge myself truthfully.

Black Kettles

Or how can you say to your brother, "Brother, let me remove the speck that is in your eye," when you yourself do not see the plank that is in your own eye? Hypocrite! First remove the plank from your own eye, and then you will see clearly to remove the speck that is in your brother's eye.

LUKE 6:42

If we see a problem with a brother or sister in Christ, we should handle it with much prayer, with gentleness, and in a spirit of love. This is because Romans 14:4 says that we should avoid judging our brethren, "Who are you to judge another's servant? To his own master he stands or falls. Indeed, he will be made to stand, for God is able to make him stand."

If it's a moral issue and we feel compelled to say something, Galatians 6:1 tells us how we are to approach the situation: "Brethren, if a man is overtaken in any trespass, you who are spiritual restore such a one in a spirit of gentleness, considering yourself lest you also be tempted."

We are very dirty pots, and looking for spots on black kettles shouldn't be our business.

SOUL SEARCH

Do I always walk in a spirit of love and gentleness? Is there someone in my life I feel I need to confront about a moral issue?

Father, help me to keep my eyes on you and on the lost.

Locker Room Talk

A good man out of the good treasure of his heart brings forth good; and an evil man out of the evil treasure of his heart brings forth evil. For out of the abundance of the heart his mouth speaks.

Luke 6:45

Nothing angers a sinful world like a Christian who says that there are no good people. But when the Bible speaks of good in the context of morality, it means moral perfection, in thought, in word, and in deed. And only God is that good.

If we want to know what is in the heart of man, we need only to listen to what comes out of his mouth. Just listening to locker room talk proves the Scripture to be true when it says: "There is none who does good, no, not one. Their throat is an open tomb; with their tongues they have practiced deceit; the poison of asps is under their lips" (Romans 3:12–13).

The Bible tells us that God's Law is both perfect and good. That's why we need it to show us our true state before our Creator. It gives us a perfect moral measuring rod, and that's good.

SOUL SEARCH

May I never lose sight of where I would be heading without the Savior.

Father, I am at a loss of words for what you did at the cross.

God's Will and Ours

But why do you call Me "Lord, Lord,"
and not do the things which I say?
LUKE 6:46

It has been said of Judas Iscariot that he never called Jesus "Lord." He merely referenced Him as a teacher. John 12:6 also says that Judas stole from the collection bag. He had been trusted as the disciples' treasurer, yet he ruthlessly stole money from their savings. He was a thief and a hypocrite.

When we convert to Christ, God's will becomes ours. We call Jesus "Lord," not only because He is the Lord of creation, but because He is Lord over our lives, and we are responsible to Him for every thought, word, and deed.

However, there are many who profess godliness but deny Him by their works. They will be part of that great multitude that will cry out to Jesus on the day of judgment, "Lord, Lord," and hear the terrifying words, "I never knew you; depart from Me you who practice lawlessness!" (Matthew 7:21–23).

Such thoughts should put the fear of God in each of us, which is the beginning of wisdom.

SOUL SEARCH

Is Jesus Lord over everything in my life? What areas do I need to surrender?

Father, today I give my all to you.

Wise Building

*Whoever comes to Me, and hears My sayings and does them,
I will show you whom he is like: He is like a man building
a house, who dug deep and laid the foundation on the rock.
And when the flood arose, the stream beat vehemently
against that house, and could not shake it, for it was founded
on the rock.*

Luke 6:47–48

There are three steps to being a wise builder. We are to come to Jesus, hear His sayings, and we are to do them. The door of salvation hinges upon obedience. We are saved by grace through faith alone, and the fruit of our salvation will be obedience because now we have a desire to walk in His statutes. This is the message of the new covenant.

Those who are soundly born again delight to do God's will. It is preeminent. They seek first the kingdom of God and His righteousness (Matthew 6:33); they build their lives upon the solid rock of the teachings of Jesus Christ (Matthew 7:24). And when the ultimate storm comes, they stand firm in Christ.

SOUL SEARCH

Do I obey God's Word, or are there some areas of secret disobedience?

Father, I want to delight to do your will. Help me to always be obedient.

Watch for the Curveball

But he who heard, and did nothing is like a man that built a house on the earth without a foundation, against which the stream beat vehemently, and immediately it fell. And the ruin of that house was great.

LUKE 6:49

Many come to Jesus at emotional and manipulative altar calls. They hear but don't obey. We can be tempted to think that these verses of warning are speaking to hardened unbelievers. But they are directed toward those who hear the sayings of Jesus but don't have an obedient heart.

It makes sense to build a house on the earth because the earth is unmovable. However, in this case, water forcibly beat upon the house, and it collapsed.

Tribulation often comes to us as a curveball and reveals our vulnerability, despite our efforts to fortify ourselves against unexpected storms. That's why we must always and only build our lives on the solid rock of Jesus Christ and His wonderful teachings.

SOUL SEARCH

Have I truly built my life on the teachings of Jesus? How am I practically doing that today?

Father, search out any hidden motives or self-deception of secret sins.

Faith Pleases God

I say to you,
I have not found such great faith,
not even in Israel!

LUKE 7:9

It's a good feeling to know that we can be trusted. Someone having faith in us makes us feel good. But in this verse we see an amazing thing. This man's childlike faith made Jesus rejoice.

Jesus marveled at the faith that this man had in Him. Imagine that! Almighty God manifest in human form was marveling at the faith of this mere man.

The Bible says without faith it is impossible to please God (Hebrews 11:6). The inference is that we can please God with our faith . . . and that's what we see happening in this passage of Scripture. Every time we pray a believing prayer, we are exercising faith. Every time we share the gospel with an unsaved person, we are trusting in God to make our words come alive and the sinner receptive. God has left the marvelous door open for us to step through, if we want to.

SOUL SEARCH

In what ways can I exercise faith in God today?

Father, may I never insult you with my unbelief.

We Don't React Like This World

Do not weep.
LUKE 7:13

Could there possibly be a more sorrowful sight than a woman who has lost both her husband and only son? This mother's grief was real and deep.

When someone is grieving, it is rather insensitive to tell them not to cry. This woman had reason to weep. Mourning is natural in the face of death; tears can help release the pain. Yet Jesus said, "Weep not."

We know why. Jesus planned to deliver this young man from death and the widow would be weeping no longer. Death, our greatest enemy, immediately bowed its cold knee to the power of His Word.

As Christians, we don't grieve at the death of those we love as the world does. Heaven rejoices at the death of His saints and so with living hope, we can say with the apostle Paul, "O Death, where is your sting!" (1 Corinthians 15:55).

What unspeakably good news we have for this dying world.

SOUL SEARCH

Do I rejoice in the fact that in Christ, death has lost its sting? Is my faith ready for the day when it's my turn to meet the Lord?

Father, thank you for the incredible victory we have over the power of death.

Nowhere Else to Go

Young man, I say to you, arise.
LUKE 7:14

When Israel was trapped at the Red Sea with Egypt biting at their heels, they had nowhere to go but to God. Moses said, "Stand still, and see the salvation of the Lord" (Exodus 14:13).

When it comes to death, we have nowhere to go but to God. Peter once said to Jesus that he had nowhere else to go because Jesus alone had the words of eternal life (John 6:68). No religion or religious leader has ever spoken even one word like Jesus. And so we stand still before Him.

When Jesus touched the casket, those carrying it stood still, and we must do the same in order to be saved from death. We are at the end of our rope with nowhere else to go and nothing we can do to save ourselves. It's only the grace of God (without works) that can rescue us from death's terrible power. And it is His grace that is sufficient to deliver us from our greatest enemy.

SOUL SEARCH

Do I ever stand still before God? Today I will do that. I will calm my mind and think of His love and power.

Father, may I never panic when things go wrong. Help me to still my heart before you.

The Nature of Repentance

Woe to you, Chorazin! Woe to you, Bethsaida! For if the mighty works which were done in you had been done in Tyre and Sidon, they would have repented long ago in sackcloth and ashes.

MATTHEW 11:21

There are those who say that they do not need to preach repentance because the Bible speaks of sinners simply believing in Jesus to be saved. However, the verses that speak only of belief are qualified by other verses that tell us to preach both "repentance unto life" and faith (Acts 11:18 KJV). Charles Spurgeon said, "Repentance is a hatred of sin; it is a turning from sin and a determination in the strength of God to forsake it."

How can any sinner have assurance of salvation if he is still serving sin? The Bible says, "Let the wicked forsake his way, and the unrighteous man his thoughts; let him return to the LORD, and He will have mercy on him" (Isaiah 55:7). That's the nature of repentance—having a change of mind about sin, then a change of direction from sin to Christ. Jesus said that if the cities of Tyre and Sidon had seen His miracles, they would have repented of their sins and (it is inferred) found forgiveness of sins.

SOUL SEARCH

When I find sin in my heart, how do I react? Do I take time to repent?

Father, let me always be quick to detect and forsake sin. Never let me be deceived by its subtleties.

True Justice

But I say to you, it will be more tolerable for Tyre and Sidon in the day of judgment than for you. And you, Capernaum, who are exalted to heaven, will be brought down to Hades; for if the mighty works which were done in you had been done in Sodom, it would have remained until this day.

MATTHEW 11:22–23

One of the major objections of modern skeptics is that God is unjust. They maintain that He is evil in sending a sweet little old lady and a mass murderer to the same place. And so they dismiss our warnings about hell as being incompatible with justice.

But here Jesus speaks of it being more tolerable for Tyre and Sidon than for Capernaum. In other words, there will be degrees of justice on judgment day. How could it be any other way? It's ludicrous to think that God will be unjust in the slightest. All His judgments will be righteous and true altogether. Despite that fact, the most tolerable place in hell will be a horror beyond words. It is better to cut off a hand or pull out an eye than to end up there (Matthew 5:30).

SOUL SEARCH

Do I rest in the fact that God is always right in His judgments?

Father, nothing you do worries me. I have complete confidence in your perfect integrity.

No Longer Called Sin

But I say to you that it shall be more tolerable for the land of Sodom in the day of judgment than for you.
MATTHEW 11:24

There was a time when homosexuality was called "sodomy," named after the city of Sodom—a city that came under God's wrath for its homosexual activity. But the sin is now called "gay" and is no longer frowned upon by the world.

The question arises, how do we share the gospel with a person who is struggling with same-sex attraction without getting into hot water? The answer is simple. First Timothy 1:8–10 tells us that the moral Law (the Ten Commandments) was made for all sinners, including those who practice homosexuality. When you meet people who say they are gay, I suggest you dismiss that bit of information and don't address this topic deliberately. Instead, take them through the Ten Commandments. Show them that we are condemned for lying, stealing, blasphemy, and lust. Lovingly show them that they are justly under God's wrath and heading for hell, whatever their particular sexual orientation. Preach Christ crucified and the necessity of repenting of all sin. Then leave the rest up to God. When that person becomes a new creature in Christ, old things will pass away and things will become new (2 Corinthians 5:17).

SOUL SEARCH

Am I confident that I could lovingly share the gospel with people who struggle with same-sex attraction? What can I do to prepare for the opportunity when it comes?

Father, help me to honor all people as your Word instructs us.

As Little Children

I thank You, Father, Lord of heaven and earth, that You have hidden these things from the wise and prudent and have revealed them to babes. Even so, Father, for so it seemed good in Your sight.

MATTHEW 11:25–26

When a lightning storm comes, experts tell us to get as low to the ground as we can. Similarly, we are all in the lightning storm of God's just wrath, and the only way to survive is to get low to the ground. Humble yourself. God resists the proud and gives grace to the humble.

God has also chosen foolish things to confound the wise of this world. He put foolish sounding stories in the Bible to confound the arrogant ungodly—stories that are similar to the story of Cinderella and her pumpkin coach. Consider these: A serpent talks to Eve, Joshua stops the sun, the children of Israel shout until the walls of Jericho come down, Jonah is swallowed by a big fish, Noah builds an ark, and a donkey speaks. These are certainly bizarre stories, and who (with any intellectual dignity) would ever stoop to believe them? Only the humble of heart, and therein is the wonderful wisdom of God. He set the door of salvation very low.

SOUL SEARCH

Am I embarrassed to say that I believe the stories of the Bible? Why?

Father, help me to be as a little child and walk in humility of heart.

One of the Biggest

All things have been delivered to Me by My Father, and no one knows the Son except the Father. Nor does anyone know the Father except the Son, and the one to whom the Son wills to reveal Him.

MATTHEW 11:27

"All" is one of the biggest words in the English language—right up there with "everything." God delivered all things to the Son. Everything. Not an atom in the universe was kept from Him because before the incarnation, Jesus made all things. John said that without Him, "nothing was made that was made" (John 1:3).

Jesus was eternally preexistent before the incarnation. He always existed with the Father. He knows the Father, and the Father knows Him.

While billions profess to know God and speak to Him daily through prayer, we only know Him intimately by going through the Son. John 14:21 speaks of this intimate relationship: "He who has My commandments and keeps them, it is he who loves Me. And he who loves Me will be loved by My Father, and I will love him and manifest Myself to him."

SOUL SEARCH

Do I know that I know Him because He has made me a new creature in Christ?

Father, I long to see you face to face.

Roses and Thorns

Come to Me, all you who labor and are heavy laden, and I will give you rest. Take My yoke upon you and learn from Me, for I am gentle and lowly in heart, and you will find rest for your souls. For My yoke is easy and My burden is light.

MATTHEW 11:28–30

This Bible verse is often interpreted to mean that Jesus will take all of our problems and give us a trouble-free life—a bed of roses without thorns. However, the Christian life is not trouble-free. Acts 14:22 says that we enter the kingdom of God through much tribulation. There are many sharp thorns along with the roses. Jesus is saying that when we come to Him heavy laden with the weight of our own sins, He gives us rest. We enter into a rest from our labors: "For he who has entered His rest has himself also ceased from his works as God did from His" (Hebrews 4:10).

No longer is the heavy weight of the Law on our shoulders as we strive to earn our way to heaven. Instead, we find that salvation is the free gift of God, and that every sin is cast as far as the east is from the west (Psalm 103:12). This is the way God demonstrates his kindness and mercy.

SOUL SEARCH

Today I will meditate on the fact that eternal life is the free gift of God. I will think of those who are tormented by fear and guilt because they don't know the truth of the gospel.

Father, burden me with the millions of unsaved. Give me no rest until my life is only about reaching them with the gospel.

Tell the Things

Go and tell John the things you have seen and heard: that the blind see, the lame walk, the lepers are cleansed, the deaf hear, the dead are raised, the poor have the gospel preached to them.

LUKE 7:22

What a joy it would have been to be alive during the time of Christ and to actually see those wonderful miracles. However, the experience of seeing the miraculous does little to overcome the power of sin or to give us the power and courage to proclaim the gospel.

The disciples had seen Jesus raise the dead, walk on water, multiply bread and fish, give sight to the blind, and open deaf ears. Yet they still deserted Jesus in the garden of Gethsemane. Until the new birth, our understanding is darkened, and we are alienated from the life of God through the ignorance that is in us because of the blindness of our hearts (Ephesians 4:18). Until that time, we are spiritually blind, lame, deaf, dead in our trespasses and sins, and in deep spiritual poverty. That's why we need to hear the gospel and come to Jesus.

SOUL SEARCH

Do I see the world's pains as rooted in the spiritual realm?

Father, use me today to minister to a lost soul.

His Name

And blessed is he who is not offended because of Me.
LUKE 7:23

No other human being in history has had his or her name adopted as a cuss word. Only Jesus. The name of Jesus is unique. It is so offensive to a sinful world that it uses His name to express disgust without a second thought. It rolls off their evil tongues as meaningless—not worthy of the slightest honor.

When asked why they would do such a thing, people often try and excuse themselves by saying that they don't realize they are doing it. His precious name means nothing to them. That's what it means to take it in vain—it is counted as worthless.

The person of Jesus is offensive to the lawless in the same way the police are offensive to the criminal world.

But, by the grace of God, we are blessed in Him. He mercifully saved us, washed us of our sins, and granted us everlasting life.

SOUL SEARCH

May I forever honor Jesus Christ as the name above all names.

Father, forgive this evil world. They know not what they do. Have mercy on them as you did on me.

Be the Same

What did you go out into the wilderness to see? A reed shaken by the wind? But what did you go out to see? A man clothed in soft garments? Indeed those who are gorgeously appareled and live in luxury are in kings' courts.

LUKE 7:24–25

Not many people crowd around to look at a reed shaking in the wind. It doesn't exactly catch the eye. Both reeds and wind are commonplace. Like Jesus, John the Baptist had nothing that was attractive to the natural eye (Isaiah 53:2). He wasn't clothed in fine garments. He didn't live in kings' courts. He was in the hot and dry desert, clothed in rough and common camel hair.

However, he was possessed by the urgent message to the world that a Messiah was coming. He was preparing the way for the One who was to bring salvation to dying humanity. He was just the voice of one crying in the wilderness (John 1:23), a burning and shining light in a dark world. We are called to be the same.

SOUL SEARCH

Is my highest purpose in life to point sinners to the Savior? Is there something I consider to be more immediately important?

Father, help me to shine in this dark world.

More Than a Prophet

But what did you go out to see? A prophet?
Yes, I say to you, and more than a prophet.
LUKE 7:26

In the Old Testament, prophets were used by God to bring particular messages to Israel at particular times. Often they called Israel to repentance because the people had forsaken God's Law and given themselves to sin. God also used prophets to speak about future events and prophesy specifically of the coming Messiah who would destroy the power of the grave.

John the Baptist was certainly a prophet—he did all those things. But Jesus said that he was more than a prophet. He was a lighthouse in a dark and dreadful storm, pointing lost sinners in the right direction—a lone voice in the wilderness telling those in danger to "prepare the way of the Lord" (Luke 3:4). He was to make His path straight. John was the forerunner to the Messiah, preparing Israel for the Lamb of God.

With the help of God, we are to prepare the world for the roaring Lion.

SOUL SEARCH

When did I last share the gospel with an unsaved person? What happened?

Father, let my priorities be the same as yours.

May

Mountain Movers

This is he of whom it is written:
"Behold, I send My messenger before Your face,
who will prepare Your way before You."

LUKE 7:27

God Himself told the Messiah through the prophet that He would send a messenger to go before Him and prepare the way. He was speaking of John the Baptist.

John prepared the way by specifically calling Israel to repentance. He said that the crowds were to make every path straight—every mountain was to be brought low, and every valley was to be filled. In other words, human beings should not let anything, whether it is a mountain or a valley, stop them from coming to Jesus Christ.

Atheism is a mountain. So is self-righteousness and religious works. We need to learn how to use the dynamite of God's Law to move those mountains. The Law in the hand of the Holy Spirit says, "Be removed and be cast into the sea" (Matthew 21:21).

A looming eternity should make every mountain an immediate molehill. There's nothing more important than our eternal salvation.

SOUL SEARCH

Do I intercede for the lost, or are my prayers mostly about myself?

Father, help me to see this world through your pure and compassionate eyes.

The Greatest Prophet

For I say to you, among those born of women there is not a greater prophet than John the Baptist; but he who is least in the kingdom of God is greater than he.

LUKE 7:28

Jesus called John the Baptist the greatest of all the prophets. He was greater than the great Moses, Abraham, Elijah, Isaiah, David, and all those whom God chose to bring a divine message to Israel.

In the eyes of the world, John the Baptist was no more than a homeless raving lunatic—a wild man living in the desert, clothed in animal skins, and eating strange foods. But he was chosen by God to be a special messenger. He had the smile of His Creator because he was faithful to his calling.

The world thinks that Christians are weirdos and laughs at what we believe about God. But we bear the reproach of Christ gladly and pray that we will be faithful in the desert in which we have been placed.

SOUL SEARCH

Am I faithful to my calling?

Father, help me to number my days and to use my time wisely.

Childish Children

*To what then shall I liken the men of this generation,
and what are they like? They are like children sitting in the
marketplace and calling to one another, saying:
"We played the flute for you,
And you did not dance;
We mourned to you,
And you did not weep."*

LUKE 7:31-32

Jesus likened His generation to children. Children believe anything, and they are infantile in their understanding.

We live in a generation that believes anything as long as it's not in the Bible. They are a generation that is wise in their own eyes but very shallow and infantile in their understanding of things that matter. They give little thought to God and even less thought to their eternity.

This is why we must confront them. We have to take the gospel to them as we've been told to (Mark 16:15). We need to love them and pray that our words will bring a sense of sobriety to this careless generation.

SOUL SEARCH

Have I ever done a study on how to reach the lost? Would now be a good time to start?

Father, give me the wisdom and the will to reach out to the unsaved.

Overzealous Ref

For John the Baptist came neither eating bread nor drinking wine, and you say, "He has a demon." The Son of Man has come eating and drinking, and you say, "Look, a glutton and a winebibber, a friend of tax collectors and sinners!" But wisdom is justified by all her children.

LUKE 7:33–35

The Bible calls Satan the "accuser of the brethren" (Revelation 12:7–12), and he has many a willing mouthpiece in the world. People are quick to accuse believers of the slightest of sins. They accused John the Baptist of being demon possessed because he didn't drink wine, and if he had drunk wine, they would have accused him of being a wino.

Some people are like an overzealous referee. They run around blowing their little whistles, pointing their fingers when they see what they think is a transgression, and insisting on some sort of penalty. People accused Jesus of all sorts of sin as well, and they will do the same with any Christian. We should never be surprised or discouraged when this happens.

SOUL SEARCH

Am I thin-skinned when judged by the world? How can I thicken my skin?

Father, help me try to be blameless in the eyes of this world for the sake of the gospel.

To the Pure

Simon, I have something to say to you.
LUKE 7:40

A woman who had a bad reputation was washing Jesus' feet. Simon, the dinner's host, reacted like any normal man would. If Jesus was surely a prophet, wouldn't he know that this woman was a sinner? What he didn't understand was that Jesus was without sin—His heart was pure. The Bible says, "To the pure, all things are pure" (Titus 1:15).

When Jesus said to Simon, "I have something to say to you," Simon had the wisdom to respond, "Master, say on."

God knows our deepest thoughts as well as our hidden motives, and when He speaks, we need to have the good sense to say, "Master, say on." It is with this attitude that we open the Word of God. We want God to speak to us, even if it's a loving rebuke. That should be the attitude of any who profess to be servants of God. We need to willingly listen to what His Word says to our hearts, which is proof of our regeneration. John Wesley said, "I have seen (as far as it can be seen) many persons changed in a moment from the spirit of horror, fear, and despair to the spirit of hope, joy, peace; and from sinful desires till then reigning over them, to a pure desire of doing the will of God."[2]

SOUL SEARCH

Am I eager to hear God's voice through His Word? Do I spend time listening?

Father, help me to have the willing ear of a servant.

Those Who Love Much

There was a certain creditor who had two debtors. One owed five hundred denarii, and the other fifty. And when they had nothing with which to repay, he freely forgave them both. Tell Me, therefore, which of them will love him more?

LUKE 7:41–42

Jesus was speaking about those who have a deep love for God—those who understand how much they've been forgiven in Christ. Others have a shallow love for God because they haven't seen the depth of their sin and grasped the fact that even though they are worthy of hell, God has given them heaven.

This brings us back to the purpose of the moral Law. When it's not used to bring the knowledge of sin, showing it to be exceedingly sinful (Romans 3:19–20; 7:7, 13), the professed convert does not see his moral depravity.

Those who lack enough love to reach out to the lost need to get on their knees and ask God for a revelation of their own sinful state. Only then will they grasp the depth of the love and mercy of God shown at Calvary's cross.

SOUL SEARCH

Do I appreciate how much I have been forgiven? Think about what your life used to be like when you were headed in the wrong direction.

Father, show me the true depth of my sin.

The Sacrifices of God

Do you see this woman? I entered your house; you gave Me no water for My feet, but she has washed My feet with her tears and wiped them with the hair of her head. You gave Me no kiss, but this woman has not ceased to kiss My feet since the time I came in.

LUKE 7:44–45

An ocean of religious works is nothing compared to one teardrop of contrition. This sinful woman had tears of contrition in her eyes because she knew that she had sinned against God.

Genuine remorse is what impresses heaven. The Bible says the sacrifices of God are a broken spirit and a contrite heart (Psalm 51:17). The way to find a place of contrition is by comparing yourself to the life and character of the Son of God. We all fall so far short of Jesus' perfect righteousness and will never measure up. That's why we need His everlasting mercy.

SOUL SEARCH

Am I a stranger to a contrite heart? Have I ever shed a tear for my sinful condition and for the mercy shown to me in Christ?

Father, help me to see Jesus in His wonderful purity.

Great Mercy

*Therefore I say to you, her sins, which are many,
are forgiven, for she loved much. But to whom little
is forgiven, the same loves little.*

LUKE 7:47

This verse tells us that Jesus was well aware of this woman's sins—He said that they were many.

Most of us tend to trivialize our sins or desperately hide them under a cloak of proud self-righteousness. But nothing is hidden from the pure and holy eyes of our Creator (Proverbs 15:3). God sees every secret transgression, and even the best of us have a multitude of sins, each one calling for the wrath of God's justice to fall.

This sinful woman wasn't forgiven because she had great love. She was forgiven because of God's great mercy and love. Her gratitude and love spilled out through her tears as she worshipped her Savior.

SOUL SEARCH

Are there sins in my life I trivialize or try to hide?

Father, may my love and gratitude match your mercy.

The Done Deal

Your sins are forgiven.
LUKE 7:48

Here we have evidence of the deity of Jesus of Nazareth. No one can forgive sins but God. Yet Jesus said to her, "Your sins are forgiven." He used the present tense—your sins are forgiven. It was a done deal.

We can't really comprehend the eternal implications of the moment we put our faith in Jesus, at least this side of eternity. It was a definite point in time where God legally allowed the guilty and condemned criminal to live. He commuted the death sentence and granted instead everlasting life. As finite beings, it is difficult to wrap our small minds around such an incredibly great and wonderful truth.

When Jesus cried "It is finished" (John 19:30), the debt had been paid for the sin of the Adamic race, and a new world was opened for dying humanity.

SOUL SEARCH

Am I ready to shout the gospel from the housetops, or am I secretly hiding in the basement?

Father, make me bold.

Peace with God

Your faith has saved you. Go in peace.
LUKE 7:50

While it is faith that saves us, it only saves us because of grace. Grace is the vehicle through which faith arrives. We are saved by grace through faith, not of works (Ephesians 2:8).

If somebody graciously gave you his life-saving parachute knowing that he himself would perish, the parachute is the means by which you are saved—but it came by the graceful hand of the person who sacrificed his life for you.

The Bible says grace came by Jesus Christ: "For the law was given through Moses, but grace and truth came through Jesus Christ" (John 1:17).

It was on the cross that God displayed His fathomless love for guilty sinners. So when we come to Jesus Christ, our faith saves us. We can go in peace because we have two types of peace—the peace that surpasses all understanding and peace with our Creator.

SOUL SEARCH

Have I the peace of God and peace with God? Has faith saved me? Do I testify to this to the unsaved?

Father, thank you for the blood of the cross.

The Seed of a Woman

A sower went out to sow his seed. And as he sowed, some fell by the wayside; and it was trampled down, and the birds of the air devoured it.

LUKE 8:5

Seed is first mentioned way back in the book of Genesis (1:29). God created a seed to be planted and to bring forth fruit after its own kind. We tend to take seed for granted. But it is miraculous that something so tiny could grow into something as massive as a tree. You and I exist because our parents joyfully planted a tiny seed.

All around us we see the genius of God's creative hand, and almost all life traces itself back to the soil.

The seed finds sustenance in the earth, grows, and bears fruit. God created man from the same dust of the earth, and to the earth he returns when he dies.

How terribly depressing life would be if Jesus hadn't been born of the seed of a woman. His life gives us eternal life, and even though our body dies, the Christian truly lives on. Our souls are eternal, and thanks be to God, they are preserved in Jesus Christ.

SOUL SEARCH

May I remember today that I am but dust and appreciate that God showed His love for me at the cross.

Father, thank you for giving me life.

Heart of Stone

Some fell on rock; and as soon as it sprang up,
it withered away because it lacked moisture.

LUKE 8:6

In the Bible, the human heart is often likened to stone (Ezekiel 26:36). Without the grace of God working in our hearts, we remain cold and selfish. We have little concern for others unless there is something to be gained personally. We fall far short of loving God with all of our heart, mind, soul, and strength, even though He gave us life and every good thing we have.

But when the kindness of God turned us from our own way and His love entered our lives, our hearts were softened toward those who face the terrible fate of death in their sins.

Through the new birth, God removes our heart of stone, and gives us a heart of flesh, making it possible for us to supernaturally love Him with all of our heart, mind, soul, and strength, and love our neighbor as ourselves.

SOUL SEARCH

Has my stony heart been replaced with a heart of flesh? How should that affect my interactions with others today?

Father, I love you and ask that you help me to love others
unconditionally.

Useless Weeds

And some fell among thorns,
and the thorns sprang up with it and choked it.
LUKE 8:7

Weeds need very little water to survive and seemingly don't need nutrients that other plants do. They burst forth through the soil like there is no tomorrow, and they choke anything in their way. They even push their way through tiny cracks in concrete and survive the heat of summer.

We know that they are part of the Genesis curse (3:18) because they are intent on choking healthy plants around them. They seem to us good for nothing except to show how fast and furious they can grow. Won't it be wonderful when the curse on the earth is lifted?

We can only begin to imagine how fruit-bearing plants will flourish then. What a wonderful hope for the future we have because we trust in God's mercy. May every cursed weed we see remind us of that glorious hope.

SOUL SEARCH

Is my life like a weed or a fruit-bearing plant?

Father, thank you for the future hope you have given us in Christ.

True and False

But others fell on good ground, sprang up, and yielded a crop a hundredfold. . . . He who has ears to hear, let him hear!

LUKE 8:8

It's a little strange to say, "He who has ears to hear, let him hear." Surely if people have ears, they should be able to hear. But it would seem that Jesus was speaking of understanding what they heard. Hearing doesn't automatically mean that we understand. Jesus told His disciples to let certain truths sink down into their ears (Luke 9:44).

The parable of the sower is the key that unlocks the mysteries of all the other parables. Once we understand that there are true and false conversions when the gospel is preached, then all the other parables—the sheep and goats, good and bad fish, the wheat and tares, and so on—begin to make sense. Such an understanding helps us to see why every church has its own struggles—murmurers, complainers, gossipers, or those resistant to evangelism. The false sit alongside the true and will be sorted out on judgment day.

SOUL SEARCH

Do I have ears that hear the Word of God? How does that play out as I read the Scriptures?

Father, may my ear always be toward heaven.

The Mystery

*To you it has been given to know the mysteries of the
kingdom of God, but to the rest it is given in parables, that
"Seeing they may not see,
And hearing they may not understand."*

LUKE 8:10

This statement was Jesus' answer to the disciple's question about
the meaning of the parable of the sower.

He said that the mysteries of the kingdom of God are hidden
from the world. The god of this world has blinded the minds of
those who do not believe. They remain willfully ignorant of the
truth, but God has promised that if we seek Him with our whole
hearts, we will surely find Him: "And you will seek Me and find Me,
when you search for Me with all your heart" (Jeremiah 29:13).

The moment any blind sinner calls upon the name of the
Lord, God (by His grace) opens the sinner's understanding to the
mystery of the gospel—which is Christ in us, the hope of glory
(Colossians 1:27). The new birth takes a sinner from darkness
into light.

SOUL SEARCH

Do I grasp the awesome truth that Jesus Christ in me, my
hope of glory?

*Father, may Christ in me be evident today in some way to this lost
world.*

The Life-Giving Seed

Now the parable is this: The seed is the word of God.
LUKE 8:11

In the beginning, in the first book of Genesis, the Word of God brought life as we know it into being. God said, "Let there be light" (1:3). And it is the seed of the Word of God that brings eternal life to dying sinners. When Lazarus heard the Word from the mouth of the Son of God, four days dead, he came out of the grave. The seed of the Word brought forth life.

We tend to see seeds as being lifeless, but when they are placed in soil and watered, what seems to be dead suddenly comes to life.

When the seed of the Word of God finds root in the good soil of an honest heart and is watered by the conviction of the Holy Spirit, eternal life is germinated. That is the new birth of which Jesus spoke in John 3:1–5.

SOUL SEARCH

Has the Word of God found root in my heart? How did it change my life?

Father, thank you for giving me a new beginning.

The Reason

Those by the wayside are the ones who hear; then the devil comes and takes away the word out of their hearts, lest they should believe and be saved.

LUKE 8:12

Disinterested sinners don't value the gospel when they hear it, so the devil is able to take the word out of their hearts. The gospel has not captured their attention, and therefore they give it no thought. A parachute is of little value to someone who doesn't believe that they have to jump ten thousand feet. But those who know they are in danger will greatly value the parachute because it will save their lives.

This is why it is essential to preach future punishment according to the Law. God commands all men everywhere to repent because He has appointed a day in which He will judge the world in righteousness (Acts 17:30). It is because of God's holiness and His love of justice that each of us needs a savior.

Those who understand and believe will embrace Jesus Christ for the sake of their very lives.

SOUL SEARCH

What part of the gospel message captured my heart?

Father, please help me to hold onto your every word.

Things That Accompany Salvation

But the ones that fell on the good ground are those who,
having heard the word with a noble and good heart,
keep it and bear fruit with patience.

LUKE 8:15

We know that the Bible says there is no one who is good
(Romans 3:10–18). No one is morally perfect in God's holy eyes.
We all fall desperately short of the standard He requires. But here
we see that the ones with the good soil receive the Word with an
honest and good heart. This doesn't mean that the soil here is
morally perfect. It means that under the light of God's Law, they
are honest about their sins. They no longer run away from God
and hide in the dark like Adam did. Rather they come out into
the light, confess, and forsake their sins.

God's Law plows the soil of the human heart so that it is able
to hear and understand the Word, which brings forth *fruit* worthy of repentance. These are the things that accompany salvation
(Hebrews 6:9–12).

SOUL SEARCH

Do I have the "things that accompany salvation"? What things
are these?

Father, help me to value the depth of my salvation and give me a
passion for the salvation of others.

Sobering Responsibility

*No one, when he has lit a lamp, covers it with a vessel,
or puts it under a bed, but sets it on a lampstand,
that those who enter may see the light.*

LUKE 8:16

The story is told of a lighthouse keeper who kindly gave away much of his oil to a desperate ship. They were in need, and he graciously helped them.

Unfortunately for him, a great storm arose, and he ran out of oil for his own lighthouse. It was because his light went out that a ship ran aground, and many lives were lost.

When sentencing him to prison, the judge spoke of the lighthouse keeper's kindness in helping that desperate ship, but also of his irresponsibility in failing to keep his own light shining.

We must never be so misguided as to let our lights go out because we are involved in other legitimate works. We must be faithful and shine the glorious light of the gospel for those who sit in the shadow of death and are in the greatest of dangers.

SOUL SEARCH

Am I living to let my light be seen by the unsaved?

Father, help me to be a light in this dark world.

Dirty Old Dirt

*The kingdom of God is as if a man should scatter seed on the
ground, and should sleep by night and rise by day, and the seed
should sprout and grow, he himself does not know how. For
the earth yields crops by itself: first the blade, then the head,
after that the full grain in the head. But when the grain ripens,
immediately he puts in the sickle, because the harvest has come.*

MARK 4:26–29

We not only take the miracle of seed for granted, we take soil for
granted also. We call it "dirt" and trample it under our feet. Think
about it for a minute. The soil miraculously gives us our food. It
nourishes the seeds and makes them grow into trees that bear
fruit. It causes the grass to grow, which provides food for cows,
who turn it into milk, which can be turned into cheese, churned
into butter, yogurt, and ice cream. It yields corn, from which
comes syrups, cereals, and bread. Jesus said that nobody knows
how a seed sprouts and grows. That was two thousand years ago,
and this miracle of life is still a great mystery.

SOUL SEARCH

Do I tend to take so much of this life for granted, or do I see
everything around me as a miracle?

Father, open my eyes wide this day, please.

Genuine and False

The kingdom of heaven is like a man who sowed good seed in his field; but while men slept, his enemy came and sowed tares among the wheat and went his way. But when the grain had sprouted and produced a crop, then the tares also appeared. So the servants of the owner came and said to him, "Sir, did you not sow good seed in your field? How then does it have tares?" He said to them, "An enemy has done this." The servants said to him, "Do you want us then to go and gather them up?" But he said, "No, lest while you gather up the tares you also uproot the wheat with them. Let both grow together until the harvest, and at the time of harvest I will say to the reapers, 'First gather together the tares and bind them in bundles to burn them, but gather the wheat into my barn.'"

MATTHEW 13:24–30

Here is the church—true and false converts sitting alongside one another until the fearsome Day of Judgment arrives when God will sort out the genuine from the false. It should make us tremble at such a thought. Fear is a friend if it brings us in genuine repentance to the foot of the cross: "By the fear of the Lord men depart from evil" (Proverbs 16:6).

SOUL SEARCH

Do I have a healthy fear of God? How will this be evidenced when I am tempted to sin?

Father, make me wise with my eyes.

Love of Justice

For nothing is secret that will not be revealed, nor anything hidden that will not be known and come to light.

LUKE 8:17

It is not only a foundational biblical doctrine that God is omniscient, but it's common sense. If God can make the eye, He can obviously see, and if He made the ear, He can hear. If He has seen and heard every crime against His Law, He must—if He is good (something we intuitively know)—bring every work to judgment. Think of it—nothing is secret. Sinners think that their sins are either not seen by God or that He sees and doesn't care. But He does care. He passionately cares about justice, and He will see to it that perfect justice will be done on the Day of Judgment.

This is what we must tell the ungodly, because as long as they hold on to their idolatry, they will have a false sense of security and won't see their need of the Savior.

This is what Paul did in Athens (Acts 17:22) when he said that God had winked at past sins, but now He commands all men everywhere to repent because He has appointed a day in which He will judge the world in righteousness.

SOUL SEARCH

Do I live with judgment day in mind? How does this play out daily?

Father, thank you for saving me from your wrath.

Within the Church

Therefore take heed how you hear. For whoever has, to him more will be given; and whoever does not have, even what he seems to have will be taken from him.

LUKE 8:18

There are many who sit within the Body of Christ who seem to be part of the true church. But they are like Judas, who seemed to be a genuine disciple. The problem they have is that they lack the things that accompany salvation. They don't have the evident fruits that they have passed from death to life.

These are false converts—goats among the sheep, foolish virgins among the wise, bad fish among the good, and tares among the wheat.

These professing Christians are the workers of iniquity of whom Jesus spoke, saying that there would be a great company who would cry out to him, "Lord, Lord," but He would say to them, "Depart from me, you workers of iniquity" (Luke 13:25–27). We need to examine ourselves and see if we are in faith. If we are not, then we should make our calling and election sure, today, because we may not have tomorrow.

SOUL SEARCH

Have I examined myself for biblical fruit to see if I'm in the faith? Is there any hypocrisy in my life?

Father, search me daily and show me if any secret sin has a place in my heart.

Let Them See

A prophet is not without honor except in his own country and in his own house.

MATTHEW 13:57

The religious leaders were amazed at the wisdom of Jesus. It had been evident even as a twelve-year-old when He spoke with the elders in the temple (Luke 2:41–52). But this Man wasn't just a wise man. Someone greater than Solomon was here (Luke 11:31). It was God manifest as a human being, and His words were with power—they were spirit and life. But instead of embracing Him as the Messiah, they hated him and rejected His words.

We often find the same thing with our loved ones. We are without honor in their eyes, and so they reject our words, much to our heartbreak. But God hasn't left them without a witness of some sort. When we can't reach those closest to us with our words, we can reach them with our works. If you want your loved ones to listen to your words, first let them see your works. Buy them gifts for no reason. Let them see your genuine love by your continual kindness, and your actions will speak louder than your words.

SOUL SEARCH

Is my invisible faith seen by my visible works?

Father, show me how I can show love for my loved ones.

They Are Ready

The harvest truly is plentiful, but the laborers are few.
MATTHEW 9:37

We may doubt that the harvest truly is plentiful, but it's not so difficult to believe that the laborers are few. Church outreach teams are often nonexistent. For whatever reason, we are hesitant to believe that there are masses of people in the world who are ready to be saved. It's true. All they need to know is that they have violated the moral Law and that God's wrath abides upon them. God has given us weapons of warfare that are not carnal but mighty through Him to the pulling down of strongholds (2 Corinthians 10:4).

Plead with God to make your words come alive, and then use the Law to bring the knowledge of sin. Jesus said they are ready. Believe Him. Don't wait. Do you sense the urgency? Every day people are dying in their sins, and when that happens, they will end up in hell. This fact should drive us to prayer and motivate our feet to take the gospel to this dying world while we still have time.

SOUL SEARCH

Do I believe that sinners are ready to come to the Savior and that all they need is the knowledge of sin for the gospel to make sense to them? Am I ready to share with them today?

Father, once again I ask you to replace my fear with your love.

Labor Shortage

Therefore pray the Lord of the harvest
to send out laborers into His harvest.
MATTHEW 9:38

The fields are ready for harvest, and we must pray for laborers. We are lacking workers. Ask those who are actively involved in evangelism, and they will tell you that this is true. It seems that almost everyone in the Body of Christ is busy doing everything but what we've been commanded to do—to go into all the world and preach the gospel to every creature (Mark 16:15).

It leaves us wondering what Bible they are reading or whether or not they truly believe its terrible warnings about hell. Or perhaps their image of God is wrong and they think that He is going to compromise on judgment day and let sin go unpunished.

It is because of the shortage of laborers that Jesus said "therefore." We should be praying to the Lord of the harvest to raise up more laborers.

SOUL SEARCH

When did I last obey the command of Jesus to pray for laborers?

Father, I plead with you today to raise up laborers. Use me to reach the lost.

The Name of Jesus

And blessed is he who is not offended because of Me.
MATTHEW 11:6

The beautiful name of Jesus is an offense to this God-hating world. How can that be? There has never been such a wonderful, kind, loving, and forgiving human being who walked on this earth.

Jesus told us what causes the offense. It's His words. He said, "The world cannot hate you, but it hates Me because I testify of it that its works are evil" (John 7:7). He spoke against their sins—adultery, lying, stealing, covetousness, hatred, murder, greed, and hypocrisy.

People are only offended at Jesus if His name is used in truth. It carries no offense if it is used in vain.

Police officers are murdered by criminals, not because of who they are, but because of what they stand for. They uphold what is right, good, and just, and that's the reason sinners hate the Savior. But blessed are those guilty sinners who are not offended because of Him.

SOUL SEARCH

Is the name of Jesus sweet to my ears? Am I overwhelmed by the love that was expressed at the cross? Do I show that I love Him by taking His love to the unsaved?

Father, keep my eyes on Jesus today in a world filled with distractions.

The Local Attraction

What did you go out into the wilderness to see? A reed shaken by the wind? But what did you go out to see? A man clothed in soft garments? Indeed, those who wear soft clothing are in kings' houses. But what did you go out to see? A prophet? Yes, I say to you, and more than a prophet. For this is he of whom it is written: "Behold, I send My messenger before Your face, who will prepare Your way before You."

MATTHEW 11:7–10

John the Baptist was a local attraction. He hit the Judean headlines, compelling the crowds out into a hot desert to see him and hear what he had to say. What they saw wasn't too impressive. He surely didn't dress very well. But what he said was impressive. He spoke with power and passion about the coming One, telling his hearers to prepare the way for the Lord's coming.

The church should be similar. We are not impressive, but our message certainly is. We proclaim the everlasting gospel—that Jesus Christ has abolished death and brought life and immortality to those who believe. May multitudes flock to hear that message!

SOUL SEARCH

Do I see how powerful the message is that God has entrusted us with? How has that same gospel transformed me?

Father, set me apart as you did John the Baptist.

Violent Sinners

Assuredly, I say to you, among those born of women there has not risen one greater than John the Baptist; but he who is least in the kingdom of heaven is greater than he. And from the days of John the Baptist until now the kingdom of heaven suffers violence, and the violent take it by force. For all the prophets and the law prophesied until John. And if you are willing to receive it, he is Elijah who is to come. He who has ears to hear, let him hear!

MATTHEW 11:11–15

What does it mean when Jesus said that the kingdom of heaven suffers violence? We don't see people violently trying to enter into the kingdom of God. If anything, we see apathy. Sinners are generally unconcerned about their eternal salvation.

The answer is in Jesus' words that follow: "For all the prophets and the law prophesied until John." In other words, the Law was doing its job in Israel. Multitudes were flocking to John to confess their sins and to be baptized. The Law brought the knowledge of sin and made them hunger and thirst after righteousness (Matthew 5:6). A man who doesn't believe he's drowning will not seek to be rescued. But if he understands that he is about to die, he will become desperate. May we see the day when sinners are desperate to be saved.

SOUL SEARCH

Is that my testimony? Did I call upon the name of the Lord, desperately crying out, "What must I do to be saved?" (Acts 16:30).

Father, this day I call upon you to not only save me, but to fill me with a love that will run after perishing sinners.

Childlike Faith

But to what shall I liken this generation? It is like children sitting in the marketplaces and calling to their companions.
MATTHEW 11:16

The Bible says that atheists profess to be wise, but in truth they are fools (Romans 1:22). They hide behind the skirts of science and look down their noses at those who see the genius of God's hand in His creation.

Believers become as little children in attitude. They are filled with wide-eyed awe and a childlike trust in the precious promises of our heavenly Father. But the atheists are childish in their understanding, clinging to silly theories, denying the obvious. They are like children in the marketplace who are only interested in having fun. They are children of wrath (Ephesians 2:3), and children of disobedience (Colossians 3:6).

Oh, how we must pray for them and reach out to them that they would come to their senses before God gives them their just deserts.

SOUL SEARCH

Am I childlike in my faith? Do I believe all the promises of God deep down in my heart?

Father, help me to have pure childlike trust in you today.

Just Do It

My mother and My brothers are these
who hear the word of God and do it.
LUKE 8:21

This was the opportunity for Jesus to put His blessing on the Roman Catholic doctrine concerning Mary. They believe that she was conceived without sin, that she remained a virgin (despite having other children, according to the Bible), that God took her into heaven, and that she is interceding for sinners.

But Jesus didn't teach that doctrine. He said, rather, that His mother and His brethren are those who hear the Word of God and do it. He included her with all ordinary believers. The Bible says that only God is to be worshiped. We are not to worship any other person living or dead.

Notice also that Jesus is once again saying (as He did many times) that it's not enough to simply hear the Word of God. It must be put into practice—hear the Word and "do it." Faith without works is dead. We know that there are batteries in the flashlight because the light shines. Obedience to the words of Jesus shines from a changed life.

SOUL SEARCH

Do I ever pay homage to anyone or anything other than God?

Father, you alone are the ultimate object of my affection and adoration. It was for you that I was created.

June

It Will Happen

Let us cross over to the other side of the lake.
LUKE 8:22

It is imperative that we know what God says in His Word so when storms come, we can stand on that word and have peace.

Jesus told His disciples that they were going to cross the lake to the other side. It was absolutely going to happen because God always gets His way. When He said, "Let there be light" (Genesis 1:3), light appeared—at the speed of light. When He told bread to multiply, bread did what it was told to do. The same with fish. Death bowed the knee to His Word. Had the disciples remembered that Jesus had said they were going to cross the lake and simply believed it, they would not have become fearful for their lives when a great storm arose.

The Word of God is full of exceedingly great and precious promises. If we're not aware of them (and believe them), when trials come our way, we will lose our peace. That's why we need to soak our souls in the Word of God daily and commit Scripture to memory.

SOUL SEARCH

Do I soak myself in God's Word each day? What was the last verse I memorized?

Father, help me to search your Word as one who seeks great treasure.

Face It with Faith

Where is your faith?
LUKE 8:25

Jesus asked His disciples this question because it was evident that the storm had terrified them. Jesus had told them they were going over to the other side of the lake. Had their faith been strong, it would have been evidenced by their peace in the middle of the storm.

It's the daily storms that come to us (both small and big) that test our faith. Our great consolation is that every storm that God allows to come our way works for our good if we love Him and are called according to His purposes (Romans 8:28). Therefore, peace should remain when trials come, and (because of Romans 8:28) we can even give thanks in the midst of them.

Those who know we are going through trials should be able to see the answer to the question, "Where is your faith?" Our faith should show on our faces. It should be seen in our eyes and heard from our lips. We all go though rough times, but we will get to the other side.

SOUL SEARCH

Is my heart fixed on God for the future? How can I fortify my faith in Him?

Father, help me to trust you in the storms.

Natural Concern

Return to your own house,
and tell what great things God has done for you.
LUKE 8:39

When we are first saved, we have a natural concern for those we love. We long for the opportunity to tell our unsaved family members about the great things that God has done for us. Not only has He given us life, but through the blood of the cross, He saved us from death. He has given us immortality through the light of the gospel.

This man in Luke 8 went further than just telling his own household about the great things God had done for him. The Bible says that he went to the whole city and shared the good news.

Speaking of the Savior, Charles Spurgeon said, "You want to honor Him, you desire to put many crowns upon His head, and this you can best do by winning souls for Him. These are the spoils that He covets, these are the trophies for which He fights, these are the jewels that shall be His best adornment."[3]

May we never become tired of telling dying sinners the great news of the cross and the glorious hope of everlasting life.

SOUL SEARCH

Do I have the zeal that I had when I first came to Christ?

Father, may I always hold on to my first love.

Texas Thunder

Do you believe that I am able to do this?
MATTHEW 9:28

Jesus asked the blind men if they had faith in Him. Did they believe He was able to open their eyes? Our faith in God will be in direct proportion to our understanding of His power. The world sees God as an elderly bearded man in the sky, reaching out his finger to touch Adam. But He is nothing like what we, in our foolish ignorance, conceive Him to be.

God is the Creator of the entire universe. When God opens our eyes and we finally see His awesome power, we should be left breathless and in awe. If we're not, we need to pray that God puts us in the center of a violent lightning storm in Texas (everything is big in Texas) so that the sound of thunder shakes our bones and the massive terrifying flashes of lightning put the fear of God in our hearts.

Did you know that lightning can get as hot as 60,000°F? That's hotter than the surface of the sun! God created every incredible streak of lightning. Every atom that holds it together was shaped by Him. Perhaps if we were caught in such a storm, we would get a slight understanding of how powerful our God is and never doubt His ability to do the impossible.

SOUL SEARCH

Do I need a terrifying thunderstorm in my life to help me fear God?

Father, smash erroneous thoughts that I have of you and replace them with the truth.

Our Unworthy Worth

Who touched Me?
LUKE 8:45

The whole crowd was pushing in to touch Jesus, and yet He said, "Who touched me?" God knows each of us as individuals, even though millions are reaching out to Him in prayer. We want to touch Him with our requests. He knows when we sit down, and He knows when we stand up. The Bible says that every hair on our heads is numbered by God, and sinful though we are, each of us is of great worth to Him.

How much are we worth in God's eyes? Look to the cross where the ultimate price was paid so we could spend eternity with Him. He wanted us to be with Him. He took on human form and was crucified for the sin of the world. While we are not worthy of our salvation, the cross proves our worth in His eyes and the depth of His love for us.

When He asked who it was who touched Him, the desperate woman stepped forward and confessed that it was she. And during that moment of contact, she was healed.

"Draw near to God and He will draw near to you" (James 4:8).

SOUL SEARCH

Do I realize God's personal love for me? How does knowing God loves me change my behavior?

Father, I am ever grateful for your personal love for me.

The Fullness of God

Somebody has touched Me:
for I perceive that virtue is gone out of Me.
LUKE 8:46

When Jesus walked among a crowd of people reaching out and touching him, he stopped and said, "Somebody has touched Me: for I perceive that virtue is gone out of Me."

Even though there was a multitude around Him, Jesus was aware of one individual person. The power of God flowed out of Him the moment she reached out and touched His robe. The same thing happened to us the moment we reached out in repentance and faith. The virtue of God flowed into us, and this is evidence that the fullness of God was in Jesus of Nazareth (Colossians 2:9). His miraculous life was without precedent. No other person in history had the virtue of God flow through them at someone else's touch!

Never let the cults or other religions tell you that Jesus was merely a prophet, a great teacher or *a* god. The Creator became a human being for the purpose of reconciling the world to Himself, and the day will come when every knee will bow to Jesus Christ as Lord of the universe.

SOUL SEARCH

Is Jesus the center of my Christian walk?

Father, thank you for bringing the light into my darkness.

Unconditional Invitation

Daughter, be of good cheer;
your faith has made you well.
Go in peace.
LUKE 8:48

Salvation comes to us when we reach out to touch the Lord. He promises that if we seek Him, we will find Him: "And you will seek Me and find Me, when you search for Me with all your heart" (Jeremiah 29:13).

God gives an open invitation to all of humanity when He promises, "Whoever calls on the name of the Lord shall be saved" (Romans 10:13). *Whoever* is without condition.

Just as this woman's disease caused her to reach out and touch the Savior, when we see the disease of sin in our own hearts, it causes us to reach out for the mercy that is in Christ alone.

In Jesus we find good comfort. In Him we find peace and rest for our souls. It is in Christ and Christ alone that we find wholeness.

Jesus told this woman to go in peace, and He tells us to go into all the world and preach this glorious gospel of peace to every creature.

SOUL SEARCH

Am I whole in Christ, or am I still craving for the things of this world?

Father, may the sunshine of your love be my light and life.

The Weight of Fear

Do not be afraid; only believe, and she will be made well.
LUKE 8:50

Jairus, ruler of the synagogue, was facing the most devastating situation any parent could ever face. This man's precious daughter was dead. It was all over. Hope was gone. Death had taken her.

Who of us would not feel the power of fear in such a hopeless situation? But Jesus said to him, "Do not be afraid; only believe, and she will be made well." Faith is the antidote to fear. Fear is like an elephant that sits on our shoulders suffocating and rendering us helpless. Faith, however, takes concerted effort. We have to shrug off the negative weight of fear from when we say, "I will not fear," and replace it with the positive, "I will trust in God!"

D. L. Moody rightly said, "Real true faith is man's weakness leaning on God's strength." When we fully trust in God's promises, we lean on God's strength to remove the elephant.

Little did this father know that the One who was speaking to him was "the resurrection and the life" (John 11:25)—the same One who spoke life into being in the very beginning.

SOUL SEARCH

When have I let fear steal my faith?

Father, help me to trust you in the tough times.

Delivered from Death

Do not weep; she is not dead, but sleeping.
LUKE 8:52

These words would have been nothing but a slap in the face to the grieving parent if Jesus had not been able to raise the child from the dead. He said she was just asleep. It was no big deal. He said a similar thing about Lazarus.

If Christianity can't deliver us from death, it's a slap in the face of all who hope in Jesus. But Jesus did deliver Lazarus and this little girl from death, and we have more than God's Word that He will deliver us from death's grip. We have been sealed with the Holy Spirit as a token of the surety of God's promise (Ephesians 1:3).

The Bible says of Jesus that death could not hold Him (Acts 2:24). Timothy said that Jesus Christ has abolished death in order to bring life and immortality to the world (2 Timothy 1:10). In the book of Revelation Jesus said, "I am He who lives and was dead, and behold I am alive forevermore. Amen. And I have the keys of Hades and of Death" (Revelation 1:18).

Truly, never a man spoke like this Man because there never was a man like this One. He confirmed His Word with power.

SOUL SEARCH

How would I behave in this dying world if I truly believed that Jesus Christ has abolished death?

Father, increase my love for the lost.

In His Hand

Little girl, arise.
LUKE 8:54

Christianity is unique among the religions in that it portrays the Creator as being gentle, loving, and kind. Jesus took her by the hand. The moment we come to Christ, He takes us by our hand and leads us on the path of righteousness. He is no longer our just enemy pointing His holy finger at our transgressions. Rather, He is our closest friend, one who guides us through our daily trials and tribulations:

> What a friend we have in Jesus,
> all our sins and griefs to bear!
> What a privilege to carry
> everything to God in prayer!
> O what peace we often forfeit,
> O what needless pain we bear,
> all because we do not carry
> everything to God in prayer![4]

The most consoling word in this tiny verse is that in Christ, God will also tell us to "Arise." Death could not hold Him, and it can no longer hold those asleep in Jesus because they belong to Him.

SOUL SEARCH

Is my hand purposefully in the hand of Jesus today?

Father, thank you for your gentleness with me.

Our Needs Will Be Supplied

Take nothing for the journey, neither staffs nor bag nor bread nor money; and do not have two tunics apiece.

LUKE 9:3

The Bible promises that God will supply all of our needs according to His riches in glory by Christ Jesus (Philippians 4:19).

Each of us is on the journey of a lifetime. During our lifetime we are going to have daily needs, and we have God's promise that He will take care of us if we seek first His kingdom and His righteousness (Matthew 6:33). Keep in mind that we are trusting God to give us only what we need. Sometimes He will withhold giving us something we think we need because (in His infinite wisdom) He knows that we don't need it. We merely want it.

In another passage, Jesus said to consider the fowls of the air and the flowers of the earth. They don't concern themselves with whether or not tomorrow will have problems. Jesus said that if our heavenly Father takes care of birds and flowers, how much more will He take care of His precious children? Then He diagnosed our problem: "O you of little faith" (Luke 12:22–28).

If you have a genuine need today, trust Him to take care of it.

SOUL SEARCH

Have I given my daily needs to God?

Father, this day I reaffirm my trust in you to supply all that I need.

Even the Dust

*Whatever house you enter, stay there, and from there depart.
And whoever will not receive you, when you go out of that
city, shake off the very dust from your feet as a testimony
against them.*

LUKE 9:4–5

When the world refuses to listen to the gospel, we can do nothing but shake the dust from our feet and seek others who will listen. We are not responsible for people's salvation. Our responsibility is to simply tell them the truth in love.

However, if someone seems to have a hard heart as you are trying to sow the seed of God's Word, take the time to break up the soil with the plough of the Law of God. Take them through the Ten Commandments to bring the knowledge of sin, which will show them their need for God's mercy. If they continue to reject the Savior, don't be concerned. Simply trust God to watch over His Word, and commit that person to His care.

The words of Jesus have a deeper meaning. We are to shake even the dust from our feet, because of the wicked nature of sin. The world is permeated by evil, and we are to separate ourselves from its wickedness before that day of wrath so that not even a hint of residue clings to us.

SOUL SEARCH

Am I living in holiness, separated from this sinful world?

Father, please tell me if the dust from this world is clinging to me.

Be of Good Cheer

Be of good cheer! It is I; do not be afraid.
MATTHEW 14:27

When the disciples saw Jesus walking on water, they thought they were seeing a ghost, and they cried out in fear. When life scares us, we can be of good cheer because what is happening to us is never as bad as it seems. Even if our trial is real and not imaginary, the risen Lord Jesus is with us.

The disciples saw Jesus walking on water. They saw what skeptics demand to see—a miracle. They witnessed the supernatural, and it terrified them.

Jesus' admonition is the same to us as it was to those fear-filled disciples. We are to look to Jesus and be of good cheer. Spurgeon preached, "David says, 'I am afraid.' Admire his honesty in making this confession. Some men would never have admitted that they were afraid. They would have blustered and said they cared for nothing! Generally there is no greater coward in this world than the man who never will acknowledge that he is afraid."[5]

SOUL SEARCH

Are there times when I let fear overtake me? Why does this happen? Have I determined to trust the Lord this day, no matter what happens?

Father, today I say with the psalmist, "When I am afraid I will trust in You" (Psalm 56:3).

Walking on Water

Come . . . O you of little faith, why did you doubt?
MATTHEW 14:29-31

The question that Jesus asked was rhetorical. He asked, "O you of little faith, why did you doubt?" It didn't require an answer.

But let's answer the question anyway. The Bible tells us, "But when he saw that the wind was boisterous, he was afraid; and beginning to sink he cried out, saying, 'Lord, save me!'" (Matthew 14:30). He was terrified of the boisterous wind. Isn't that our problem when uncertain circumstances make us afraid? Instead of looking to Jesus, the author and finisher of our faith, we naturally look to those around us.

So the next time the winds blow, look beyond those around you. Look to Jesus and His ability and integrity to keep His word. He will cause all things to work together for good (Romans 8:28). Instead of sinking in fear, get a good grip on yourself and trust Him. Jesus will lift you up.

Being a Christian means that we walk hand-in-hand with God, live above our circumstances, and therefore keep our heads above water.

SOUL SEARCH

What winds am I afraid of? How can I rid myself of that fear?

Father, sometimes I am so lacking in faith. My fears reveal that. I need you to be my strength today and forever.

Godly Priorities

Most assuredly, I say to you, you seek Me, not because you saw the signs, but because you ate of the loaves and were filled. Do not labor for the food which perishes, but for the food which endures to everlasting life, which the Son of Man will give you, because God the Father has set His seal on Him.

JOHN 6:26–27

We are naturally carnal. We are drawn more to the natural than to the spiritual. Our sin nature is a downward descent, and it's a continual uphill battle to walk in the Spirit. We prefer bread that fills us now to the everlasting bread that heaven offers. That's why we continually need the help of the Holy Spirit. When we don't even know how to pray, He is there to help us: "Likewise the Spirit also helps in our weaknesses. For we do not know what we should pray for as we ought, but the Spirit Himself makes intercession for us with groaning which cannot be uttered" (Romans 8:26).

He stirs our conscience when we become complacent about feeding on the Word, praying, fellowshipping, or caring about the fate of the lost. This is why we must cultivate a tender conscience and walk in the fear of the Lord. Without a tender ear we will be easily distracted into laboring for the bread that perishes.

SOUL SEARCH

Am I distracted by temporal things? Today I will discipline myself to remember the eternal.

Father, today please help me keep my eyes on what really matters.

The Work of God

This is the work of God,
that you believe in Him whom He sent.
JOHN 6:29

Skeptics often accuse God of hiding Himself. In one sense they are right. He hides Himself from the proud heart. He resists them. However, the atheist has no excuse when it comes to believing in the existence of God because He has revealed Himself through the genius of His handiwork.

> The heavens declare the glory of God;
> And the firmament shows His handiwork.
> Day unto day utters speech,
> And night unto night reveals knowledge.
> (Psalm 19:1–2)

Creation testifies to the existence of a Creator, so He hasn't hidden Himself in that respect. When Jesus speaks of finding Him, He is talking about finding a relationship with Him. That relationship begins through repentance and faith in the one God sent to suffer for the sin of the world. When we trust in the Son, we are doing the work of God. So if anyone is hiding, it is the sinner—who, like Adam, is hiding from Him because of his guilt.

SOUL SEARCH

Am I doing "the work of God?" Do I fully believe in Him whom God sent? Is that my message to this world?

Father, I want to do your work.

Thank the Teacher

Most assuredly, I say to you, Moses did not give you the bread from heaven, but My Father gives you the true bread from heaven. For the bread of God is He who comes down from heaven and gives life to the world.

JOHN 6:32-33

Moses didn't divide the Red Sea. God did. Neither did Moses bring water out of the rock, nor bring quail from the heavens. God did those things.

Moses—or rather the Law of Moses—doesn't provide food. It starves us. The Law has no benefit other than to strip us of self-righteousness and leave us hungering for righteousness. It leaves us longing for the Bread of Life. The Bible calls it a schoolmaster that brings us to Christ (Galatians 3:24). The Law came by Moses, but grace and truth came by Jesus Christ.

We must never fall into the trap of nullifying, even despising God's Law, as some do—saying that it has no purpose. We should never despise the teacher who brought us through to graduation; rather, we should be thankful for that teacher. And so we are grateful to God, not only for using the Law to bring us to Christ, but for providing a tool for us to use as a schoolmaster to bring others to the Savior.

SOUL SEARCH

Do I appreciate the purpose of the moral Law? Was it the schoolmaster that brought me to Christ? If not, from where did I get the knowledge of sin so that I could repent?

Father, make me a skilled worker for your kingdom.

The End of Religion

I am the bread of life. He who comes to Me shall never hunger, and he who believes in Me shall never thirst. But I said to you that you have seen Me and yet do not believe.

JOHN 6:35–36

Trusting in Jesus means an end to religion. No more trying to please God through religious works. We have thrown off the heavy burden of sin and guilt and exchanged it for the yoke that is easy and the burden that is light (Matthew 11:30). We cling only to the Savior. He alone is our hope of salvation, and that hope is steadfast—an anchor for the soul.

Jesus said, "Whoever comes to me." We come to Him because there is no one else to whom we can go. Buddha can't forgive sins and neither can Mohammad, the pope, the priest, or the pastor. Only Jesus has the authority on earth to wash away our sins. He told the religious leaders, "The Son of Man has power on earth to forgive sins" (Matthew 9:6). Actually, we are more than forgiven in Christ—we are justified and made righteous in His sight.

SOUL SEARCH

Is there anything in me that trusts in my works to save me? Is my faith entirely in Jesus?

Father, thank you for drawing me to yourself.

The Power of Rejection

All that the Father gives Me will come to Me, and the one who comes to Me I will by no means cast out. For I have come down from heaven, not to do My own will, but the will of Him who sent Me.

JOHN 6:37-38

Most of us intensely dislike rejection. It is one of the fears that stops us from sharing the gospel. We are afraid of looking foolish and being mocked. The world is full of people who have been rejected by others, and consequently they carry hurts that have festered into bitterness. Some are rejected by family—brothers reject sisters, fathers their children, and wives their husbands. Employers fire employees, coaches are tossed from losing teams, and girlfriends reject boyfriends. That's life, and it hurts.

But here Jesus promises that He will never reject those who come to Him. He is able to save all who come to God through Jesus. When Jesus accepts and embraces lost sinners, He is doing the will of the Father. God stretched out His welcoming arms in Christ on the cross and said, "This is how much I love you." The cross is a picture of the Prodigal's loving father running to his lost son and embracing him (Luke 15:11–32). It is the ultimate sign of love and acceptance.

SOUL SEARCH

Have I felt the pain of rejection? How did it make me feel? Have I completely forgiven those concerned?

Father, because of your grace, I am totally accepted in the beloved.

Do We See Him?

This is the will of the Father who sent Me, that of all He has given Me I should lose nothing, but should raise it up at the last day. And this is the will of Him who sent Me, that everyone who sees the Son and believes in Him may have everlasting life; and I will raise him up at the last day.

JOHN 6:39-40

Being a Christian means having total assurance that I am saved—without a doubt. We know that we have passed from death to life. This confidence isn't based on our feelings or circumstances. Rather it is based on God's trustworthiness. Jesus said that of all the Father has given Him, He should lose nothing. Notice the words *all* and *nothing*. There is no wiggle room. He said that *everyone* who sees the Son and believes in Him has everlasting life.

Do you see the Son?

Do you see Him as the only begotten Lamb of God?

Do you see Him purposefully sent to be crucified?

Do you see Him as the conqueror of death, holding its keys in His nail-pierced hands?

Do you trust Him entirely for your eternal salvation?

Then believe His wonderful words with all your heart. He will never disappoint you because you have immutable promises from the One who cannot lie.

SOUL SEARCH

If I truly see the Son, it will change everything I see and do.

Father, help me to glorify you in everything I look at, listen to, and say today.

Murmuring and Complaining

Do not murmur among yourselves. No one can come to Me unless the Father who sent Me draws him; and I will raise him up at the last day.

JOHN 6:43–44

Murmuring is annoying. It is a manifestation of a disgruntled heart, the opposite of gratitude and thankfulness. Think of Jesus in the darkest hours of the crucifixion. He had every reason to murmur and complain, but He didn't utter even one dissenting word.

The religious leaders had hated and rejected Him. Every one of the disciples had forsaken Him. He had been humiliated, impaled on a cross, and was in unprecedented agony. His hands were nailed to the cross, yet He kept reaching out—to the unsaved thief beside Him, to his mother by asking John to take her in. In His agony, He pleaded with the Father for the forgiveness of His murderers.

And just before He dismissed His spirit, He cried out, "It is finished!" (John 19:30). He was thinking of you and me. Oh, what love He displayed! He had finished His task of purchasing eternal salvation for sinners.

In the light of such love, may we never be guilty of murmuring or complaining.

SOUL SEARCH

Do I ever murmur when things don't go my way? Am I a complainer?

Father, help me to be truly thankful and never guilty of murmuring and complaining.

Our Earnest Prayer

It is written in the prophets, "And they shall all be taught by God." Therefore everyone who has heard and learned from the Father comes to Me. Not that anyone has seen the Father, except He who is from God; He has seen the Father.

JOHN 6:45–46

"It is written in the prophets." Perhaps today's equivalent would be, "It is written in stone." In other words, it will surely come to pass.

The words "they shall be taught by God" are a reference to the unsaved because Jesus said, "Therefore everyone who has heard and learned from the Father comes to the Son." Jesus didn't forget about the unsaved. So how could we? How could those of us who claim to have the love of God dwelling in us forget that we are surrounded by people who are still under the power of death and will go to hell if they die in their sin? It should be our earnest prayer that the Father uses us to teach sinners because He has chosen the foolishness of preaching to save those who are perishing.

This should be our life's work. We are to instruct sinners, using the Law to point them to Jesus—specifically Christ crucified for the sin of the world. Everything else we do in life, important though it may be, pales in comparison to this task. May God help to keep this truth our priority.

SOUL SEARCH

As a Christian, I am a follower of Jesus Christ. Am I following Him in His example of seeking and saving that which is lost?

Father, consume me with the desire to imitate Jesus.

The Foundation

Most assuredly, I say to you, he who believes in Me has everlasting life. I am the bread of life. Your fathers ate the manna in the wilderness, and are dead.

JOHN 6:47–49

Look at what Jesus is saying to the religious leaders. He is saying that Moses left their fathers dead. Moses didn't give them everlasting life. All Moses does is show us the nature of our sins and give us the death sentence. The Israelites ate manna from heaven, but they still died. Jesus is the Bread of Life, and the sustenance He gives overcomes death.

Charles Spurgeon said:

> It is of the utmost importance to those of you who have spiritual life that you should feed upon the Lord Jesus. It is well to know everything that is revealed, for every word of God is good, and has its uses, and all Scripture is profitable, but the daily household bread, the substantial meat on which we must be nourished if we would grow strong for God and holiness, is Christ Himself.[6]

SOUL SEARCH

Is Jesus my *life* right at this moment? If I succumbed to death, is my trust entirely in Him?

Father, help me always be ready to see you face to face.

The Mother of Knowledge

This is the bread which comes down from heaven, that one may eat of it and not die. I am the living bread which came down from heaven. If anyone eats of this bread, he will live forever; and the bread that I shall give is My flesh, which I shall give for the life of the world.

JOHN 6:50–51

Repetition is said to be the mother of all learning. Let me repeat that. Saying something again drives the point home. Jesus used this technique with the religious leaders because He was talking to fellow human beings about the most important subject on earth.

We tend to miss the fact that Jesus spoke out of His love for people—the same love He manifested on the cross. Only God knows how many of the three thousand who came to faith on the day of Pentecost were those who earlier had heard His gracious words.

We must never tire of repeating the same gospel to sinners, even though we have heard it ten thousand times. Those who have made evangelism a way of life know how their energy is renewed when a sinner sincerely asks about the Savior. It's like giving food to a starving child who is at a point of death, and seeing life come into his eyes.

SOUL SEARCH

Do I get tired of sharing the gospel?

Father, your Word says that when I received the Holy Spirit, I received power. Let that power be evident today.

Tasting the Goodness of God

Then Jesus said to them, "Most assuredly, I say to you, unless you eat the flesh of the Son of Man and drink His blood, you have no life in you."

JOHN 6:53

There are some who take these words literally. Yet Jesus qualified them by saying that the words He spoke were spirit and life (John 6:63). He was making a spiritual statement. He isn't speaking of physical cannibalism. Rather, it is a reference to the new birth that Jesus teaches Nicodemus about in John 3 (being born of the Spirit) when we "taste and see that the LORD is good" (Psalm 34:8).

When we trust alone in Jesus, we taste of His goodness. As long as sinners trust in unbiblical church traditions, they will ignore the Bread of Life and the new birth, which is necessary to enter heaven (John 3). It is important that we don't get caught up in arguments over church doctrine as we attempt to share the gospel. Simply take people through the Law to show them that nothing they can do on their own will save them, and then present the biblical gospel. When people are truly born again, the Holy Spirit will lead them into all truth, and they will trust in Jesus alone rather than in their church tradition.

SOUL SEARCH

Do I find myself getting caught up in heated arguments over doctrine? What can I do to avoid doing that?

Father, help me to "be gentle to all" (2 Timothy 2:24–26).

Taking Communion

Whoever eats My flesh and drinks My blood has eternal life, and I will raise him up at the last day. For My flesh is food indeed, and My blood is drink indeed. He who eats My flesh and drinks My blood abides in Me, and I in him. As the living Father sent Me, and I live because of the Father, so he who feeds on Me will live because of Me. This is the bread which came down from heaven—not as your fathers ate the manna, and are dead. He who eats this bread will live forever.

JOHN 6:54–58

As we participate in communion and remember the cross in all its horror, we should examine ourselves. This is a time to remember what God has forgotten and blotted out forever—our past sins. We should never forget what we deserve and what grace has done for us. God should have given us hell, but instead He gave us heaven. Such thoughts magnify mercy, ignite gratitude, and should become a great motivation for us to reach out to the lost.

SOUL SEARCH

Do I understand what I have been forgiven in Christ? Does gratitude consume me as it should?

Father, since I can't put my gratitude into words, may I put it into my works.

The Fogged Mirror

Why do you also transgress the commandment of God because of your tradition? For God commanded, saying, "Honor your father and your mother"; "He who curses father or mother, let him be put to death." But you say, "Whoever says to his father or mother, 'Whatever profit you might have received from me is a gift to God'— then he need not honor his father or mother." Thus you have made the commandment of God of no effect by your tradition.

MATTHEW 15:3–6

The religious leaders shredded the Commandments of God by their tradition. They didn't bother to honor their parents because they figured out a way to get out of their parental obligations. In doing so, they stripped the moral Law of its power to show them their need for mercy. Their traditions fogged the mirror so that they couldn't see their own reflection. And so they were left believing that all was well between them and God. That's the tragedy of nullifying the Law.

At the root of this tradition was their erroneous image of God, an image that allowed them to hold onto sin. Idols don't give sinners any moral directives. Had they had a biblical image of God, they would have feared Him and listened to the Law, which would have acted as a schoolmaster to bring them to Christ.

SOUL SEARCH

Do I regularly judge myself by looking into the perfect Law of Liberty (James 1:5)?

Father, help me to always be without guile.

Spotting Guilt

Hypocrites! Well did Isaiah prophesy about you, saying:
"These people draw near to Me with their mouth, and
honor Me with their lips, but their heart is far from Me.
And in vain they worship Me, teaching as doctrines the
commandments of men."

MATTHEW 15:7–9

The religious leaders were hypocrites, and while hypocrisy can be a stumbling block to the world, it is not a legitimate reason to reject the gospel. An atheist will point to pickpocket televangelists with their bottomless collection bags or to perverted pedophile priests, and think that their hypocrisy justifies their own rejection of the Savior.

No criminal should think that a judge will let him go based on others' guilt. Scripture warns, "And do you think this, O man, you who judge those practicing such things, and doing the same, that you will escape the judgment of God?" (Romans 2:3).

SOUL SEARCH

Do I ever justify myself or feel righteous by pointing at the sins of others?

Father, forgive me for any self-righteousness.

Out of the Mouth

Hear and understand: Not what goes into the mouth defiles a man; but what comes out of the mouth, this defiles a man.
MATTHEW 15:10–11

The world is consumed with what goes into the mouth. It is forever talking about what we should and shouldn't eat. It strains at the gnat and swallows the camel (Matthew 23:24).

But those who hear and understand know that what we eat will be irrelevant when it really matters on the day of judgment.

On an airplane, we should be more concerned about whether there is an adequate parachute on board than what food they plan to serve. The parachute could save a life.

Such sobering thoughts help us to prioritize what matters and what doesn't. The godly know that eating food has no moral consequences. What does matter is guarding our hearts and lips with all diligence because it is out of the heart that come the issues of life (Proverbs 4:23).

SOUL SEARCH

Am I overly careful about what I should and shouldn't eat but careless about my heart?

Father, may morality take precedent over calories.

Blind Leaders

Every plant which My heavenly Father has not planted will be uprooted. Let them alone. They are blind leaders of the blind. And if the blind leads the blind, both will fall into a ditch.

MATTHEW 15:13–14

It is very helpful to study the parable of the sower in order to understand that there are true and false converts sitting together within the Body of Christ. The Bible calls them tares among the wheat, foolish virgins among the wise, bad fish among the good, and goats among the sheep—and these will be sorted out on judgment day.

The true converts are those who have been born of God. They are the planting of the Lord, and those not planted by the Lord will be uprooted. This is why contemporary evangelism that manipulates and plays on human emotion is so dangerous. Many of today's professed converts are born of the will of man rather than by the will of God, evidenced by the fact that up to 90 percent of present-day converts fall away from the faith.[7]

Jesus warned that many would say to Him on judgment day, "Lord, Lord," and yet will be cast out of heaven into hell (Matthew 7:21–24).

SOUL SEARCH

Have I ever been guilty of leading someone to a decision for Christ who ended up stillborn rather than being born of God?

Father, keep me from interfering with your work when it comes to the salvation of the lost.

July

Take Hold of Understanding

Are you also still without understanding? Do you not yet understand that whatever enters the mouth goes into the stomach and is eliminated? But those things which proceed out of the mouth come from the heart, and they defile a man.
MATTHEW 15:16–17

When David took Bathsheba to himself and became entangled in a web of sin, he did so without understanding. He didn't consider that the eye of the Lord is in every place, beholding the evil and the good. He didn't think about how God will bring to judgment every secret thing whether it is good or evil. Neither did he understand his own heart.

We can learn from David's experience. The problem wasn't Bathsheba—it was his heart. She revealed that lust was burning in the king:

> The heart is deceitful above all things,
> And desperately wicked;
> Who can know it? (Jeremiah 17:9)

David should have taken note of Joseph's story. When Potiphar's wife called, he ran. So should we. Run from sin.

SOUL SEARCH

Do I understand how wicked my own heart is? Do I ever make provision for the flesh?

Father, help me to walk in the fear of the Lord today and to glorify your name by everything I think and look at.

The Law is Spiritual

For out of the heart proceed evil thoughts, murders, adulteries, fornications, thefts, false witness, blasphemies. These are the things which defile a man, but to eat with unwashed hands does not defile a man.

MATTHEW 15:19–20

The Bible says that sin is a transgression of the Law (1 John 3:4). The Ten Commandments show us the nature of sin and at the same time reveal to us the character of God.

Notice how many of the Ten Commandments are named as Jesus defines the nature of sin. He named the sixth, the seventh, the eighth, the ninth, and the third. He also included fornication and added that lustful thoughts, hatred, and thoughts of covetousness violate the Law.

These are the things that defile a man, and these are the issues with which men and women need to be confronted. Therefore, learn to open up the spiritual nature of the Ten Commandments as Jesus did in the Sermon on the Mount.

SOUL SEARCH

Do I understand the nature of sin today? Do I love righteousness?

Father, cause me to walk in truth this day and be aware that I am surrounded by people who are going to hell if they die in their sins.

The Advantage

I was not sent except to the lost sheep of the house of Israel.
MATTHEW 15:24

Jesus was sent by God to the Jew first. The apostle Paul reiterated that the gospel was to go to the Jew first. This wasn't because they were morally superior to the other nations. The reason the gospel went to the Jew first was because Israel had the Law: "What advantage then has the Jew, or what is the profit of circumcision? Much in every way! Chiefly because to them were committed the oracles of God" (Romans 3:1–2).

When the gospel came to the Jews, they were able to understand that a holy God was providing the sacrifice and providing the payment that the Law required.

No one is going to accept a cure unless they are first convinced that they have a disease. We must follow that pattern. When we speak to Gentiles we must use the Law to bring the knowledge of sin, as Jesus did in Mark 10:17, so that they can understand the gospel's message—that Christ was made a curse for us in order to redeem us from the curse of the Law.

SOUL SEARCH

Do I fully understand the advantage that I have in using the moral Law to bring the knowledge of sin to unbelievers? How can I begin to incorporate this tool in my witnessing?

Father, give me wisdom when I share the gospel.

Crumbs of the Bread of Life

*It is not good to take the children's bread
and throw it to the little dogs.*

MATTHEW 15:26

This Gentile woman cried out, "Have mercy on me, O Lord, Son of David! My daughter is severely demon-possessed" (Matthew 15:22).

To those lacking understanding, Jesus' reply seems harsh. But it wasn't. Jesus was without sin; His words didn't discourage her in the slightest. Instead, they provoked her to say, "Yes, Lord, yet even the little dogs eat the crumbs which fall from their masters' table" (v. 27).

How wonderful it is that God didn't confine the gospel to the Jews. The Holy Spirit was also given to the Gentiles. The gospel is good news for all the nations, for all peoples.

The Bible gives an open invitation by saying whosoever will may come: "Ho! Everyone who thirsts, come" (Isaiah 55:1). "Whoever calls on the name of the Lord shall be saved" (Romans 10:13). The door to everlasting life swung wide open the moment that Jesus rose from the dead.

This is deliriously good news for Muslims, Hindus, Buddhists, agnostics, atheists, and religious people who are trying to earn their way to heaven by their works.

SOUL SEARCH

Am I delirious with joy that death has been conquered? Fill your prayers with thanksgiving today.

Father, let me be as the disciples who could not help but share what they had seen and heard.

Make Him Marvel

O woman, great is your faith!
Let it be to you as you desire.
MATTHEW 15:28

Jesus' seemingly harsh response to the woman's plea would probably have removed hope from most but not this mother. She wasn't discouraged. Her desire to have her prayer answered increased.

Without faith, it is impossible to please God, which conversely means that with faith, we can please Him. Look at Jesus' reaction to this woman's faith. He said, "O woman." In another place when a man trusted in Him, the Bible says that Jesus "marveled" at his faith. How amazing that faith made Jesus marvel.

Our deepest desire should be to please God. We can't please him by our own works, but we can please Him in Christ by trusting in His promises.

Trust in God can make us marvel as well. We can have perfect peace in the lion's den. We can sleep in the storm because we trust the Lord from the heart "that all things work together for good to those who love God, to those who are called according to His purpose" (Romans 8:28). And that is marvelous.

SOUL SEARCH

Am I going to walk above my circumstances today, because of my faith in God? Make God marvel today.

Father, this day I choose to trust you with all of my heart.

The Hidden Enemy

For this saying go your way;
the demon has gone out of your daughter.

MARK 7:29

There's an irony when it comes to the demonic realm. This sinful world revels in the occult but ignores the Bible's warnings about serving the dark side: "Be sober, be vigilant; because your adversary the devil walks about like a roaring lion, seeking whom he may devour" (1 Peter 5:8).

As Christians, we know that we wrestle not against flesh and blood but against principalities and powers, spiritual wickedness in high places (Ephesians 6:12–20). When the world has its own diagnosis of a man who hears multiple voices telling him to murder, we know better. When we read in the news each day of killing, stealing, and destroying, we know that the thief comes only to kill, steal, and destroy. We know that those who serve sin serve the devil.

But here's the greatest tragedy of serving sin: "But even if our gospel is veiled, it is veiled to those who are perishing, whose minds the god of this age has blinded, who do not believe, lest the light of the gospel of the glory of Christ, who is the image of God, should shine on them" (2 Corinthians 4:3–4).

SOUL SEARCH

Do I have a fascination with horoscopes, Halloween, horror movies, palm reading, and the like? Identify any areas of temptation and bring them to the cross.

Father, deliver me from every work of darkness.

Be Opened

Ephphatha.
MARK 7:34

The New Testament was written in Greek and translated into English. However, here Mark gives us the original Aramaic word spoken by Jesus and then kindly gives us the meaning: "Be opened." The man was deaf and had a speech impediment. Jesus took him aside from the crowd, put His fingers in his ears, spat and touched his tongue. Then, looking up to heaven, He sighed and said, "Be opened."

What a transformation that took place in this man's life! He could now hear the sounds of the wind in the trees, the human voice, music, laughter, and the song of birds. He could speak clearly; he could express himself freely.

Jesus took us aside from this world and opened our ears to His voice. He also opened the eyes of our understanding so that we can see all things clearly. In addition, He touched our tongues and healed our speech. We can now speak clearly about the mystery of life and of the kingdom of God.

The gospel opened a whole new world to us.

SOUL SEARCH

Do I realize that I can now speak clearly of the kingdom of God? Open your mouth and speak of His wonders!

Father, open a whole new world to me as I step out in faith and plead with the lost.

Entering into Suffering

I have compassion on the multitude, because they have now continued with Me three days and have nothing to eat. And I do not want to send them away hungry, lest they faint on the way.

MATTHEW 15:32

Compassion comes with a cost. If we have the virtue of compassion, it means that we feel for those who are suffering. We weep with those that weep. It is deeper than a distant sympathy because compassion enters into the sufferings of others. It feels the hunger.

In this passage, we see Jesus entering into the hunger of the multitudes. He could never be accused of being so heavenly minded that He was of no earthly use. His feet were planted firmly on the ground as evidenced by His concerns about the daily problems of this life.

We must also enter into the suffering of others and do all we can to help those who are sick and hungry and clothe those who are naked. When we are regenerated, our compassion should deepen. The thought of the suffering of those who will be damned in their sins and the terrible pains of hell should motivate us to preach the love of God in Christ.

SOUL SEARCH

Do I ever take the time to meditate on the fate of the ungodly? Does concern for the unsaved grip my soul?

Father, help me to have the depth of compassion that will reach out to lost sinners with the gospel.

The Good Seed

How many loaves do you have?
MATTHEW 15:34

This was the question Jesus asked His disciples as they looked at the hungry multitude. All that could be found was a boy's lunch comprised of only five loaves and two fish. Jesus took what they gave Him and multiplied it miraculously.

What can you and I give to God? We may not be able to sing, dance, write, or be creative. Perhaps we're not able to teach or preach. We may not be super intelligent or eloquent or have a good grasp of the English language. We may consider ourselves a little boring, and perhaps we are. But that doesn't matter because God doesn't want talent. He wants us. He can take our lack of ability, our nothingness, and multiply it to reach multitudes.

We may not have abilities, but we have the gospel—the most powerful, dynamic, and wonderful message this world could ever hope to hear. A farmer may not have any skills, but if he has high quality seed and takes the time to prepare the soil, he's going to see fruit for his labors.

SOUL SEARCH

Have I been looking at my abilities rather than the power of the gospel? Have my inadequacies hindered me from reaching out to the unsaved?

Father, thank you for the glorious gospel of Jesus Christ. It is the power of God unto salvation.

The Sign of Jonah

When it is evening you say, "It will be fair weather, for the sky is red"; and in the morning, "It will be foul weather today, for the sky is red and threatening." Hypocrites! You know how to discern the face of the sky, but you cannot discern the signs of the times. A wicked and adulterous generation seeks after a sign, and no sign shall be given to it except the sign of the prophet Jonah.

MATTHEW 16:1–4

One of the best things I ever purchased was a digital clock that beams the time onto our bedroom ceiling. Anytime I wake up in the darkness, I instantly know the time because it's written in large numbers above my dozing head.

Bible prophecy is a beam of light in the darkness. If anyone wants to know if the Bible is the Word of the Creator, all they need to do is study biblical prophecy—particularly the history of the nation of Israel.

However, the greatest sign any of us can ever have is that Jesus Christ was swallowed by death for three days but then rose from the grave, stripping it of its power. That's the gospel, and that message has the power to instantly transform any sinner. That's the greatest of signs.

SOUL SEARCH

Do I sometimes get caught up in arguments and forget to share the simplicity of the gospel—Christ crucified for the sin of the world?

Father, help me to always preach Christ crucified.

Puffed with Pride

*Take heed and beware of the leaven
of the Pharisees and the Sadducees.*

MATTHEW 16:6

The disciples were confused as to what Jesus meant when He spoke of the leaven of the Pharisees. Jesus explained that He was talking about their doctrine. One obvious property of leaven is that it causes bread to rise—it puffs up. The Pharisees were puffed up with pride. They considered themselves to be experts on the kingdom of God, but look what knowledge can do: "Now concerning things offered to idols: We know that we all have knowledge. Knowledge puffs up, but love edifies. And if anyone thinks that he knows anything, he knows nothing yet as he ought to know" (1 Corinthians 8:1–2).

In their pride they despised others, extolling their own virtues. They were puffed up by their giving of alms, their public praying, teaching, and preaching when in reality, they were in transgression of the first of the Ten Commandments. Their image of God was erroneous. They didn't believe that God required truth in the inward parts but believed that He was happy looking at the outward appearance. However, Jesus said they were like an odious graveyard in the eyes of God.

SOUL SEARCH

Do I strive to walk in humility of heart? Consider your attitude toward others—is there any underlying arrogance in your heart?

Father, give me knowledge and help me to stay low as I grow.

Leaven

O you of little faith, why do you reason among yourselves because you have brought no bread? Do you not yet understand, or remember the five loaves of the five thousand and how many baskets you took up? Nor the seven loaves of the four thousand and how many large baskets you took up? How is it you do not understand that I did not speak to you concerning bread?—but to beware of the leaven of the Pharisees and Sadducees.

MATTHEW 16:8–11

Charles Spurgeon said about this passage:

> He used a parabolic expression, which they would readily have understood, had not their minds been already absorbed by their lack of bread. He saw that in them, too, there would soon be a desire for a sign, now that they needed bread; and He feared the influence of both the Ritualism of the Pharisee, and the Rationalism of the Sadducee upon His little church. Hence His double word, "Take heed, and beware." The warning is needed today as much as in our Lord's time. "Pharisees and Sadducees" are both leavening the churches.[8]

SOUL SEARCH

Do I strive to ensure that everything I believe has a sound basis in the Word of God?

Father, please keep my doctrine pure.

Taking the Initiative

You give them something to eat.
LUKE 9:13

God has given us the word of reconciliation—condescending to use the foolishness of preaching to save those who believe. He has trusted us to take the initiative, step out in faith in any way possible to reach the lost.

Paul said that he would use any means to reach the unsaved (1 Corinthians 9:22). When Jesus said to give the multitudes something to eat, the Bible says He was testing Peter to see what he would do (John 6:6).

The Scripture says not to despise the day of small beginnings (Zechariah 4:10). Many a small lunch has ended up feeding multitudes simply because someone cared enough to take the initiative and do the right thing, and God added His blessing.

While you and I are called to feed the physically hungry, we are also called to give them the Bread of Life. Yet when we look at the multitudes in the valley of decision, the task can seem overwhelming. There are just too many people. However, our confidence is that God will multiply the meager loaves and fishes we have in our hands.

SOUL SEARCH

Do I ever feel overwhelmed because I look at the problem rather than to the Lord?

Father, may I always look past the problem to you.

The Wisdom of God

Make them sit down in groups of fifty.
LUKE 9:14

This was a dangerous situation. When a crowd of five thousand people have gone for three days without eating, they are likely to become agitated if they suddenly see food. This would be especially true if they were able to smell supernaturally fresh-baked bread wafting through the air. If people at the back surged forward, others could have been trampled to death.

Jesus dealt with this danger by breaking the crowd into a hundred groups of fifty and then had them sit down. The crowd was now in manageable small groups who couldn't press forward because they were seated. In Mark 6:39, we are given even more information: "Then He commanded them to make them all sit down in groups on the green grass."

Perhaps the verse gives us the color of the grass because the color red makes us angry, blue gives us a sense of well being, but the color green gives us a sense of peace. That's precisely what you want when you are dealing with five thousand hungry people.

SOUL SEARCH

Do I daily seek God for His wisdom on all things? Make a habit of praying first.

Father, help me to understand hidden truths in your Word.

Who is He?

Who do the crowds say that I am?
LUKE 9:18

If you ask the world who they think Jesus was, you will get a variety of answers. Some say He was delusional; others say that He was a great teacher. Those who are really confused say that He didn't exist. They tend to forget the fact that time is determined from the year of His birth. Their answers reveal their ignorance of what the Scripture teaches.

To say that Jesus was delusional is nonsensical. Historians and experts agree that the Sermon on the Mount is uniquely superb in its content. These are not the words of someone who is deranged. If someone else said the words Jesus said, people would search him out, fall at his feet, and worship him as Lord. Neither was Jesus merely a great teacher. Those who believe that take little notice of His great teachings.

The Bible teaches that our eternity as individuals depends upon how we answer the questions: Who is Jesus? Is He the Christ? Do you know Him as Lord and Savior? Are your sins forgiven because you are trusting Him?

SOUL SEARCH

Do I uphold the biblical revelation of Jesus to this sinful and dying world? Am I convinced myself that He is the Christ, the Son of the living God?

Father, may I always rightly reflect the light of the Savior.

Who is He to You?

But who do you say that I am?
LUKE 9:20

It is overwhelming to think of the number of people who have walked this earth—each a unique individual, living his or her own life. Yet God knows every one. He knows every thought of every human heart and every individual hair on every individual head. The mind of God goes even deeper. He knows every individual atom in every person. And He says to each of us, "Who do you say that I am?"

It is the greatest of biblical truths to say that our Creator loves us. This love was proven when God Himself provided the only begotten Savior to deliver us from the power of death. Scripture says that there is salvation in no other name under heaven given among men (Acts 4:12). Salvation comes from embracing Jesus Christ, and to embrace Him, we must acknowledge who He is.

Romans 10:9 says that if we confess with our mouths that Jesus Christ is Lord and believe that God has raised Him from the dead, we shall be saved. This must happen to each of us personally to be saved. That's why Jesus said to Peter and each of us, "Who do you say that I am?"

SOUL SEARCH

Do I confess that Jesus is the Christ of God? Who can I share that with today?

Father, never let me be ashamed of the exclusivity of Christianity.

The Suffering Savior

The Son of Man must suffer many things, and be rejected by the elders and chief priests and scribes, and be killed, and be raised the third day.

LUKE 9:22

As with every other human being, Jesus was born to die. His death, however, was going to be different. He was going to suffer for the sin of the world, then rise again on the third day. It wasn't enough for Him to merely die—resurrection had to happen!

Jesus said that He must suffer these things; there was no way of escape. Can you imagine living life knowing that such unspeakable horror awaited you? It is because of His great love that you and I can look forward to what happens after death because death has lost its sting.

This terrifying nightmare turns into a wonderful dream for those who repent and trust in the Savior. As we take comfort in the promises of God, we should have mixed emotions. How can we rest and take comfort when so many don't have what we have in Christ?

"Lost! Lost! Lost! Better a whole world on fire than a soul lost! Better every star quenched and the skies a wreck than a single soul to be lost!"[9]

SOUL SEARCH

Have I so grown in my trust in God that I can boldly declare I have no fear of my own death? I have certainty of eternal life in heaven.

Father, for me to live is Christ. To die is gain.

Self-Denial

If anyone desires to come after Me, let him deny himself,
and take up his cross daily, and follow Me.

LUKE 9:23

There is that wonderful word again in a different form: anyone. Other places in Scripture say whosoever will may come. God welcomes anybodies, everybodies, and nobodies. With outstretched arms He says, "Follow me." In order to follow Him, we must deny ourselves and take up the reproach of the cross. That's the only path to everlasting life.

We are selfish creatures by nature. Denying ourselves doesn't come easy, whether it be denying ourselves food so that we can pray and learn self-control or denying ourselves certain legitimate pleasures because we want to do the will of God. But He gives us the grace we need and helps us to follow Him.

Self-denial means that we refuse the constant pull of the sins of the flesh, the attractions of the sinful world, and the whispering of the devil. Instead of living for the praise of the world, we live for the praise of heaven, and in doing so, we daily carry the cross. We do this not to merit eternal life but because we have eternal life. We look for a city. We look to Him who is invisible and see eternity.

SOUL SEARCH

In what ways do I deny myself daily?

Father, help me today to restrain my appetites and guard my eyes and thoughts.

Letting Go and Holding On

For whoever desires to save his life will lose it,
but whoever loses his life for My sake will save it.
LUKE 9:24

When we come to Christ, we give up our lives. We say, with Paul, "I have been crucified with Christ and I no longer live, but Christ lives in me" (Galatians 2:20 NIV). He is the source of life and His residence within us is the evidence that we belong to God.

We can learn a sobering lesson from Lot's wife. As the family fled for their lives, she looked back longingly at Sodom. May God help us refuse the temptation to even glance back at this wicked world with any sense of affection. Scripture warns that if we follow the inclinations of the flesh, we shall die. But if, with the help of the Holy Spirit, we crucify the flesh, we shall live.

The story is told of a rich man who fell overboard from a ship while wearing a money belt filled with gold. He refused to let go of the precious gold, and it dragged him down to his death. Such is the way of sin.

Being a Christian means a daily letting go of sin and resolving to hold fast to God's gift of salvation and eternal life.

SOUL SEARCH

In what areas of my life am I vulnerable to temptation? What can I do to strengthen my resolve to hold fast to the truth?

Father, open my dull mind to that which you have given me in the gospel.

Profit or Loss

For what profit is it to a man if he gains the whole world,
and is himself destroyed or lost?
LUKE 9:25

This is the ultimate example of a rhetorical question. It doesn't need an answer because the answer is so obvious. No one benefits if a man loses himself or is cast away. Our most precious possession is our life, and if we lose that, we have nothing.

For many years, I have asked sinners if they would sell one of their eyes for a million dollars. Some would, but no one in his or her right mind would sell both for any amount. Yet the eye is merely the window of the soul. We look out of the windows we call eyes. The point I am making is that if eyes are priceless, how much more valuable is the soul?

What a tragedy it is to live a life devoid of any reference to God. Everything we have comes from His gracious hand. We have the ability to enjoy the beauty of His creation, taste the wonderful food He generously provides, and hear the beautiful music He gave us the ability to produce. And yet the ungodly refuse to give God praise or even be thankful for all these blessings.

And so on their deathbed, if they are fortunate enough to have one, the unbelievers take nothing with them from this world and end up lost and cast away forever.

SOUL SEARCH

What am I especially thankful for today?

Father, forgive me for any ingratitude I may have.

His Offensive Words

For whoever is ashamed of Me and My words, of him the Son of Man will be ashamed when He comes in His own glory, and in His Father's, and of the holy angels.

LUKE 9:26

The Bible tells us that God is no respecter of persons (Acts 10:34). This is illustrated by the word "whoever." It doesn't matter who we are. If we are ashamed of the Lord, He will disown us on the day of judgment.

Notice that Jesus included those who are ashamed of His words. The world is full of professing Christians who are not ashamed of the historical Jesus, but they are ashamed of His words. They merely have an image of Jesus as being a good man with some good teachings.

However, when we quote what He actually said, they are offended. His words shatter their idol. The Jesus revealed in Holy Scripture rebuked hypocrites. He boldly spoke against sin, talked of judgment, and talked of the holy and just character of God. He said that our Creator is angry at humanity. He told us that lust was adultery in His morally perfect eyes, condemned divorce, and spoke of cutting off hands and plucking out eyes if they caused us to sin. Most importantly, He warned of the reality of hell.

If we want to be true and faithful witnesses, we must never be ashamed of Jesus' words.

SOUL SEARCH

Am I ever hesitant to speak of sin for fear of offending sinners?

Father, may I never be ashamed of the words of Jesus.

The Coming Kingdom

But I tell you truly, there are some standing here who shall not taste death till they see the kingdom of God.
LUKE 9:27

As this world grows darker and the birth pangs of travail increase, we long for the kingdom of God even more. The Bible says that we groan within ourselves, waiting for the coming kingdom: "We know that the whole creation has been groaning as in the pains of childbirth right up to the present time. Not only so, but we ourselves, who have the firstfruits of the Spirit, groan inwardly as we wait eagerly for our adoption to sonship, the redemption of our bodies" (Romans 8:22–23 NIV).

The time will come when God's kingdom will come to this earth, and God's will will be done on the earth as it is in heaven. We will inherit this whole amazing earth! And there will be a new heaven and a new earth without the Genesis curse.

There will be no more suffering, disease, death, dentists, or dandruff. God Himself will wipe away every tear from the eyes of those who love Him. And so we say with the apostle John, "Come quickly, Lord Jesus" (Revelation 22:20). Then add a little prayer, *Please save the lost before that day.*

SOUL SEARCH

If Jesus came today, would I be ashamed of anything in my life?

Father, pour out your Holy Spirit upon the lost. Raise up laborers. Use me to reach them.

Remove Hindrances

Indeed, Elijah is coming first and will restore all things. But I say to you that Elijah has come already, and they did not know him but did to him whatever they wished. Likewise the Son of Man is also about to suffer at their hands.

MATTHEW 17:11-12

Jesus was making reference to his cousin, John the Baptist. John was a burning and shining light. He was a voice in the wilderness, preparing the way of the Lord and making His paths straight.

You and I should be a burning and shining light to those who sit in darkness and in the shadow of death. We too are telling sinners to prepare for the way of the Lord and make every path straight. If riches are a hindrance, toss them aside. If love of sports, love of a man or a woman, love of family, or love of the praises of men get in the way, we must push them aside and give God His rightful place in our lives.

The first time Jesus came, it was as a harmless sacrificial lamb. The second time He comes, He will be coming as a roaring lion to judge this world in righteousness. John's diet was locusts and wild honey. Our message should be the plague of Moses' Law and the sweet honey of the gospel. It is only when sinners see their terrible danger that they will cry out for the mercy of God.

SOUL SEARCH

Does God have His rightful place in my life today? Is there anything that is a hindrance?

Father, you are my primary affection. You gave me my life. I give it back to you.

Perverse Generation

O faithless and perverse generation, how long shall I be with you and bear with you? Bring your son here.

LUKE 9:41

Jesus called His hearers (and His whole generation) faithless and perverted. His testimony was true.

Do you ever look at this faithless and perverted world and wonder why God bears with us? It is because He is rich in mercy and abundantly patient. After speaking about the fearful judgment of God upon wicked men, the Scripture says, "with the Lord one day is as a thousand years, and a thousand years as one day. The Lord is not slack concerning His promise, as some count slackness, but is longsuffering toward us, not willing that any should perish but that all should come to repentance" (2 Peter 3:8–9).

The words Jesus spoke about His generation are applicable to this generation. We live in an unbelieving, skeptical, faithless, and very perverse generation who will gladly have faith in anything but the Word of God. They have twisted almost everything that is holy and right and just, from the institution of marriage to music to child-rearing to religion. May God have mercy on them as He did on us.

SOUL SEARCH

Do I pray for this generation? Include a prayer for your lost generation in your next quiet time.

Father, please send light into the darkness of this world.

Preparing Fish

What do you think, Simon? From whom do the kings of the earth take customs or taxes, from their sons or from strangers? . . . Then the sons are free. Nevertheless, lest we offend them, go to the sea, cast in a hook, and take the fish that comes up first. And when you have opened its mouth, you will find a piece of money; take that and give it to them for Me and you.

MATTHEW 17:25–27

Once you establish the fact that God is supernatural and that Jesus Christ is God in human form, there is nothing too hard for Him. He made every scale on that fish. He made its brain and its thoughts, and if He can turn the hearts of kings, He can move the thoughts and fins of a fish.

The most avid skeptic must admit that this is a great way to make a point. If you think you are God, command some random fish among the billions of fish in the ocean to swallow a coin that somebody has dropped on the ocean floor. Then have that fish swim with the coin in its stomach, find the hook that Peter has lowered into the ocean, and bite the bait. Impossible? Yes, unless you were Almighty God in human form.

Having faith in Jesus opens the door to every impossibility the mind can imagine.

SOUL SEARCH

Do I ever think deeply about what I read in the Bible? Meditate on Psalm 1.

Father, help me dig deeply into your wonderful Word.

Dull of Hearing

Let these words sink down into your ears, for the Son of Man is about to be betrayed into the hands of men.

LUKE 9:44

Many of us have trouble internalizing information. It may be heard but doesn't really sink in. We are especially dull of hearing when it comes to spiritual truths—our understanding seems darkened. So, we must make a special effort to let the message of the cross really sink in and pray for understanding.

The disciples were rejoicing at all that Jesus had done. Little did they know what was ahead. The darkest hours were to come and would cast an evil black shadow over those lighthearted days of miracles. The cross is the ultimate oxymoron. It was evil yet good. It was gross darkness but glorious light.

If we let the love expressed on that cross sink deeply into our hearts, we will have the light of the glorious gospel of Jesus Christ when dark days come. It was for us that the Son of Man was delivered into the hands of men, so we could have everlasting life. Such thoughts are lights of consolation in our darkest hours.

SOUL SEARCH

Does the glorious light of the cross carry me through the dark hours? Remember a time when you experienced God's sustaining grace through a difficult circumstance.

Father, help me to joyfully accept the thorns.

Children are People Too

Whoever receives this little child in My name receives Me; and whoever receives Me receives Him who sent Me. For he who is least among you all will be great.

LUKE 9:48

It's easy to forget that children are people and should be treated with respect. Ill-spoken words by an adult have scarred many little ones for life. Kids never forget. For Christians, this is even more important because Jesus said that when we embrace a child in His name, we embrace Him. As strange as this may sound to the world, we know that God is the Creator of all things and that includes children. When we honor a child, we honor His handiwork.

The kingdom of God is a mystery to this world. Our main message, the preaching of the cross, is foolishness to them (1 Corinthians 1:18). If we seek to save our lives, we lose them. If we make ourselves small in our own eyes, we become big in God's eyes. In the kingdom of God, the way down is the way up. And when we receive a little child in the name of Jesus, we receive the Savior.

SOUL SEARCH

Was I scarred as a child by the harsh words of an adult? Am I respectful to children?

Father, help me to share your love and kindness with everyone, including children.

Birds of a Feather

Do not forbid him, for he who is not against us is on our side.
LUKE 9:50

It is true that birds of a feather flock together. Sparrows don't hang out with doves. Neither do hawks with hummingbirds. They stay with those that look and sound like they do.

As human beings, we tend to do something similar. We gather in our own little flocks and think we have it right. But there are millions who love God that have different feathers and sing a different song than you. They sometimes act, dress, and worship differently. However, God doesn't look upon each of us through the doors of a particular denomination. He looks upon the heart, and the Bible says His foundation stands sure, having this seal, the Lord knows those that are His (2 Timothy 2:19).

It is therefore wise for us not to want to call fire down from heaven upon those we disagree with about nonessential doctrines. We should instead love and pray for them.

SOUL SEARCH

Do I think I'm right and look condescendingly upon those with different beliefs within the Body of Christ?

Father, help me to see other Christians as you see them.

Sons of Wrath

You do not know what manner of spirit you are of.
LUKE 9:55

The context of this rebuke from Jesus was the occasion when the disciples saw those with whom they disagreed and wanted to call fire down from the heavens and kill them.

Jesus told them that that spirit was the evil spirit that works within the sons of disobedience. Before we came to the Savior, the devil was our father, and we were held captive by him to do his will. We do his will when we are bitter and angry without cause and when we lie, steal, kill, commit adultery, hate, lust, rape, and murder.

As Christians, we now have the wisdom of the Word, a tender conscience, and the indwelling Holy Spirit to restrain us from evil. But before we were saved and people ran contrary to us, we acted like spoiled children who can't have their way. We would gladly call fire down from heaven just like the disciples wanted to do. That's the spirit that works within the world. Road rage isn't confined to the road: "Therefore put to death your members which are on the earth: fornication, uncleanness, passion, evil desire, and covetousness, which is idolatry. Because of these things the wrath of God is coming upon the sons of disobedience, in which you yourselves once walked when you lived in them" (Colossians 3:5–7).

SOUL SEARCH

Is love and kindness at the core of everything I do?

Father, let your love shine through me today.

Mercy There was Great

For the Son of Man did not come to destroy men's lives
but to save them.

LUKE 9:56

The book of Psalms puts great emphasis upon the mercy of God. Although our Creator is just and holy and, therefore, wrathful against our sins, the Bible says that He is rich in mercy (Ephesians 2:4).

The richness of that mercy is seen in the patience Jesus had with His disciples—their unbelief, their fears, their sectarianism, and their attempts to keep little children away from Him. Even His harsh rebuke of the Pharisee's hypocrisy was clothed in mercy. Justice could have rightly been displayed from heaven, but mercy held it back.

The wonderful life-giving mercy was best displayed for all to see at the cross when Christ suffered and died for our sins. This is because the Son of Man did not come to destroy men's lives but to save them. His lovingkindness and His mercy cannot be separated: "Have mercy upon me, O God, according to Your lovingkindness; according to the multitude of Your tender mercies, blot out my transgressions" (Psalm 51:1).

SOUL SEARCH

Is my life a lighthouse in this dark world? What can I do to express mercy toward others?

Father, let the light of your mercy shine through me.

The Gauntlet

My doctrine is not Mine, but His who sent Me. If anyone wills to do His will, he shall know concerning the doctrine, whether it is from God or whether I speak on My own authority. He who speaks from himself seeks his own glory; but He who seeks the glory of the One who sent Him is true, and no unrighteousness is in Him.

JOHN 7:16–18

The old adage is true—the proof of the pudding is in the tasting. "O taste and see that the LORD is good" (Psalm 34:8). If anyone will obey the gospel, they will discover that the words Jesus spoke were from God. His doctrine wasn't His own but of the One who sent Him. God was in Christ, reconciling the world to Himself.

We are not naturally inclined to repent and trust in Jesus. We are like cockroaches in the night. When a light comes on, we scurry back into hiding. This is why the Law plays such a significant role in bringing us to the gospel. The criminal will only come out of the darkness with his hands raised in surrender if he knows that he has no other way of escape. The Law does that convincing. It enables us to understand our danger: "But before faith came, we were kept under guard by the law, kept for the faith which would afterward be revealed."

SOUL SEARCH

Do I use the Law as Jesus did, to bring the knowledge of sin to sinners? How can I incorporate the Law into my witnessing?

Father, teach me to "teach sinners in the way" (Psalm 51:13).

August

Lawbreakers

*Did not Moses give you the law, yet none of you
keeps the law? Why do you seek to kill Me?*
JOHN 7:19

Here is the root of the error made by the religious leaders. They
had been given the Law of Moses, continually violated its precepts, and yet they accused Jesus of breaking the Law. They went
even further and wanted to kill Him for His supposed Lawbreak-
ing. This evil intention was directed toward the Just One, the only
human being who had ever kept the Law perfectly, in thought,
word, and deed.

When we are found guilty, we can either react in humility and
contrition or act proudly in anger. Jesus accused them of breaking the Law and asked why they had murder in their hearts. Ste-
ven said almost identical words to the Pharisees. On speaking of
what they did to Jesus, he said, "Of whom you now have become
the betrayers and murderers, who have received the law by the
direction of angels and have not kept it" (Acts 7:52–53).

Then they killed him.

Despite these two extreme precedents, never be afraid to take
a sinner through the moral Law. If they honor the Law and have
an honest heart about their state before God, they will not only
listen to you, but they will also understand the gospel.

SOUL SEARCH

Am I hesitant to preach against sin for fear of the consequences? Bring your fear to the Lord and ask for divine courage.

Father, never let me fear anything but you.

Marvelous Work

I did one work, and you all marvel. Moses therefore gave you circumcision (not that it is from Moses, but from the fathers), and you circumcise a man on the Sabbath. If a man receives circumcision on the Sabbath, so that the law of Moses should not be broken, are you angry with Me because I made a man completely well on the Sabbath?

JOHN 7:21–23

One Sabbath day, Jesus angered the religious leaders by healing a man who had been lying in misery for thirty-eight years. This was a marvelous thing to do. It was a divine miracle and an expression of love and kindness. Instead of seeing it that way, the religious leaders, professed representatives of the God of Israel, accused the perfect Son of God of sin.

If you are doing a good work for the Lord, you can be sure those same accusatory demons will point their fingers at you, either through flesh and blood or through negative thoughts. Like bloodsucking mosquitoes, they hang around for an opportunity to poison.

Your best repellent is to watch, pray, and slap the pests with the Word of God.

SOUL SEARCH

Have I ever been persecuted for the name of Jesus? Am I doing anything that would attract the scorn of this world?

Father, today, help me to keep my eyes on you.

How to Judge

Do not judge according to appearance,
but judge with righteous judgment.
JOHN 7:24

It's normal for us to judge by appearance, but God looks upon the heart. When Samuel was looking for the next king of Israel, he was impressed with one of the sons of Jesse. Listen to what God told him: "Do not look at his appearance or at his physical stature, because I have refused him. For the Lord does not see as man sees; for man looks at the outward appearance, but the LORD looks at the heart" (1 Samuel 16:7).

As Christians, we must try and see the world through the eyes of God. That means judging according to the standards of the Word of God.

One of the most misquoted Bible verses used by skeptics is "Judge not lest you be judged" (Luke 6:37). In context, Jesus was saying that as believers we should not judge one another. But we are certainly free to make judgments, and when we do, we are to judge according to God's righteousness. Every time we hear of rape, murder, theft, lying, or any other transgression and say that these actions are morally wrong, we are making legitimate judgments.

SOUL SEARCH

Am I ever guilty of prejudging people or of being prejudiced?

Father, help me to hold back when I'm tempted to prejudge people.

The Fear of the Lord

You both know Me, and you know where I am from; and I have not come of Myself, but He who sent Me is true, whom you do not know. But I know Him, for I am from Him, and He sent Me.

JOHN 7:28–29

The continual accusations of the religious leaders did not come from a sincere desire to do the will of God but came from evil hearts that hated the light. From the moment Jesus opened His mouth, they wanted to kill Him. The apostle Paul said to his hearers: "Men and brethren, sons of the family of Abraham, and those among you who fear God, to you the word of this salvation has been sent. For those who dwell in Jerusalem, and their rulers, because they did not know Him, nor even the voices of the Prophets which are read every Sabbath, have fulfilled them in condemning Him" (Acts 13:26–27).

The gospel is only understood by those who fear God. Until the fear of the Lord dawns in the human heart, the good news makes no sense. The Law produces this necessary fear, and it is the fear that causes people to let go of their sin: "In mercy and truth atonement is provided for iniquity; and by the fear of the LORD one departs from evil" (Proverbs 16:6).

SOUL SEARCH

What evidence is there in my life that I fear the Lord?

Father, may I never fail to tremble when I think of your holiness and power.

Known Future

*I shall be with you a little while longer,
and then I go to Him who sent Me.
You will seek Me and not find Me,
and where I am you cannot come.*

JOHN 7:33–34

God is never thrown into confusion. He never has a senior moment. From the second that Jesus was conceived in the womb of Mary until He ascended into the heavens, every moment of His divine life was planned by God. He was not caught off guard by the betrayal of Judas Iscariot, by the mockery of Herod's guards, or by the Roman nails that pierced His gracious hands and beautiful feet.

Jesus knew what the future would bring. He would go to the cross, suffer for the sin of the world, rise from the dead after three days, and then ascend into the heavens. He would be with His disciples a little longer, and then He would go to the Father who had sent Him and be seated at the right hand of God. This was the immediate dwelling place of Almighty God, where no human being had ever been nor could go without being consumed by the just wrath of His perfect holiness.

SOUL SEARCH

Do I long for the coming kingdom? Will it be in my thoughts today?

Father, I groan for the redemption of my body. Save the lost and then come quickly.

The Required Thirst

If anyone thirsts, let him come to Me and drink. He who believes in Me, as the Scripture has said, out of his heart will flow rivers of living water.

JOHN 7:37–38

If anyone thirsts. Anyone. Black, white, rich, poor, happy, sad, wise, fool. Whosoever will may come, but with one condition: He must "thirst." "'Ho! Everyone who thirsts, come to the waters; and you who have no money, come, buy and eat'" (Isaiah 55:1).

A sinner must come to the Savior thirsting for righteousness. Riches will be worthless on the Day of Wrath, but righteousness will deliver us from death (Proverbs 11:4).

One of the properties of salt is that it creates thirst. Jesus called us "the salt of the earth" (Matthew 5:13). With the help of God, we can enable sin-loving sinners to have a change of heart and begin to thirst for righteousness. All we need to do is what Jesus did when he counseled the rich young ruler in Mark 10: open up the divine Law to show them that without righteousness they are going to perish on the day of wrath.

SOUL SEARCH

Am I causing sinners to desire the righteousness that will deliver them from God's wrath?

Father, help me to be the salt of the earth.

Written with His Finger

He who is without sin among you,
let him throw a stone at her first.

JOHN 8:7

These wonderful words came on the heels of the woman caught in adultery. The religious leaders called for her blood, but Jesus ignored their accusations. Instead, He bent down and wrote with His finger in the sand.

We don't know what He wrote, but I would suggest that it was the Ten Commandments because of what happened to His listeners. Their consciences were smitten, and they began to leave from the oldest to the youngest. That's what the Law does. It accuses of sin; it smites the human conscience. It brings the knowledge of sin and shows us that our personal sins are exceedingly sinful in the sight of God. The Law is the stone that Jesus said would fall on unrepentant sinners and grind them to powder. When something is ground to powder, a thorough job is done.

It would seem that Jesus wrote the Commandments that day. After all, what else does God write with His finger? Scripture says that the Commandments were written in stone with the finger of God. Now they were being written in sand so that they could be easily erased by the grace of God. In Christ, our sins are easily washed away.

SOUL SEARCH

Am I quick to throw stones? Have I forgotten what I've been forgiven in Christ?

Father, never let me forget your mercy.

Sin No More

Woman, where are those accusers of yours?
Has no one condemned you? . . .
Neither do I condemn you; go and sin no more.
JOHN 8:10–11

Go and sin no more. This is the essence of repentance and this is the message of the cross the world needs to hear.

"Cleanse your hands, you sinners; and purify your hearts, you double-minded. Lament and mourn and weep! Let your laughter be turned to mourning and your joy to gloom. Humble yourselves in the sight of the Lord, and He will lift you up" (James 4:8–10).

When we are truly repentant and trust in Jesus alone, our sins are completely forgiven. Our hearts are purified.

The Bible says that there is no condemnation from God to those who are in Christ Jesus (Romans 8:1–2). And as evidence of genuine repentance and faith in Jesus, by His grace, they sin no more. This does not mean that they will not fall into sin, but it does mean that they will not dive into it. How could this woman caught in the very act of adultery and so close to a terrible death ever go back to adultery? After shown such mercy, never. And how could we ever go back to sin after seeing the cross? Such a thought is loathsome.

SOUL SEARCH

Have I truly seen the incredible sacrifice Jesus made on the cross for my sins? Can I carry the wonder of it with me daily and share it with others?

Father, never let me look back at the world.

The Light of the World

I am the light of the world. He who follows Me shall not walk in darkness, but have the light of life.

JOHN 8:12

The adulterous woman had violated the seventh commandment, and she felt the wrath of the Law calling for her blood. She couldn't justify herself. She was guilty and had no hope of salvation outside of falling at the feet of the Savior.

This is the way of salvation for guilty sinners. We realize that our sin has been discovered and that the Law rightly calls for justice. Our mouths are stopped (Romans 3:19–20), and we cannot justify ourselves. So with no hope, we fall at the feet of the Savior where we find mercy. It is in the darkness of the Law that we see the light of the Savior.

When God gave His Law there was blackness and darkness: "For you have not come to the mountain that may be touched and that burned with fire, and to blackness and darkness and tempest, and the sound of a trumpet and the voice of words, so that those who heard it begged that the word should not be spoken to them anymore" (Hebrews 12:18–19).

In the darkness of the Law's wrath we see the light of the glorious gospel of Jesus Christ. And so begins the new life of those who follow Jesus, the Light of the world.

SOUL SEARCH

Have I ever heard the thunder of the Law demanding justice for my sin? Have I fled to the light of the Savior?

Father, help me to stay in the light today.

The Appointment

Even if I bear witness of Myself, My witness is true, for I know where I came from and where I am going; but you do not know where I come from and where I am going. You judge according to the flesh; I judge no one. And yet if I do judge, My judgment is true; for I am not alone, but I am with the Father who sent Me.

JOHN 8:14-16

Unlike Jesus, skeptics don't know where they came from or where they are going. They have no idea of their origin, their purpose, or where they will spend eternity. Some even say there is no after-life, as if they had inside information. To the rest of the ungodly (who are honest), death remains the ultimate mystery.

Many years ago, the rock group Blood, Sweat & Tears sung a famous song in which they said that they were sure that there was no heaven but prayed that there was no hell. Then they ended with the words, "But . . . only my dying will tell."

We don't have to die to know the truth. We can know it this side of death. Jesus said that if we truly became His disciples by continuing in His Word, we would know the truth and the truth would make us free (John 8:31–32).

SOUL SEARCH

Do I know the truth? What words would I use to share the truth with others?

Father, overlook my weaknesses, and use me to take the truth of your Word to the lost.

True and Faithful Witness

It is also written in your law that the testimony of two men is true. I am One who bears witness of Myself, and the Father who sent Me bears witness of Me.

JOHN 8:17–18

A witness is someone who is called upon in court to testify about what they have seen and heard. If you are concerned that you are not gifted or eloquent enough to be a witness for Jesus Christ, consider this thought: the last thing a judge wants in a trial is for a witness to wax eloquent: "The cool breeze seemed to splash across the skin on my warm brow like the fresh aroma of Brazilian coffee beans on the dark and stormy night of the crime."

He would probably rebuke you and tell you to keep it simple. When we testify to others about our experience with Christ, we don't need to use impressive words or be particularly eloquent. We just talk about what we have seen and heard: "And I, brethren, when I came to you, did not come with excellence of speech or of wisdom declaring to you the testimony of God. For I determined not to know anything among you except Jesus Christ and Him crucified … [so] that your faith should not be in the wisdom of men but in the power of God" (1 Corinthians 2:1–5).

SOUL SEARCH

Have I excused myself from the task of evangelism by saying that I'm not gifted? Determine to stop making that excuse and bring your inadequacies to God.

Father, help me to lay aside every excuse and do what I know I should.

Jesus Is God

You know neither Me nor My Father. If you had known Me,
you would have known My Father also.

JOHN 8:19

Jesus Christ is the exact representation of the God who created every atom in the universe. When He cleared the temple of the money changers, He was expressing God's hatred of hypocrisy. When He walked on water and calmed the storm, He was revealing the sovereignty of God over His creation. When He raised people from the dead, He was showing us the power of God over the grave. When He wept at the graveside of Lazarus (four days dead) and shed tears over Jerusalem, He was expressing the compassionate heart of His Father:

> He is the image of the invisible God, the first-born over all creation. For by Him all things were created that are in heaven and that are on earth, visible and invisible, whether thrones or dominions or principalities or powers. All things were created through Him and for Him. (Colossians 1:13–16)

SOUL SEARCH

Do I correctly exalt Jesus in my theology?

Father, I honor Jesus as I honor you, according to your Word (John 5:23).

Dying to Sin

I am going away, and you will seek Me,
and will die in your sin.
Where I go you cannot come.
JOHN 8:21

Better to lose both of your eyes than to die in your sin. Better to lose your arm or leg than to die without the forgiveness of God in Christ because it means you will be damned with no way out of hell. It means that you will stand before the Judge of the universe and give an account for every idle word you have spoken. You will answer for every sinful thought you have ever had, every wicked deed ever done, every failure to be thankful for, and every blessing God showered upon you.

In addition, every word spoken in unjust anger will be proof of your guilt. Oh, please, don't entertain sin for a second because it demands payment for the pleasure it affords. The payment is your eternal soul—your most precious possession: "If your right eye causes you to sin, pluck it out and cast it from you; for it is more profitable for you that one of your members perish, than for your whole body to be cast into hell" (Matthew 5:29).

SOUL SEARCH

Have I contemplated the cost of my sin? Do I guard my heart with all diligence?

Father, let my fear of you be real today. Help me to reckon sin dead.

Two Kingdoms

You are from beneath; I am from above. You are of this world; I am not of this world. Therefore I said to you that you will die in your sins; for if you do not believe that I am He, you will die in your sins.

JOHN 8:23-24

There are only two kingdoms. We are either in the kingdom of darkness or we are in the kingdom of light. Until we come to the Savior, we are born from beneath. We are children of the kingdom of darkness. Children of wrath. Children of disobedience. And if we are friends with this world, we are enemies of God (Romans 5:10).

When the love of God came like a beam of light breaking through the dark clouds, we were translated from the kingdom of darkness into the kingdom of light. Now we are born from above. We are not of this world. We are no longer enemies of God. We have the divine smile. We don't think like this world, don't speak or act like this world, and will not perish like this world. This is all because of the grace of Almighty God.

It is because of the cross that we will not die in our sins. God, who cannot lie, promised us everlasting life.

SOUL SEARCH

Today I will think like the child of the King. This world is not my home.

Father, lead me and guide me today according to your promise.

The Enduring Love

Just what I have been saying to you from the beginning.
I have many things to say and to judge concerning you,
but He who sent Me is true; and I speak to the world those
things which I heard from Him.

JOHN 8:25-26

The incarnation was a mystery. God Almighty, who fills the universe with His presence, limited Himself to the body of one tiny baby in a common manger in the little town of Bethlehem. As Jesus grew, the Bible says that He grew in knowledge. As He read the Scripture and heard from the Father, His true identity must have gradually dawned on Him. What an overwhelming thought!

We really don't know if He knew about His coming suffering from studying the Scripture or if God spoke directly to Him. Whatever the case, Jesus knew that He had been born for the purpose of suffering.

He was the Lamb of God whose blood had to be shed for the sin of the world. We must never for a moment forget that breathtaking sacrifice. Because in remembering, we will be reminded how much God loves us, and it will help us to endure our daily trials and this world's hatred: "For consider Him who endured such hostility from sinners against Himself, lest you become weary and discouraged in your souls" (Hebrews 12:3).

SOUL SEARCH

If I ever become weary in my soul it may be because I'm not considering the suffering of my Savior.

Father, keep my mind on Jesus today.

The Revelation of the Cross

When you lift up the Son of Man, then you will know that I am He, and that I do nothing of Myself; but as My Father taught Me, I speak these things. And He who sent Me is with Me. The Father has not left Me alone, for I always do those things that please Him.

JOHN 8:28–29

The crowds gathered to watch the agonizing spectacle of Jesus of Nazareth being nailed to the cross. They witnessed the horror of seeing and hearing nails being driven into His hands and feet. They saw the blood stream from His gaping wounds. As He died, they witnessed a great earthquake. Even the centurion confessed that Jesus of Nazareth truly was the Son of God.

No doubt the centurion was not the only one who witnessed the Son of man being lifted on that cross and suddenly realized that He was who He said He was—the Messiah.

We are to paint that dark scene for sinners. We are to gather them together to gaze at the spectacle of the cross and may the same realization fall upon them as the Holy Spirit opens the eyes of their understanding of what actually took place two thousand years ago.

Our great hope is that they will whisper, "Truly this was the Son of God."

SOUL SEARCH

May I realize that today is an opportunity to reach sinners with the message of everlasting life.

Father, please give me someone today who will listen.

Daily Food

If you abide in My word, you are My disciples indeed. And you shall know the truth, and the truth shall make you free.
JOHN 8:31–32

I often ask Christians I meet if they are reading the Word daily. The most common answer is that they are "trying to." That's when I ask them if they try to have breakfast each morning. Do they try to have lunch and then try to have dinner? Of course not! Food is such a priority that they don't try to eat—they just eat.

The enemy could care less if we eat ten meals a day, but he will fight us tooth and nail to stop us from feeding on the Word daily. He knows that God's Word nourishes us, makes us strong, and causes us to grow in Christ.

The Bible says of Job that he esteemed the words of God's mouth more than his necessary food (Job 23:12). That's how you and I should be with our Bible reading. We need to read it daily. No Bible, no breakfast. No read, no feed. We esteem the Word of God more than necessary food. This is what a disciple is, and this is what a disciple does. We abide in the Word. The fruit of such discipline is the knowledge of the truth that sets us free.

SOUL SEARCH

Have I been lazy when it comes to feeding on the Word daily? How can I change my schedule to make time for devotions?

Father, help me to esteem your Word more than my necessary food.

Sin's Partner

Most assuredly, I say to you, whoever commits sin is a slave of sin. And a slave does not abide in the house forever, but a son abides forever. Therefore if the Son makes you free, you shall be free indeed.

JOHN 8:34–36

Jesus often uses "most assuredly." As we have seen, this is the urgency we need to convey every time we speak with the lost. The truth we share is utterly sobering, and what Jesus is saying here could never be overemphasized. Most assuredly, if we serve sin, we are its slave.

As a son or daughter of the living God, you are not a slave of sin. The moment you came to Christ, your chains fell off. Jesus unlocked them so that you could be free from its power. Always remember: sin is married to death. You can't have one without the other. The Bible speaks of the law of sin and death. If we are married to sin we will be married to the ice-cold bed partner of death.

Never let sin deceive you. Never allow its allurements to attract your eyes or its whisperings entice your ears. Be deaf and blind to its seductions. The only way to do this is to walk in the fear of the Lord. Cultivate it. Read and believe the Bible's revelation of God's holy character and let it make you tremble.

SOUL SEARCH

Today I will meditate on God's holiness.

Father, this day help me see you as you really are.

Their True Identity

I know that you are Abraham's descendants, but you seek to kill Me, because My word has no place in you. I speak what I have seen with My Father, and you do what you have seen with your father.

JOHN 8:37–38

Over the next few verses, Jesus used the words "your father" four times. At first He didn't tell them who their father was. They assumed that God was their father because they were Abraham's descendants. However, when they did not accept the words that Jesus spoke, they proved themselves to be children of the devil.

Millions throughout the world assume that God is their Father and that they are His children, but when they finally see their own sin, suddenly God becomes distant as the thunder of His wrath against sin is heard.

When the world practices their religion, they assume that they are doing the will of God, but the apostle Paul says differently: "Rather, that the things which the Gentiles sacrifice they sacrifice to demons and not to God, and I do not want you to have fellowship with demons" (1 Corinthians 10:20).

If they were serving God, they would accept Jesus Christ as their Messiah. He was the litmus test of their spirituality.

SOUL SEARCH

May I never be cavalier in my walk with God. May I never be overly familiar with Him or take anything for granted.

Father, give me the wisdom I need to reason with those who don't know you.

An Eye on Eternity

If you were Abraham's children, you would do the works of Abraham. But now you seek to kill Me, a Man who has told you the truth which I heard from God. Abraham did not do this. You do the deeds of your father.

JOHN 8:39–41

Once again Jesus makes reference to their father without revealing his identity. No doubt they thought that Jesus was referring to the God of their forefathers. But if God was their father, and they were truly walking in the steps of their father Abraham, they would not have entertained thoughts of murder. They sought to kill Jesus for simply saying he had heard from the God they professed to love.

The statement "Abraham did not do this" was perhaps a reference to the theophany Abraham experienced in Genesis 18. Abraham was quick to show his love and hospitality to the strangers who came to him. If these people had been Abraham's seed, they would have treated Jesus with respect.

Abraham had his eyes on eternity. He saw Him who is invisible. Charles Spurgeon said, "Can we live through this transient span of time and never remember that we have to live forever?"[10]

SOUL SEARCH

Do I walk in the steps of Abraham? Is my faith entirely in God today and my eye on eternity?

Father, I trust you with all my heart because you are faithful.

The Future

If God were your Father, you would love Me, for I proceeded forth and came from God; nor have I come of Myself, but He sent Me. Why do you not understand My speech? Because you are not able to listen to My word.

JOHN 8:42–43

Jesus reiterated His words because the religious leaders were dull of hearing. If God was truly their Father, they would have embraced Jesus because He proceeded from God. He didn't speak His own words; He spoke the words of the Father. He had been sent down as light from heaven by Almighty God who "Gave His only begotten Son, that whoever believes in Him should not perish but have everlasting life" (John 3:16). Still, they did not understand because they did not mingle His words with faith. Sin makes us unable to hear from God. It deafens, blinds, deludes, and deceives.

Those who deliberately stiffen their necks in unbelief close their ears to the words of everlasting life. They are not able to listen because of their stubborn pride and their love for sin. Oh, how our hearts should break for such foolish people. There are so many! What does the future hold for them if they don't come to saving faith? Death without trust in Christ is terrifying because hell awaits.

SOUL SEARCH

Is my heart broken for the unsaved? Does love overcome my fears and drive me to reach out to them? I determine today to step out of my comfort zone and share the good news with someone.

Father, help me to do something today to reach the unsaved.

The Truth in Love

You are of your father the devil, and the desires of your father you want to do. He was a murderer from the beginning, and does not stand in the truth, because there is no truth in him. When he speaks a lie, he speaks from his own resources, for he is a liar and the father of it.

JOHN 8:44

If you don't want to win a popularity contest, tell those who think they are serving God that they're serving the devil. Tell them that God is not their father and that they are actually children of disobedience.

There is a way to make such distasteful words palatable though. The religious leaders had the moral Law and as we have seen, they had nullified it through unbelief and tradition. More than likely, those to whom you and I speak are not guilty of this. When you take people through the Commandments, their consciences may be tender and their hearts humble. When we show sinners that lust is adultery and hatred is murder in the eyes of God and that all liars will end up in the lake of fire, the thought that God isn't their coddling Father will be more believable. Instead of being their friend, He is their enemy. Such thoughts will prepare them for the revelation of His love displayed at the cross.

SOUL SEARCH

Does the thought of talking about sin to the lost make me feel uncomfortable? Why?

Father, help me to always speak the truth in love.

Sinless Savior

But because I tell the truth, you do not believe Me. Which of you convicts Me of sin? And if I tell the truth, why do you not believe Me? He who is of God hears God's words; therefore you do not hear, because you are not of God.

JOHN 8:45–47

While the world would have no trouble accusing you and me of being sinners, we can never do that with Jesus. He was squeaky clean. He was without sin and walked in perfect righteousness. Neither the world nor the Law could accuse Him.

If you asked a skeptic if Jesus ever did anything wrong, he would probably point a finger at His anger when He cleared the buyers and sellers from the Temple. But who cannot rejoice at the thought of God clearing out the televangelists of His day? If He wasn't angry at evil, He wouldn't be good. Wrath against evil is evidence of the goodness of God.

The world often complains about hypocrisy, but we cannot charge Jesus with that sin. None of His accusers could find fault with Him, so why didn't they believe His words? Jesus once again put His finger on the problem. They were not of God. They were children of the devil, and it was his works they were doing.

SOUL SEARCH

Have I ever experienced righteous anger? Do I ever feel angry at evil?

Father, make me more like Jesus.

The Life Source

I do not have a demon; but I honor My Father, and you dishonored Me. And I do not seek My own glory; there is One who seeks and judges. Most assuredly, I say to you, if anyone keeps My word he shall never see death.

JOHN 8:49–51

Jesus said that anyone who obeys what He says will never see death. This is equivalent to a man saying that he will put the noonday sun in his pocket. It sounds insane. Everyone sees death.

When sinners are born of the Spirit, the eternal life-source enters them, and the presence of eternal life overcomes death in the same way that light overcomes darkness. This knowledge should give us a passion to share the gospel:

> So when this corruptible has put on incorruption, and this mortal has put on immortality, then shall be brought to pass the saying that is written: "Death is swallowed up in victory."
>
> "O Death, where is your sting? O Hades, where is your victory?" The sting of death is sin, and the strength of sin is the law. But thanks be to God, who gives us the victory through our Lord Jesus Christ. (1 Corinthians 15:54–57)

SOUL SEARCH

What can I do to remind myself to dwell on the miracle of eternal life?

Father, never let me forget for one moment your unspeakable gift.

The Honor of God

If I honor Myself, My honor is nothing. It is My Father who honors Me, of whom you say that He is your God. Yet you have not known Him, but I know Him. And if I say, "I do not know Him," I shall be a liar like you; but I do know Him and keep His word. Your father Abraham rejoiced to see My day, and he saw it and was glad.

JOHN 8:54-56

The world seeks honor from the world. From sports to politics to business and in almost every human interaction, we seek the praise of man. We dress, talk, and act to impress others. When we come to Christ, our greatest desire is to seek the praise that comes from God in all things. We honor Him in our thoughts, dress, and by our desires. We say with the psalmist, "Let the words of my mouth and the meditation of my heart be acceptable in your sight, O LORD" (Psalm 19:14).

Perhaps the greatest way we can honor God is to point the world to the gospel of Jesus Christ. It is in the cross that God is most honored. It is there that we see His righteousness revealed from faith to faith, and His great love is displayed to the whole world. What an honor it will be to have God Himself say to the faithful laborer, "Well done you good and faithful servant" (Matthew 25:23).

SOUL SEARCH

Are there any areas in my life where I still seek the honor of men?

Father, may I seek the honor that comes from you alone.

Claiming the Name

Most assuredly, I say to you, before Abraham was, I AM.
JOHN 8:58

Of all the breathtaking and fantastic claims made by Jesus of Nazareth, this arguably has to be near the top. He made other amazing and incredible claims, and He declared He was the only way to God—no one could get to the Father without Him (John 14:6). He also said that the day would come when the dead billions that are in their graves would hear His voice and would be raised from the dead to stand before Him in judgment. He said that He was the resurrection and the life, and He was preexistent and had come down from heaven to do the will of God.

But here He claims to be the same I AM who revealed Himself to Moses in the burning bush. When Moses asked God for His name, He replied, "I AM."

And God said to Moses, "I AM WHO I AM." And He said, "Thus you shall say to the children of Israel, 'I AM has sent me to you'" (Exodus 3:14).

That name tells us that He is ever present in time and that He is the same yesterday, today, and forever. Here, Jesus said that before Abraham existed, He was eternally present. He was Almighty God.

SOUL SEARCH

How do I react when I hear the name of Jesus used in blasphemy?

Father, may I never dishonor your holy name.

God's Judgments

Neither this man nor his parents sinned, but that the works of God should be revealed in him. I must work the works of Him who sent Me while it is day; the night is coming when no one can work. As long as I am in the world, I am the light of the world.

JOHN 9:3–5

How quick we are to judge others and conclude that they are under the judgment of God or at least that they have lost His favor.

For example, when someone is struck by lightning, it would be easy to say God was judging him. After all, we know that God is in charge of electricity. However, only about twenty-seven people die each year in the United States from lightning strikes. If God is judging people with lightning, He's not hitting as many as He did back in the 1940s when 432 people died from lightning. The drop in numbers is attributed to education, particularly the phrase "When thunder roars, go indoors."

Even though the man and his parents in this story were sinners, his blindness had nothing to do with their moral state before God; rather, Jesus said it was an opportunity for the work of God to be revealed in him. And it was. He opened the eyes of a man born blind, and we are still talking about it two thousand years later.

SOUL SEARCH

Am I quick to make judgments about what may or may not be God's judgments?

Father, remind me to lay my hands upon my mouth when I'm not sure of the facts.

Come Back Seeing

Go, wash in the pool of Siloam.
JOHN 9:7

This blind man groped his way to the pool of Siloam and washed. It was an act of faith and obedience. He had no doubt washed himself a thousand times before, but this time was different. Jesus had told him to go and wash.

And he came back seeing!

We have a similar message for this blind world that is stumbling through life. When Paul addressed his hearers in Athens, he said, "So that they should seek the Lord, in the hope that they might grope for Him and find Him, though He is not far from each one of us; for in Him we live and move and have our being, as also some of your own poets have said, 'For we are also His offspring'" (Acts 17:27–28).

We need to tell the spiritually blind that if they go to the Light of the World, He will open the eyes of their understanding. While the gospel is good news, it is ineffective for sinners without faith and obedience. They must exercise God-given repentance and place their trust alone in Jesus Christ as Lord and Savior. The gospel is backed up by the power of God, and all who go to Him will receive their sight.

SOUL SEARCH

Is this my experience? Did I come back seeing when I obeyed the words of Jesus? What was I blind to before?

Father, thank you for opening my blind eyes.

Another Miracle

Do you believe in the Son of God? . . . You have both seen
Him and it is He who is talking with you.
John 9:35-37

Do you believe in the Son of God? That's perhaps the most important question that you and I will ever be asked.

Sadly, many in the world don't understand what it means to believe in Jesus. When the Bible speaks of this, it doesn't mean believing in Him intellectually as a historical figure or even as a great religious teacher. When the Bible speaks of "belief" in Him, it means an implicit reliance upon Him as our sin-bearer. We trust Him alone for our eternal salvation.

This blind man had his eyes opened to the physical world. For the first time in his life, he saw amazing light, beautiful color, the vastness of the heavens, and human faces to go with the familiar voices. However, he needed more than physical sight; he needed another miracle. He needed to see his desperate need for the mercy of God. When that revelation comes to the human eye, we see clearly for the first time.

SOUL SEARCH

Do I see spiritually? Has my understanding been enlightened? Can I truly say, "Once I was blind, but now I see?"

Father, help me today to see your hand in everything.

Blinding Pride

For judgment I have come into this world, that those who do not see may see, and that those who see may be made blind.
JOHN 9:39

Jesus often spoke in riddles, so some of the things He said were hard to understand. Those proud hearts that delight in finding contradictions will find them here.

Jesus had said that He had not come to judge the world, and yet here He speaks of coming into the world for judgment. However, Jesus is speaking here about a special judgment that comes to those who are hardened in their sins. Romans 1 speaks of God giving these people over to a reprobate mind. The apostle Paul later spoke about God sending a strong delusion because they preferred to believe a lie rather than embrace the truth (2 Thessalonians 2:11).

Charles Spurgeon said, "We are all by nature blind and poor. It is true we account ourselves able enough to see; but this is but one phase of our blindness. Our blindness is of such a kind that it makes us think our vision perfect; whereas, when we are enlightened by the Holy Spirit, we discover our previous sight to have been blindness indeed."[11]

SOUL SEARCH

Do I regularly ask God to keep me from blinding pride? Am I sensitive to the Spirit's conviction in this area?

Father, I humble myself today. Help me to walk in truth.

Many Trials

Foxes have holes and birds of the air have nests,
but the Son of Man has nowhere to lay His head.
LUKE 9:58

This verse flies in the face of the prosperity preachers. Jesus was saying that even though animals had a place to stay at night, He had no place to lay His head.

While the promise is that God will supply all of our needs according to His riches in glory, we are not guaranteed a bed of roses. Rather, there is the promise of many thorns for the Christian. We enter the kingdom of God through much tribulation. Life for us is often trial after trial. But look at these wonderful promises: "Blessed is the man who endures temptation; for when he has been approved, he will receive the crown of life which the Lord has promised to those who love Him" (James 1:12).

In addition, when we have nowhere to lay our head or no food on the table or gas for the car, we know that all things are working together for our good because we love God and are called according to His purpose (Romans 8:28). It is in His permissive will that He allows tribulation to come to us because He has the end product in mind.

SOUL SEARCH

Do I fully believe that all things work together for my good, and do I rejoice in that fact? Recall the times when God has used a negative circumstance for a positive outcome.

Father, help me to always thank you for the good and for what may seem to be bad at the time.

September

Follow Me

Follow Me.
LUKE 9:59

Until we follow Jesus, we are lost. We are going nowhere, held firmly in the prison cell of sin and death. What a sad, depressingly hopeless state we are in until Jesus opens the prison door and says, "Follow me." Yet millions choose to stay in the cell, not understanding what awaits them. To choose death above life and hell above heaven is insane. The first second in hell will bring instant remorse.

What a sad thing that the man to whom Jesus spoke these words had an excuse. Had he followed Jesus during the incarnation, he would have entered into the most exciting adventure that any human being could ever have. Had he followed Jesus, he would have seen the sick healed, the blind given sight, and people raised from the dead. He would have had the privilege and honor of hearing life-changing words pour from the lips of the Son of God.

Today, millions have excuses for not following Jesus Christ. The bottom line is that people love sin. They love darkness rather than light because their deeds are evil, neither will they come to the light lest their deeds should be exposed (John 3:19–20).

SOUL SEARCH

When did I begin following Jesus? Am I still following Him daily as enthusiastically as I did at first?

Father, let me have the adventure of serving you.

The Father's Priority

Let the dead bury their own dead,
but you go and preach the kingdom of God.
LUKE 9:60

Here is the heart of the Savior and the heart of God. Evangelism is God's priority.

In those challenging words, we sense the urgency for the proclamation of the gospel. It is the message of everlasting life to those who not only sit in the shadow of death but will end up in hell unless they have their sins forgiven. This is why we must plead with the ungodly to get right with God today. Only God knows how many plan to repent and trust the Savior tomorrow, and only He knows how many will be too late.

As Christians we have a tremendous moral obligation to reach out to the lost. This is why the apostles said, "For we cannot but speak the things which we have seen and heard" (Acts 4:20). We are like doctors with a cure for cancer. It seems that most of the contemporary church has forgotten about the existence of hell because they are busy doing everything but reaching out to the lost. Oswald J. Smith said, "Oh, my friends, we are loaded down with countless church activities while the real work of the church, that of evangelizing and winning the lost, is almost entirely neglected."

SOUL SEARCH

Am I busy doing everything but reaching out to the unsaved? Make a list of the activities that consume your time. Would a shift in priorities be wise?

Father, help me to have love enough to warn the lost.

Examine Yourself

*No one, having put his hand to the plow,
and looking back, is fit for the kingdom of God.*
LUKE 9:62

How could anybody in their right mind follow Jesus and then turn back to the sinful world? Who, other than the insane, would rip off a parachute, knowing that they must jump ten thousand feet?

The answer is obvious. Those we commonly call "backsliders" aren't followers of Jesus at all. They didn't backslide because they didn't slide forward in the first place. They didn't just look back; they went back to the world. These are false converts with stony and thorny hearts who fall away in a time of temptation, tribulation, and persecution.

How can we make sure we are genuine in our faith? The key is to make sure that we are "fit" for the kingdom of God. The word "fit" in the Greek means "ready for use." We need to make sure that we have genuinely repented with no concealed or secret sin in our hearts. Such are those with good soil—those who have the seed of the gospel fall on a good and honest heart.

SOUL SEARCH

Am I hiding secret sins and deceiving myself?

Father, search me today and see if there is wickedness in my heart and lead me in the way everlasting.

Special Prayer

The harvest truly is great, but the laborers are few; therefore pray the Lord of the harvest to send out laborers into His harvest.

LUKE 10:2

It is true that many hands make light work. The more help we have, the easier the task. Just ask anyone who has had to move his or her household.

The task of reaching the lost is daunting. There are so many unsaved who have never heard the biblical gospel.

The verse above is a command from Jesus to pray for laborers to enter the harvest fields. He said the harvest truly is great. In other words, there are multitudes who are dead in their sins and few laborers to take the words of life to them.

We are told to pray for more laborers. If you're not a laborer, you won't have a concern for the salvation of others. You won't bother to pray for laborers because your conscience will condemn you if you do. The enemy then gets a double victory. Not only is there a shortage of laborers, but there is also a shortage of those who are praying for laborers.

Please change that today by asking God to give you love enough to reach out to the lost and to pray earnestly for more laborers.

SOUL SEARCH

Am I praying for laborers as I am commanded? What can I do to remind myself?

Father, please raise up laborers.

True Converts

Go your way; behold, I send you out as lambs among wolves.
LUKE 10:3

One of the great delusions of contemporary Christianity is the belief that you can live like the devil and still have assurance of salvation. Some believe that they can be practicing sin—living in adultery, lying, stealing, and blaspheming—and still be saved because they once gave their hearts to Jesus.

The issue is resolved when we have a biblical understanding of true and false conversion. True converts live in holiness. They have "the things that accompany salvation" (Hebrews 6:9). They are fruit bearers, and they are the ones who can (and should) have assurance that they are saved: "Now unto Him that is able to keep you from falling, and to present you faultless before the presence of His glory with exceeding joy" (Jude 24); "Being confident of this very thing, that He which hath begun a good work in you will perform it until the day of Jesus Christ" (Philippians 1:6).

Jesus was able to send his lambs out among wolves because they were genuinely converted. A true convert, one whose seed fell on good soil, will send his roots deep when tribulations and temptations come rather than fall away from the faith. The heat of the sun doesn't kill a healthy plant; it simply causes it to send its roots deep into the soil.

SOUL SEARCH

Do trials make me stronger or weaker in my faith?

Father, may I always be honest before you.

Our Priority

*Carry neither money bag, knapsack, nor sandals;
and greet no one along the road.*

LUKE 10:4

Nothing should distract us from preaching the gospel of everlasting life to a dying world. This should be the number one priority of the church. This was the priority of the early church in the book of Acts.

If the enemy can't discourage us, he will certainly try and distract us, and many things can distract Christians from reaching out to the lost.

We could be involved in fascinating prophecy, hermeneutics, worship, Bible study, and a million and one other legitimate and praiseworthy activities. However, someone once said that there is nothing wrong with straightening the furniture in your house but not while the house is on fire. These godly activities are wonderful, but we must never do them at the neglect of reaching out to the lost.

If there was no hell, it would make sense that the church has more important matters than evangelism. Nonetheless, it does exist, and the reality of hell should help us order our priorities and do what Jesus said to do: Go into all the world and preach the gospel to every creature.

SOUL SEARCH

Is my number one priority to do the will of God?

Father, give me a desperate compassion for the unsaved.

True Peace

But whatever house you enter,
first say, "Peace to this house."
LUKE 10:5

Very few in today's generation truly appreciate what it means for a nation to be at peace. After the end of the Second World War—five years of horrifying war and the loss of over sixty million lives—the world was able to enjoy and appreciate peace.

However, the Bible speaks of another peace—the peace of God that passes all understanding. It is the sort of peace that we can possess in the midst of noise, in a storm, and even in the middle of a war.

There is yet another peace of which the Bible often speaks, and this is the most important. It is peace with God that was purchased by Jesus on the cross. We were at war with our Creator; we were enemies of God in our minds because of what the Bible calls our "wicked works." But God's love came to us with a plan of peace that through the cross, we could have the peace of God and peace with God through trusting in our Lord Jesus.

SOUL SEARCH

Do I appreciate peace with God, and do I keep my peace in the storm?

Father, thank you that the war between you and me is over.

Worthy of Wages

And remain in the same house, eating and drinking such things as they give, for the laborer is worthy of his wages. Do not go from house to house.

LUKE 10:7

The Bible says to honor all men, but we are to give double honor to those who labor for the Lord (1 Timothy 5:17). We should generously pay ministers of the gospel. Paul covers this in Romans 9, by saying that they who preach the gospel, shall live by the gospel (v. 14).

The Bible says of Jesus in Luke 8:1–3 that certain women followed Him and "provided for Him from their substance." In other words, they graciously supplied Him with food and other necessities as He traveled. It is sad to see or hear of missionaries who are not taken care of by those on the home front. Churches should be active in supporting those who have the faith and courage to step out and share the gospel with the unsaved.

Pastoring is a difficult task. Preaching to the same people every week can be laborious and, at times, disheartening. Pray for your pastor. Love him. Be generous in your giving. Give him double honor.

SOUL SEARCH

Am I supporting my pastor in prayer? Do I give him double honor?

Father, let me be a home missionary to this dying world.

True Thanksgiving

Whatever city you enter, and they receive you,
eat such things as are set before you.
LUKE 10:8

Hospitality is a wonderful thing. It's an expression of love and honor. A dinner invitation is an appropriate way to honor our friends and neighbors.

It seems that some are only thankful to God for the provision of food and other blessings on one day each year: Thanksgiving. Others are thankful, but their thanksgiving is directed at "mother nature" or something called "providence." Thanksgiving should be perpetual, and it should be directed to our Creator. He is the One who gives us our daily bread, and shame on us if we eat our meals with an ungrateful heart.

There is a way to cultivate true thanksgiving. Fast. Fast a couple of meals each week, and when you sit down to eat, the familiarity that breeds contempt won't be there. You will thank God for all your food and enjoy it all the more.

SOUL SEARCH

Am I always thankful to God for daily food and other blessings? Take some time today and express your thanksgiving to God—be specific.

Father, never let me have a familiarity that takes any of your blessings for granted.

The Irrelevant Cross

And heal the sick there, and say to them,
"The kingdom of God has come near to you."

LUKE 10:9

Every time somebody hears the biblical gospel, the kingdom of God comes close to them. However, most don't value this "pearl of great price." The reason they don't value it is because they don't understand its value.

Most of us wouldn't value a parachute that sits at the back of the plane while we are eating delicious food and watching an interesting movie. If the flight is smooth and all is well onboard, why should we give it a second thought? The parachute is irrelevant.

However, if we were told that we had to jump out of the plane, suddenly the parachute would have more value to us. It would become the most important thing on the plane.

Christ's death on the cross is of little value to sinners who are enjoying the pleasures of sin. The cross is irrelevant to them. Once they understand they have to face a holy God on the day of wrath, and only Jesus can forgive their sins and grant them the gift of everlasting life, suddenly the gospel becomes a personal life-and-death issue. Now it is the most important thing in life.

"But God forbid that I should boast except in the cross of our Lord Jesus Christ, by whom the world has been crucified to me, and I to the world" (Galatians 6:14).

SOUL SEARCH

Do I value the work of the cross in my life?

Father, thank you for the unspeakable gift.

The Unclean

But whatever city you enter, and they do not receive you, go out into its streets and say, "The very dust of your city which clings to us we wipe off against you. Nevertheless know this, that the kingdom of God has come near you."

LUKE 10:10–11

The unsaved have no idea that God has made us pure through the righteousness of Christ. We are completely clean of sin, made morally perfect by the grace of God, and on the day of judgment, He will separate the clean from the unclean.

God looks on sin as we look on leprosy. The leper was told to call out that he was unclean. Similarly, sinners will be seen as unclean on the day of judgment (Leviticus 13:45). The book of Jude addresses this when we are told what our attitude should be to the unsaved: "And on some have compassion, making a distinction; but others save with fear, pulling them out of the fire, hating even the garment defiled by the flesh" (Jude 22–23).

We must remember that the lost are facing a terrible day and do what Christ commands us to reach them. We must have compassion on them and speak to them of the cleansing of the gospel. As we do, we must keep our own heart free from sin.

SOUL SEARCH

Do I appreciate being made clean, and do I try and stay clean from the filth of this world?

Father, help me to have compassion.

God's Perfect Justice

But I say to you that it will be more tolerable in that Day for Sodom than for that city.

LUKE 10:12

The world often accuses God of being unjust. It wrongly assumes that God will treat everyone the same in judgment. It comes in the form of saying that the sweet old lady who dies in her sins will get the same judgment as people like Hitler. She didn't slaughter millions of innocent people, but they maintain that God will treat her the same as someone who did. They use their presuppositions as an excuse to reject the gospel.

It's not true that God will be unjust. He will judge according to perfect righteousness. "The judgments of the LORD are true and righteous altogether" (Psalm 19:9).

Our key verse tells us that on the day of judgment, the cities that reject the gospel will be judged more severely than the city of Sodom. God will only execute perfect justice on that frightful day—no more and no less. He will give Hitler exactly what he deserves, and He will give the sweet little old lady what she deserves. Both have a lifetime of clocking up a multitude of sins and storing up God's wrath.

SOUL SEARCH

How does the righteous justice of God affect my decisions?

Father, let my life express my gratitude for your mercy in Christ.

Unearned Favor

Woe to you, Chorazin! Woe to you, Bethsaida! For if the mighty works which were done in you had been done in Tyre and Sidon, they would have repented long ago, sitting in sackcloth and ashes. But it will be more tolerable for Tyre and Sidon at the judgment than for you.

LUKE 10:13-14

Job sat in sackcloth and ashes. Life had struck him a terrible and fatal blow. He had lost his ten children to tragedy; his wife and friends didn't comfort him. He was understandably miserable.

As time passed, he demanded to speak to God about what he perceived as his ill treatment. After God spoke to him, he responded by saying, "I have heard of you by the hearing of the ear, but now my eye sees you. Therefore I abhor myself, and repent in dust and ashes" (Job 42:5–6).

There is wonderful irony in contrasting God's perfection and our unworthiness, and it is this: God loved us and saved us anyway. He owed us nothing but wrath, but He reached out while we were yet sinners and saved us from death. His love is not performance-driven. We don't have to earn His favor. It is ours because He is love itself. Our salvation isn't driven by anything we do. We are saved by grace and grace alone.

SOUL SEARCH

Do I bask in God's love in Christ as I do in the warmth and light of the sun?

Father, your love is my light in the darkness of this world.

The Fear of Man

*And you, Capernaum, who are exalted to heaven,
will be brought down to Hades.*
LUKE 10:15

I prefer not to speak of Hades. I use the word hell when speaking of the place of punishment because the world knows exactly what I mean. The reality of hell is probably the most offensive of all contemporary Christian doctrines. Preach it and a sin-loving world will despise you. It is understandable why so many popular preachers avoid its mention. It's no doubt for fear of offending their hearers.

However, it is infinitely better for a sinner to hear of hell than for him or her to feel it. The world will forever despise a preacher who failed to warn them of its reality. May every one of us be faithful and live to hear the words, "Well done, you good and faithful servant" (Matthew 25:23).

We should rather have the frown of the world because we preach hell than the frown of God because we didn't. It is the fear of God and love for sinners that motivates us to warn every man that we may present every man perfect in Christ Jesus.

SOUL SEARCH

When has the fear of man stopped me from being faithful to God?

Father, help me to always be faithful with your gospel.

Rejection

*He who hears you hears Me, he who rejects you rejects Me,
and he who rejects Me rejects Him who sent Me.*
LUKE 10:16

What an honorable privilege we have! We represent Almighty God—we are ambassadors for Christ (2 Corinthians 5:18–20).

Jesus came to His own, and they rejected Him (John 1:11), yet He showed them His love anyway from the agony of the cross. Perhaps our greatest fear when it comes to the task of evangelism is that same rejection. Our greatest weapon against that fear is the same love that God showed us through the cross. If God loved us that much, we can love this evil world in spite of its rejection.

The Bible gives us the specifics of why unbelievers have such hatred toward God: "The mind of the flesh [with its sinful pursuits] is actively hostile to God. It does not submit itself to God's law, since it cannot, and those who are in the flesh [living a life that caters to sinful appetites and impulses] cannot please God" (Romans 8:7–8 AMP). It's because they hate His Law. It forbids everything they live for: sin.

SOUL SEARCH

Is it hard for me to endure persecution personally? In what ways have I been persecuted?

Father, help me to rejoice in persecution and love my enemies.

The Silliness of Conceit

I saw Satan fall like lightning from heaven.
LUKE 10:18

We need to continually remind ourselves of the fact that we don't wrestle against flesh and blood. Our battle is spiritual, against a very real demonic world that is the essence of evil. Still, evil forces are subject to us through faith in the name of Jesus. They tremble at His name because He is the Holy One.

However, it seems that the seventy disciples in Luke 10 were rejoicing not in the power of His name but in their own power in using it. May we never become puffed up with what we may see as our own ability.

If we can sing and dance, we can only do so because God created every atom of our bodies; even our coordination comes from Him. No matter what ability we have—jump, run, preach, or teach—each one traces itself back to our Creator. Why does pride puff out its silly little chest?

Perhaps the greatest revelation any of us can have is that God is the source of everything we have, and to Him is the glory alone.

"This I say, therefore, and testify in the Lord, that you should no longer walk as the rest of the Gentiles walk, in the futility of their mind" (Ephesians 4:17).

SOUL SEARCH

Am I genuinely humble of heart? Think through your unique abilities. Do you see God as the source of each of them?

Father, remind me as I go through today that everything I have comes from your gracious hand.

Seeming Contradiction

Behold, I give you the authority to trample on serpents and scorpions, and over all the power of the enemy, and nothing shall by any means hurt you.

Luke 10:19

Here is fodder for the skeptic. Jesus warned that His disciples would be hated, and some would even be killed for His name's sake: "They will put you out of the synagogues; yes, the time is coming that whoever kills you will think that he offers God service" (John 16:2).

So this is a seeming contradiction. Jesus tells His disciples that nothing would hurt them and then says that some would be murdered. History tells us that almost all the disciples were horribly slaughtered for their faith.

Obviously there is a deeper meaning to His words. Jesus was speaking of their eternal salvation and preservation of their souls. The day will come where we will see every Christian who has died in the faith safely on the other side of death. Not one hair on their heads will perish. Then there will be no doubt—God keeps His word.

SOUL SEARCH

Do I use the authority given to me in prayer and preaching?

Father, help me to trust in you and be used by your Holy Spirit.

The Object of Our Joy

Nevertheless do not rejoice in this,
that the spirits are subject to you,
but rather rejoice because your names are written in heaven.
LUKE 10:20

It takes discipline to keep our eyes on heaven. It is so easy to allow the circumstances in the here and now to determine our joy. We tend to rejoice on the mountaintop and be gloomy in the valley. Living in such a way is precarious. Mountaintops can be more dangerous than the valleys. A new baby, a new car, the love of your life, money in the bank, mortgage paid off, and good health can be legitimate sources of rejoicing, but all these things can quickly disappear. Death, bank collapse, earthquakes, tornadoes, and sickness can take the joy from us in an instant.

We need to, therefore, look beyond earth to heaven and make sure it is the joy of the Lord that is our strength. If we continually rejoice because our names are written in the Lamb's Book of Life and we are saved forever, our joy is truly from the Lord. We will have joy in the lion's den, at the edge of the Red Sea, and while in chains in a Philippian jail; we will sing hymns. Nothing and no one can take our joy from us.

SOUL SEARCH

Is heaven the primary reason for my joy? Are there other people or circumstances I rely on to have joy?

Father, please help me keep my eyes on you, even in the lion's den.

Foolish Things

I thank You, Father, Lord of heaven and earth,
that You have hidden these things from
the wise and prudent and revealed them to babes.
Even so, Father, for so it seemed good in Your sight.

LUKE 10:21

God thought it was good to hide the way of salvation from the proud, arrogant, and the wise of this world. He did so by choosing foolish things to confound them. The Bible is filled with crazy-sounding stories like Noah and the ark, Jonah and the big fish, talking donkeys, people turning into salt, and other stories that rival Cinderella's pumpkin coach.

These stories require humility to believe. Who in this world with any intellectual dignity would ever stoop to believe such childish stories? Jesus warned that unless we become as little children, we will not enter the kingdom of God (Matthew 18:3). Little children believe anything; they have an innocent trust. That's the essence of faith in God.

So the proud are left out because the door to everlasting life is set very low. Only those who believe and become as little children will enter. Such is the wisdom of God.

SOUL SEARCH

Is my faith in God like that of a trusting little child, or do I struggle with doubts and unbelief?

Father, I trust you today with all of my heart.

His Identity

All things have been delivered to Me by My Father,
and no one knows who the Son is, except the Father,
and who the Father is, except the Son,
and the one to whom the Son wills to reveal Him.

LUKE 10:22

Jesus of Nazareth is the most famous person in history. No one compares to Him. Hundreds of millions call Him Lord and pray to Him daily. He is even esteemed by millions who don't call Him Lord. They merely see Him as a religious teacher or a great prophet. Comparatively few, however, know that He is the Creator. This is because flesh and blood doesn't reveal His identity. That revelation comes directly from God.

The Gospel of John begins by telling us, "All things were made through Him, and without Him nothing was made that was made" (John 1:3).

Jesus is the Christ, the chosen One. This is a truth Jesus told Peter, and one we could only know if the Father revealed it to us: "Jesus answered and said to him, 'Blessed are you, Simon Bar-Jonah, for flesh and blood has not revealed this to you, but My Father who is in heaven'" (Matthew 16:17).

SOUL SEARCH

Do I believe that Jesus is the Christ, the Son of the living God?

Father, I believe in Jesus with all my heart and trust alone in Him for my eternal salvation.

Treasure beyond Words

Blessed are the eyes which see the things you see . . .
LUKE 10:23

What is most precious to you in this world? Is it money, gold, silver, pearls, or diamonds? Men and women have killed for these things. Wars have been started, friendships ended, and couples divorced over them because they are considered to be precious. But a mountain of pearls or hills of gold or diamonds mean nothing to a dying person. They can offer no comfort.

The riches of this world pale in significance to what we have in Christ. Paul called Jesus a treasure in earthen vessels (2 Corinthians 4:7). John said that in Him we have "life," and he added that he had actually seen and handled it (1 John 1:1).

Jesus of Nazareth was the unspeakably precious jewel of life itself. He was the life-fountain, and His incarnation meant that dying human beings could drink of the waters of immortality. There are no words to describe such precious blessedness. The apostle Paul called what we have in Him "the unspeakable gift" (2 Corinthians 9:15). Even he couldn't find the words.

SOUL SEARCH

Do I realize what I have in Jesus? Take a moment to revel in the wonder of knowing Jesus.

Father, open my blind eyes.

The Treasure

For I tell you that many prophets and kings have desired to see what you see, and have not seen it, and to hear what you hear, and have not heard it.

Luke 10:24

The prophets and kings of the Old Testament looked forward to the time when God would destroy death. Jesus said that Abraham looked forward with rejoicing to the day that the Messiah would be manifested (John 8:56). We look back and read the Gospel accounts, and in doing so, we are greatly blessed.

We see the Christ, the chosen one, born of a virgin in the Bethlehem stable. We see Him appear as a grown man, who conquered disease and death (as in the case of Lazarus and others). We see the love of God expressed on the cross and the knowledge that eternal life is a free gift of God through simple trust in Jesus.

Kings and prophets didn't have what we have in the New Testament. The Bible is a great treasure given by God to humanity. May we never take it for granted.

SOUL SEARCH

Do I highly value the Bible?

Father, thank you for your precious Word. It's a lamp to my feet and a light to my path.

What is Written?

What is written in the law?
LUKE 10:26

Jesus often used the word "behold" as an attention-getter—a trumpet announcing something important. Perhaps it was because this person had asked the ultimate question any human being can ask. What is it that we should do to inherit eternal life?

We can learn big lessons from this verse. One key lesson to learn is how to approach God. We should not approach Him with a proud, arrogant self-righteousness as though we are testing Him.

This man stood up and tempted Jesus. The Bible tells us that God resists the proud and gives grace to the humble. Those who desire to know how to obtain everlasting life must come with childlike faith and humility of heart, seeking the truth about salvation. There is no other way.

It was because of his pride that Jesus pointed him to the Law. It humbles us so that we can understand the mercy of God revealed in the gospel.

SOUL SEARCH

May I never approach God with an arrogant attitude.

Father, remind me of my frailty and of your majesty and power.

Our Interpretation

What is written in the law? What is your reading of it?
LUKE 10:26

When this lawyer (a professing expert in the Law) asked how to inherit eternal life, Jesus asked him how he read the Law. How we interpret God's Law is essential to our understanding of our condition before God.

Many see the Commandments as a helpful standard for life, but it is much more than that. Its purpose is to reveal our guilt before God and drive us to the foot of the cross. For that to happen, we must set aside proud bias and approach the Law with humility of heart.

The lawyer then gave his perspective on the excellence of the moral Law—to love God with all our heart, mind, and soul and to love our neighbor as much as we love ourselves.

When we are closely examined by the spiritual nature of the moral Law, each of us falls infinitely short of its demands. The best of us are unthankful, unholy, ungrateful, rebellious, self-righteous, sin-loving sinners. It is the light of the Law in the hand of the Spirit that reveals to us our true state. The Law brings us the knowledge of sin.

SOUL SEARCH

Did the moral Law show me my true state before a holy God?

Father, thank you for the Law and its function as a "schoolmaster to bring us to Christ."

Do This and You Shall Live

You have answered rightly;
do this and you will live.
LUKE 10:28

If we want everlasting life, all we need to do is keep the moral Law. If we don't violate its perfect precepts in spirit—that is, in thought, word, or in deed—love God with all of our heart, mind, soul, and strength, and love our neighbors (every other human being) as much as we love ourselves, we will live. Violate one precept, and we will die.

The function of the Law is to reveal the knowledge of sin and show it to be exceedingly sinful (Romans 3:19–20; 7:7, 13). The Law pulls back the curtain and lets the early morning sunlight reveal dust on what was thought to be a clean tabletop. It exposes us for what we are and causes us to try and justify ourselves. When the Law has done its wonderful work in the hand of the Spirit, our mouths are stopped. We are caught with our hands in the cookie jar with no excuse. The Law humbles us and prepares our hearts for the grace, and once we see ourselves in truth, the sacrifice of the cross makes sense. It's no longer foolishness.

SOUL SEARCH

Do I ever try and justify myself when I know that I have sinned?

Father, thank you for your patience with me.

Passing By

A certain man went down from Jerusalem to Jericho, and fell among thieves, who stripped him of his clothing, wounded him, and departed, leaving him half dead. Now by chance a certain priest came down that road. And when he saw him, he passed by on the other side. Likewise a Levite, when he arrived at the place, came and looked, and passed by on the other side.

Luke 10:30–32

We can be quick to condemn these hypocrites for ignoring a battered and abused human being left half dead on the side of the road. I'm sure they had their excuses. But don't we do the same? There are sinners around us that the thief is killing, stealing, and destroying, leaving them dead in their sins, and we look the other way. I'm sure we have our excuses too.

We can look the other way by keeping ourselves very busy—doing what we believe are legitimate things. However, when we neglect the unsaved, we're like a firefighter who polishes his engine while people around him are burning to death. Evangelism should be our number one consuming priority.

SOUL SEARCH

Do I ever look the other way to avoid the irksome task of evangelism?

Father, take away my heart of stone.

The Selfish Gene

But a certain Samaritan, as he journeyed, came where he was. And when he saw him, he had compassion. So he went to him and bandaged his wounds, pouring on oil and wine; and he set him on his own animal, brought him to an inn, and took care of him. On the next day, when he departed, he took out two denarii, gave them to the innkeeper, and said to him, "Take care of him; and whatever more you spend, when I come again, I will repay you." So which of these three do you think was neighbor to him who fell among the thieves?

LUKE 10:33–36

This parable shows us how far we have fallen short of the demands of the moral Law. Who of us (in our unregenerate state) ever loved our neighbor to this degree? Rather, we were self-willed, self-centered, and self-righteous.

The essence of the Law is a standard by which we may measure ourselves. It is a moral mirror, and what it reveals is not pleasant.

SOUL SEARCH

Now that my sins are forgiven, do I love my neighbor to this degree? What can I do to begin loving my neighbor?

Father, help me to love my neighbor as myself and be as concerned for his or her salvation as I would be for mine.

Life's Busyness

Martha, Martha, you are worried and troubled about many things. But one thing is needed, and Mary has chosen that good part, which will not be taken away from her.

LUKE 10:41-42

Martha was seriously mistaken. She was busy doing legitimate things, but she didn't make time to sit at the Master's feet.

Never before has life been this easy for most of us. We take the convenience of transportation for granted—whether cars or planes. Communication is instantaneous around the world. Air conditioning, fast foods, automatic doors, iPads, and microwaves all make life so much easier. Still, we are stressed and busy.

No matter how busy or how necessary our endeavors may be, nothing should come before our relationship with God. He is our first love.

Have you a busy day ahead? Then get up early and sit at the feet of Jesus. Read His Word. Still your heart. Give Him your requests; give Him your love. Seek first the kingdom of God and His righteousness. Choose the "good part" because this one thing is needed.

SOUL SEARCH

Have I set time aside today? Have I made the time to sit at His feet?

Father, every day, remind me of the cross.

Our Father

When you pray, say: Our Father in heaven.
LUKE 11:2

Prayer isn't an option. Jesus didn't say "if" you pray. He said "when." The Bible is God speaking to us, and when we respond back to God, it becomes a prayer. Most of us don't know how to pray as we should, and here Jesus gives us a blueprint.

It is sad that what is commonly referred to as "The Lord's Prayer" is often repeated as though God is some sort of machine that won't respond unless a password is parroted. Instead, the spirit of this prayer tells us that God can be approached as we would approach a loving father who cares for our smallest needs. He is our "Abba Father."

The word Abba is an Aramaic word that translates as "Daddy." It gives us a picture of a loving father with his little child sitting on his knee rather than an unapproachable, austere, and distant father. This is extremely consoling because it means we can pour our hearts out to Him, knowing that He cares.

SOUL SEARCH

Is God my "Daddy?" Do I approach Him as such?

Father, although you are the Almighty God, the Creator of the universe, thank you for allowing me to call you "Father."

That Name

Hallowed be Your name. Your kingdom come.
LUKE 11:2

May we never forget that even though we call God our Father, His name is holy. How grievous it is to hear His holy name used in vain. It rolls off the sinful tongue as though it is meaningless. It is given less honor than to a dog.

But to the godly, that name is to be given the utmost honor because it is holy. We sit on His knee and gaze up at Him with a love that is mingled with a holy fear. The cross helps us to do that. We speak His name with awe and reverence.

The ungodly use His name to swear because they have no fear of God. They speak contemptuously about God, not knowing that they will be held accountable for every idle word, and how much more for blasphemy? The Lord will not hold him guiltless who takes His name in vain. The psalmist says, "Your enemies take Your name in vain" (Psalm 139:20). This should both grieve our hearts and make us tremble. We must pray that God in His mercy opens sinners' blind eyes before the day of judgment.

SOUL SEARCH

Do I use God's name with reverence and fear? Do I tremble when I think of sinners facing the God they hate?

Father, please have mercy on this wicked world.

October

New World Coming

Your will be done on earth as it is in heaven.
LUKE 11:2

Atheists often complain about the God in whom they don't believe. They point to children with cancer or the many who are starving and say that God is evil for creating such suffering.

There is much irony here. Not only do they *not* believe in God, but they also deny His explanation for suffering. As a result, they are left with no God to blame and no explanation.

The Bible says that we live in a fallen creation. It was when sin entered the world through Adam that it brought with it disease, suffering, and death. Everywhere we look we see evidence of the Genesis curse.

Fortunately, because of the cross, we have a glorious and wonderful hope. It is because the coming kingdom will have no sin; there will be no suffering. Ever. No disease, no tears, and no pain. We will inherit this whole earth without the curse and will have pleasures forevermore. That's when we will see God's will be done on earth as it is in heaven.

"Nevertheless we, according to His promise, look for new heavens and a new earth in which righteousness dwells" (2 Peter 3:13).

SOUL SEARCH

Do I ever dwell on the joys of the coming kingdom? Take a few minutes and think about the glorious hope we have in Christ.

Father, please send a worldwide revival, then hasten your coming.

The Blessing of Bread

Give us day by day our daily bread.
LUKE 11:3

Bread is called the staple of life. It was in biblical times, and no matter how you slice it, it still is today.

Jesus broke bread with His disciples. He was tempted by the devil to turn stones into bread, and He even called Himself the "Bread of Life," saying that His body would be broken for us. Bread is also linked to God's Word. Jesus said that man doesn't live by bread alone, but by every word that proceeds out of the mouth of God (Matthew 4:4). He was saying that we need both to live.

Charles Spurgeon said:

> Bread such as we get from the baker is in itself dead, and if you put it to dead lips, there are two dead things together, and nothing can come of the contact. But our Lord Jesus Christ is living bread, and when He touches the dead lips of an unregenerate sinner, life comes into them.[12]

SOUL SEARCH

Do I ever doubt that God will supply my every need? Can I think of a time when God failed to meet my needs?

Father, thank you for giving me my daily bread—both physical and spiritual.

Escape the Corruption

And forgive us our sins,
For we also forgive everyone who is indebted to us.
And do not lead us into temptation,
But deliver us from the evil one.

LUKE 11:4

Las Vegas is called "Sin City" for a reason. To the world, "sin" is another word for bright lights, excitement, and pleasure. Vegas is built on a foundation of fornication, greed, adultery, homosexuality, blasphemy, and, of course, lust.

The Bible says that Christians have escaped the corruption that is in the world through lust (2 Peter 2:20). We are drawn to the specific sin of sexual lust as a moth is drawn to a flame. One of the greatest revelations any of us can ever have is that sin is always married to death. The city of lights has a very dark side. Death is sin's wages. However, its full payment isn't seen this side of the grave. The Bible speaks of the second death and the agony of hell.

In Christ the marriage between sin and death is over. We are divorced from it. And so we are quick to confess any sin—lest we fall into its grasp.

We are also quick to forgive because if we refuse to forgive, we fall into sin and are in danger of serving the evil one.

SOUL SEARCH

Is there anyone that I secretly resent?

Father, please let the fear of you keep me from even being tempted by the evil of sin.

Persistent Prayer

Which of you shall have a friend, and go to him at midnight and say to him, "Friend, lend me three loaves; for a friend of mine has come to me on his journey, and I have nothing to set before him"; and he will answer from within and say, "Do not trouble me; the door is now shut, and my children are with me in bed; I cannot rise and give to you"? I say to you, though he will not rise and give to him because he is his friend, yet because of his persistence he will rise and give him as many as he needs.

LUKE 11:5–8

Jesus is still teaching us how to pray, and He's using this illustration to tell us to be persistent. Never be discouraged. Don't give up. God is faithful, and we should be faithful also by believing His Word and fully trusting Him.

When we pray, we should keep the word *push* in mind. We can use it to create a powerful acronym to remind us to be persistent:

P – pray
U – until
S – something
H – happens

Push is what we say to a mother in the final stages of labor. Push until you give birth to your requests of your Father.

SOUL SEARCH

Am I persistent in prayer or do I give up easily?

Father, may the Holy Spirit help me to pray with importunity.

Prayer's Qualifications

So I say to you, ask, and it will be given to you; seek, and you will find; knock, and it will be opened to you. For everyone who asks receives, and he who seeks finds, and to him who knocks it will be opened.

LUKE 11:9–10

The ungodly often accuse God of failing to keep His promises because they don't interpret Scripture with Scripture. From the above verses it would seem that anyone can get anything they want from God. However, there is a qualification. "Everyone" is confined to those who ask in faith, according to the will of God: "Now this is the confidence that we have in Him, that if we ask anything according to His will, He hears us" (1 John 5:14).

Our requests must be without a sinful motive: "You ask and do not receive, because you ask amiss, that you may spend it on your pleasures" (James 4:3).

These verses are not a blank check. Rather, they simply tell us to exercise importunity. We are to knock and keep on knocking, seek and keep on seeking, and God will answer our prayer—keeping in mind that the answer may be no.

SOUL SEARCH

Do I ask in faith, without a selfish motive, nothing wavering?

Father, help me always pray according to your will.

The Shadow

If a son asks for bread from any father among you, will he give him a stone? Or if he asks for a fish, will he give him a serpent instead of a fish? Or if he asks for an egg, will he offer him a scorpion? If you then, being evil, know how to give good gifts to your children, how much more will your heavenly Father give the Holy Spirit to those who ask Him!

LUKE 11:11-13

Here Jesus reveals the character of God. He is showing us that the Creator of the universe—who showed Himself to be holy and wholly terrifying so often throughout the Old Testament—is like a loving father. He is the prodigal's father, who fell on his son's neck, kissed him, and called for a joyous celebration.

This is a picture of God's endearing and steadfast love. The Prodigal Son story doesn't have the father making any sacrifice for the son as evidence of his love, but our Father demonstrated His love to us on the cross. It is our continual reminder. It says, "This is how much I love you."

We are, therefore, to approach Him in the shadow of that cross, knowing that He will never deceive us. Ever.

SOUL SEARCH

Am I determined to live today in the shadow of the cross?

Father, if you said it, I will believe it and trust you with all of my heart.

The Great Priority

Every kingdom divided against itself is brought to desolation, and a house divided against a house falls. If Satan also is divided against himself, how will his kingdom stand? Because you say I cast out demons by Beelzebub. And if I cast out demons by Beelzebub, by whom do your sons cast them out? Therefore they will be your judges.

LUKE 11:17–19

We have a divided church. There is contention about water baptism, salvation, tithing, free will, prophecy, and hundreds of other issues. Doctrines divide Christians when we get our eyes off our goal—to seek and save the lost. Sound doctrine is essential to the life of any church, but it shouldn't overshadow the Great Commission. Firefighters should be fighting fires, not each other. If they let people burn because they are arguing, they are betrayers of their profession.

When the siren of an emergency vehicle sounds, all other traffic must pull over to let it through. So it should be with the emergency vehicle of evangelism.

SOUL SEARCH

Do I give the task of reaching the lost its necessary priority?

Father, help us to be unified in the evangelistic endeavor.

The Power of God

But if I cast out demons with the finger of God, surely the kingdom of God has come upon you.

LUKE 11:20

There is no adequate analogy to illustrate the power of the finger of God. The foot of an elephant crushing a tiny ant is infinitely inadequate because the power of the Creator is infinite. There are no words to describe it. They all fall short of His glory. Awesome, magnificent, wonderful, incredible, and powerful combined won't do it. The only word that comes close is "indescribable."

The Bible even uses a rhetorical question to give us a glimpse of His power. It says, "If God is for us, who can be against us?" (Romans 8:31).

Jesus used anthropomorphism to describe His power to His unthinking critics. God isn't like a man, and He doesn't have fingers, but if the mere finger of the Father's power was with Jesus then nothing in the universe could stop Him from fulfilling His Father's will.

Jesus concluded The Lord's Prayer by reminding us who it is that possesses the power: "For Yours is the kingdom and the power and the glory forever. Amen" (Matthew 6:13).

SOUL SEARCH

Do I catch a glimpse of the immensity of God's power? What words would I use to describe God's greatness?

Father, I am in awe of you.

The Strong Man

When a strong man, fully armed, guards his own palace, his goods are in peace. But when a stronger than he comes upon him and overcomes him, he takes from him all his armor in which he trusted, and divides his spoils.

LUKE 11:21–22

In this passage, Jesus is talking about the demonic world. Think how differently the secular world would think and act if it believed that Satan is the god of this world, that he is their father, that he came to kill, steal, and destroy, and that he blinds them to the truth of the gospel.

If they simply believed, they would be able to embrace the message of everlasting life. But they don't, so the demonic world has complete control of their lives—from the man on the street to the world's political leaders. They are the blind leading the blind to destruction.

Jesus speaks of an armed man who is strong, and because of his strength, his home and goods are safe. All it takes is someone stronger than he to overcome him. Our trust is in God, and we are, therefore, never in danger of being overcome by the demonic world.

SOUL SEARCH

Is my faith entirely in God for today? Am I completely confident in His protection?

Father, thank you that my "goods" are in peace because you are faithful.

Gathering or Scattering?

He who is not with Me is against Me,
and he who does not gather with Me scatters.
LUKE 11:23

The Bible is filled with dichotomy. We are either saved or lost, heading for heaven or hell, in the kingdom of darkness or the kingdom of light, either for Jesus or against Him, and if we are not gathering for Christ, we are scattering.

The way to be for Jesus is to surrender to Him. It is to give up the battle and yield to Him as Lord and Savior. Many profess to have surrendered, but they don't gather the lost. He said, "He who does not gather with Me scatters." We are workers with God: "For we are God's fellow workers; you are God's field, you are God's building" (1 Corinthians 3:9).

When we share the gospel one-on-one with an unsaved person, we are fellow workers with God. When we give out a gospel tract or preach to a crowd, we are working together with the Father. We have the privilege of planting, others water, and some reap, but God makes the plant grow.

SOUL SEARCH

Am I gathering or scattering for the one I call my Lord?

Father, please show me how I can gather for you.

Seven Other Spirits

When an unclean spirit goes out of a man, he goes through dry places, seeking rest; and finding none, he says, "I will return to my house from which I came." And when he comes, he finds it swept and put in order. Then he goes and takes with him seven other spirits more wicked than himself, and they enter and dwell there; and the last state of that man is worse than the first.

LUKE 11:24–26

Repentance is the removal of poison from the soul. It is a clearing of the house. The Bible says to give no place to the devil. When we invite sin in, the devil is crouching at the door. So guard the door of your heart with all diligence. Bolt it. Set the alarm. And when conscience sends out an alarm, heed it. You are in danger.

Satan came to kill, steal, and destroy.

"Be sober, be vigilant; because your adversary the devil walks about like a roaring lion, seeking whom he may devour" (1 Peter 5:8). The Bible uses the word "may" in that verse. You give him permission when you venture into his dark and evil territory. The world ignorantly walks into the lion's den, but we know better because the Word of God gives us light.

Today, be resolute to walk in the light.

SOUL SEARCH

Do I sometimes forget that we are surrounded by spiritual darkness? Am I walking in the light?

Father, keep me close to you.

The Blessed

*More than that, blessed are those who hear
the word of God and keep it!*

LUKE 11:28

Jesus spoke this in response to a woman saying that His mother was blessed, and she certainly was. However, Mary was merely the human vessel who gave birth to the Savior. Here was the perfect opportunity for Jesus to exalt her as the Virgin Mary, as the Mother of God, and have us fall at her feet in worship.

However, the Bible tells us that Mary was no longer a virgin after she bore Jesus. She had at least five other children: "'Is this not the carpenter, the Son of Mary, and brother of James, Joses, Judas, and Simon? And are not His sisters here with us?' So they were offended at Him" (Mark 6:3). More references to Jesus' siblings are made in Matthew 12:46 and 13:55, John 2:12 and 7:3, 5, and 10, Acts 1:14, 1 Corinthians 9:5, and Galatians 1:19.

When blessing was offered to Mary, Jesus said that those who hear the Word of God and keep it were blessed. This is because they are saved through the gospel and being born again is the way of entry into everlasting life.

May the many millions who have a form of godliness (but lack the new birth) hear the words of Jesus in John 3, obey them, and be blessed.

SOUL SEARCH

Have I been truly born again? Am I a new creation in Christ?

Father, I pray that the unsaved listen to the gospel and obey it.

The Sign

This is an evil generation. It seeks a sign, and no sign will be given to it except the sign of Jonah the prophet. For as Jonah became a sign to the Ninevites, so also the Son of Man will be to this generation.

LUKE 11:29–30

When people asked for some sort of a "sign," Jesus said that they were evil. They needed evidence that Jesus was the promised Messiah—the Savior of the world. We are no different. The book of Romans tells us that all of humanity knows that God exists because of creation, and they are therefore without excuse (Romans 1:18–20).

No one would reject Jesus if they believed Moses. The Law is the clear signpost to the Savior, and they don't need any more signs. Sinners close their ears and shut their eyes because they love their sins.

The world can know that Jesus Christ is the Son of God by looking to the cross. As Jonah was swallowed by a large fish and resurrected onto the shore, so Jesus was swallowed by death and rose on the third day. When the cross is appropriated and our lives are transformed by the power of the gospel, we receive the only sign needed. We pass from death to life.

SOUL SEARCH

Am I content to live by faith until I see Him as He is? When have I doubted Him?

Father, may I fully trust your exceedingly great and precious promises until I pass into your glorious presence.

The Wisdom of Solomon

The queen of the South will rise up in the judgment with the men of this generation and condemn them, for she came from the ends of the earth to hear the wisdom of Solomon; and indeed a greater than Solomon is here.

LUKE 11:31

Solomon was extremely wise, filthy rich, and politically powerful. When the Queen of Sheba saw his wealth and his wisdom, she was overwhelmed and said she hadn't been told the half of it (1 Kings 10:7).

As the Bride of Christ, we've caught a glimpse of the Savior through the pages of Holy Scripture. In Him we have access to the manifold wisdom of God, have true and everlasting riches in Christ, and have been invited to participate in the power of prayer. Through the medium of believing prayer, we can move the hand of God and govern the destiny of nations.

Hudson Taylor said, "The prayer power has never been tried to its full capacity . . . if we want to see mighty wonders of divine power and grace wrought in the place of weakness, failure and disappointment, let us answer God's standing challenge, 'Call unto me, and I will answer thee, and show thee great and mighty things which thou knowest not.'"

SOUL SEARCH

Do trials cloud eternity from my eyes? Do I seek your wisdom through believing prayer?

Father, help me to have peace and joy by believing you have my eternity in your hands.

Swallowed by Fear

The men of Nineveh will rise up in the judgment with this generation and condemn it, for they repented at the preaching of Jonah; and indeed a greater than Jonah is here.

LUKE 11:32

The men of Nineveh repented when Jonah preached to them. How wonderful to be used by God in such an amazing way. Jonah, however, didn't run to the blessed task; he ran from it. He was told by God to preach the gospel—the good news of His mercy and grace. But Jonah was fearful, and he fled in the opposite direction.

Most of us can identify with cowardly Jonah. We have been told to preach the good news of the gospel as well, repentance to all nations, and we want to run in the other direction. Jonah couldn't get away from God, and because of his disobedience, he ended up depressed.

Can we learn a lesson from Jonah? We will end up in the same condition if we resist the will of God. One evidence that we have truly been born again is that we joyfully say, "I delight to do Your will, O my God" (Psalm 40:8). "For this is the love of God, that we keep His commandments. And His commandments are not burdensome" (1 John 5:3). We let love swallow our fears rather than allowing fear to swallow us, leaving us feeling guilty.

SOUL SEARCH

Am I so shallow that I can let sinners go to hell without warning them?

Father, please deepen my love for you and for the lost.

This Little Light

No one, when he has lit a lamp, puts it in a secret place or under a basket, but on a lampstand, that those who come in may see the light.

LUKE 11:33

Has God lit your lamp? Have you passed from death to life? Then allow God to put you on a lampstand so that the light can be seen. We live in a dark and sinful world where the blind lead the blind and where the light of God in you is desperately needed.

The Bible says of Jesus, "And upon those who sat in the region and shadow of death, Light has dawned" (Matthew 4:16). When we share one-on-one or preach Christ crucified for the sin of the world, we give light to those who are sitting in darkness; a light that overcomes the darkness. The night always flees when the morning sun rises: "For we do not preach ourselves, but Christ Jesus the Lord, and ourselves your bondservants for Jesus' sake. For it is the God who commanded light to shine out of darkness, who has shone in our hearts to give the light of the knowledge of the glory of God in the face of Jesus Christ" (2 Corinthians 4:5–6).

Let the love of Christ shine through you today by sharing the gospel with an unsaved person.

SOUL SEARCH

Have there been times when I have hidden my light because of fear? In what situations am I afraid to let my let shine?

Father, may your light shine through me today.

The Light of the Eye

The lamp of the body is the eye. Therefore, when your eye is good, your whole body also is full of light. But when your eye is bad, your body also is full of darkness. Therefore take heed that the light which is in you is not darkness. If then your whole body is full of light, having no part dark, the whole body will be full of light, as when the bright shining of a lamp gives you light.

LUKE 11:34–36

We should tremble when we think of what the ungodly usher in through their eyes. They allow sexual perversion, terrible violence, and even scenes of horror to invade their souls—all in the name of entertainment. In doing so, they dull the inner light that is given to every person. Jesus said, "But when your eye is bad, your body also is full of darkness."

Instead, we are called the children of light. We flee the darkness to stay in the light and fill our hearts with the light of God's Word: "Finally, brethren, whatever things are true, whatever things are noble, whatever things are just, whatever things are pure, whatever things are lovely, whatever things are of good report, if there is any virtue and if there is anything praiseworthy—meditate on these things" (Philippians 4:8).

SOUL SEARCH

Is my entertainment in keeping with God's will? Would Jesus be comfortable in the activities that I engage in?

Father, may I only entertain that which I know will be pleasing in your sight.

Superficial Piety

Now you Pharisees make the outside of the cup and dish clean, but your inward part is full of greed and wickedness. Foolish ones! Did not He who made the outside make the inside also? But rather give alms of such things as you have; then indeed all things are clean to you.

LUKE 11:39-41

The Pharisees were very meticulous about their outward piety. However, God was not impressed with their religiosity. To Him, they were like a clean cup full of poison. He requires truth in the inward parts because He sees our thoughts and discerns the motives of the heart. Therefore, Jesus reasoned with them about their idolatry. The god they served was either blind to their hypocrisy, didn't care, or he didn't exist.

When God made their skin, He also made their blood and bone. His creation wasn't superficial. When He made the brain, He also created the ability to think. It shouldn't have come as a surprise to them to know that He knew their every thought. Nothing is hidden from His eyes: "And there is no creature hidden from His sight, but all things are naked and open to the eyes of Him to whom we must give account" (Hebrews 4:13).

SOUL SEARCH

Do I sometimes clean the outward and neglect the inward? Is there anything that I am hiding?

Father, help me to see you through the eyes of faith.

The Motive

But woe to you Pharisees! For you tithe mint and rue and all manner of herbs, and pass by justice and the love of God. These you ought to have done, without leaving the others undone.

Luke 11:42

"Woe unto you!" What a fearful warning of wrath to come from the gracious lips of the Son of God. These were words designed to be a whip that cleared the temple. However, there is more here than meets the eye.

We can cheer at the overturned table but easily miss the love that motivated Jesus. He rebuked the Pharisees because He loved them. At times, Jesus told His disciples to leave them alone because they were like the blind leading the blind. Here, He warned them.

We also are to reprove and rebuke this world, sometimes with strong words: "Preach the word! Be ready in season and out of season. Convince, rebuke, exhort, with all longsuffering and teaching" (2 Timothy 4:2).

If we love sinners, we will warn them. Their hypocrisy and blinding self-righteousness will only console them temporarily.

SOUL SEARCH

Does love always motivate me? Am I willing to speak the truth even though it may sound harsh?

Father, let your love fill me to overflowing.

Woe to You

Woe to you Pharisees! For you love the best seats in the synagogues and greetings in the marketplaces.
LUKE 11:43

God save us from loving the praise of men. It's so easy to do because ego-stroking can be pleasant to our proud souls. We are like blooming flowers that bask in the sunlight of applause. Who doesn't like the best seats, and who isn't encouraged when people recognize us with a warm greeting? The Pharisees, as well as being sickeningly proud and self-righteous, were condescending toward others.

Hollywood lives for adulation. It optimizes the world; it rewards itself. Such arrogance should never enter a pulpit or the pew. We live in a different world where pride is resisted, and humility is exalted.

Our world is sacred ground upon which we should remove the shoes of human pride. The praise of men should be shed like water off a proud peacock's back. It mustn't come near our flesh. There is only one seat that we should love, and that is the one at the feet of the Savior.

SOUL SEARCH

Am I no different from the Pharisees in that I seek adulation from the world? Think of a time when you stumbled over your pride.

Father, I seek only your smile. Everything else is secondary.

Our Legacy

Woe to you, scribes and Pharisees, hypocrites! For you are like graves which are not seen, and the men who walk over them are not aware of them.

LUKE 11:44

How quickly the world forgets their dead. Loved ones are remembered and greatly missed, but most who pass on into eternity are out of sight and, therefore, out of mind. Some icons do remain. Shakespeare, Napoleon, Beethoven, and a few others sit as inanimate busts on desks and in museums, standing head and shoulders above the rest. Still, billions have been forgotten, left in the dust of history.

There is something tragic when interviewers ask famous people in their final days how they would like to be remembered. It's sad to know they won't be around to know if anyone remembers them or not.

However, we are like the thief on the cross who whispered, "Lord, remember me." All those who do so will not be forgotten by God. Oh, what consolation to know that we are more than passing dust because of the love and mercy of our Creator!

SOUL SEARCH

Do I have an eternal perspective?

Father, thank you for saving me from futility.

Our Liberty

Woe to you also, lawyers! For you load men with burdens hard to bear, and you yourselves do not touch the burdens with one of your fingers.

LUKE 11:46

These lawyers weren't like modern-day defense lawyers. They were professing experts in God's Law, whose sobering and sacred duty should have been to expound the Law of Moses for Israel. They taught in the synagogues and should have been well-versed in and humbled by the Law of Moses and its precepts. Instead, they played the hypocrite by putting the weight of their useless traditions upon the shoulders of others.

Sin's burden comes off our shoulders when we come to the Savior. Paul spoke of this liberty when the Galatians were tempted to go back under the Law. He said, "Stand fast therefore in the liberty by which Christ has made us free, and do not be entangled again with a yoke of bondage" (Galatians 5:1).

May we be as biblical lawyers for this godless generation by expounding the Law, as Jesus did, and make it applicable to them. May it act as a schoolmaster to bring them to the liberty that is found in Jesus Christ.

SOUL SEARCH

Did I feel the weight of my sin before I came to the cross? Can I recall the tremendous sense of relief and joy I had when my burden was gone?

Father, help me today to be strong and courageous in my evangelistic endeavors.

Deeds of Their Fathers

Woe to you! For you build the tombs of the prophets, and your fathers killed them. In fact, you bear witness that you approve the deeds of your fathers; for they indeed killed them, and you build their tombs.

LUKE 11:47–48

The religious leaders honored the prophets, but it was merely lip service. They should have been in tears of remorse for their fathers' deeds. But they weren't ashamed. They were proud.

The Pulpit Commentary says of this passage:

> "Your fathers," he said, "killed the prophets; you complete their evil work by building tombs for these slain men of God. In other words, you pretend to make amends for the crimes of past generations by this show of ostentatious piety; … if you indeed honored, as you profess to do by this gorgeous tomb-building, the holy men of God whom they slew, would you be acting as you now are doing—trying…to take my life? Is not my life like the lives of those old murdered prophets? Are not my words resembling theirs?"[13]

SOUL SEARCH

Do I daily search my motives for my actions?

Father, you are the discerner of all thoughts and intents. Help me remember to live in the light of that knowledge.

Nothing is Impossible

Therefore the wisdom of God also said, "I will send them prophets and apostles, and some of them they will kill and persecute," that the blood of all the prophets which was shed from the foundation of the world may be required of this generation, from the blood of Abel to the blood of Zechariah who perished between the altar and the temple. Yes, I say to you, it shall be required of this generation.

Luke 11:49–51

Often skeptics look at wickedness recorded in the Bible and assume that the perpetrator got away with murder. However, time will prove them wrong. On judgment day, all creation will be silenced with the knowledge that justice will be done. Not only will murderers get their due, but men and women will also give an account of every idle word and thought. God will be vindicated and glorified.

How could God see every thought and every deed done by billions all throughout history? Think about it: God created every sinew and every bone, every drop of blood, every strand of hair on every human head, and every atom of which those things are made. Every single one of them. Such thoughts are breathtaking, but they help us to understand that with God, nothing is impossible.

SOUL SEARCH

Am I careful with my words and thoughts? Do I keep in mind that God knows my every word and deed?

Father, help me walk in the light today.

The Lost Key

Woe to you lawyers! For you have taken away the key of knowledge. You did not enter in yourselves, and those who were entering in you hindered.

LUKE 11:52

Keys have a way of getting lost. But we see in this verse that the key of knowledge was deliberately taken away by the very people who were to free the captives of sin.

The lawyers were supposed to be skilled in God's Law. They should have been expounding its precepts, showing the true nature of sin and the righteousness of God. This is what Jesus did in the Sermon on the Mount. He expanded and elevated the Law by showing that God considered lust to be adultery (Matthew 5:27–28). He also showed anger and hatred to be a transgression of the sixth commandment. The moral Law shows us how far we fall short of the glory of God. It shows us that we are sinners in desperate need of the Savior.

The lawyers weren't faithful to God or His Word. They bent the key out of shape, rendering it useless, and so left themselves and their hearers locked in the prison of sin to their own just damnation.

SOUL SEARCH

Do I ever twist Scripture to say something that it doesn't because I want to justify myself?

Father, may I always read your Word with fear and trembling.

Baking Powder

Beware of the leaven of the Pharisees,
which is hypocrisy.
LUKE 12:1

Beware of hypocrisy. It is blinding and very subtle. Jesus likened it to what we commonly call "baking powder," which is the leavening agent used in baking.

Leaven puffs up, and that perfectly described the Pharisees. They refused to look into the mirror of the Law to see what they looked like in truth, so they became inflated in their self-righteous conceit. They were proud of their appearance—their flowing robes, their flowing prayers, and how money flowed publicly from their hands into the treasury.

When the Law is used correctly, it strips us of our so-called righteousness, leaving us morally broken and humble before God. It shows us that our robes should be made of sackcloth, our prayers should be discreet, and our giving should be done in secret.

The moral Law not only brings us to the foot of the cross in humility, but it also keeps us there. It's the demands of the Law that keep us trusting in the grace of God in Christ, rather than being swollen with pride.

SOUL SEARCH

Do I "tremble at the Law I spurned" as the hymn-writer says? Is there pride anywhere in my life?

Father, thank you for saving me from the wrath of eternal justice.

The Day

For there is nothing covered that will not be revealed, nor hidden that will not be known. Therefore whatever you have spoken in the dark will be heard in the light, and what you have spoken in the ear in inner rooms will be proclaimed on the housetops.

LUKE 12:2–3

In this previous verse, Jesus warned about hypocrisy; then He gave the explanation. We should beware of hypocrisy because we may be able to fool those around us by pretending we love God, but we're not fooling Him. He is going to bring everything into judgment, including every secret thing, whether it's good or evil. Every shameful deed that has been done in the depth of darkness is going to be brought into the light. God will be the presiding Judge, and the Law will uncover every piece of damning evidence.

Such a sobering thought should motivate us to live in godly fear. We need to work out our salvation "with fear and trembling" (Philippians 2:12). It should help us to cultivate a tender conscience—confessing and forsaking any sin that creeps into our hearts. We should never be afraid of such fear. It will keep us from evil.

SOUL SEARCH

Is my heart free from hypocrisy? Am I walking in the fear of God?

Father, help me love and fear you at the same time, just as Jesus did.

Fear God

And I say to you, My friends, do not be afraid of those who kill the body, and after that have no more that they can do. But I will show you whom you should fear: Fear Him who, after He has killed, has power to cast into hell; yes, I say to you, fear Him!

LUKE 12:4–5

Notice that Jesus says this to His friends. This is an intimate, sincere, sober, and loving warning. He is describing the nature of the God that humanity has to face on judgment day. Think of what Jesus is saying. A man is coming at you with a knife, and he's going to kill you . . . and Jesus is saying not to be afraid? Of course we would be afraid. To imagine such a scenario is terrifying!

Jesus is giving us a contrast. Having someone coming at you with a knife and with murder in his eyes (terrifying though that may be) is nothing compared to falling into the hands of the living God. The killer merely takes us out of this life, but God will take us into the next—unleashing His wrath upon those found in sin on that day and casting them into hell. This is why Jesus said that we should fear God over all other things.

SOUL SEARCH

Do I really fear God? Does my attitude toward sin reflect the fear of the Lord?

Father, open my understanding so that I truly fear you.

Special Creation

Are not five sparrows sold for two copper coins? And not one of them is forgotten before God. But the very hairs of your head are all numbered. Do not fear therefore; you are of more value than many sparrows.

Luke 12:6–7

The world would have us believe that we are no better than the beasts of the field. They believe that we have a common ancestor in primates, and, therefore, we are "talking primates." The Bible tells us, however, that we are made in the image of God. We have a sense of justice and truth; we deeply care about right and wrong. This makes us unique and special among the many creatures that roam the earth.

We are not only unique in creation, but we also have great worth in the eyes of our Creator. So much so that He saw fit to come down in the person of the Savior and suffer for our sins.

If God takes note of the common sparrow, how much more is He aware of you and me? Therefore, take to heart these precious words of Jesus and never fear because we are of great value to God.

SOUL SEARCH

Do I believe that God values me? How will such a thought shape my day?

Father, thank you for the cross. It is in there that I see your love.

The Universal Call

Also I say to you, whoever confesses Me before men, him the Son of Man also will confess before the angels of God. But he who denies Me before men will be denied before the angels of God.

LUKE 12:8–9

Do we boldly confess Jesus before this sin-loving world or are we ashamed of the cross? Why would we ever be embarrassed to say that we belong to Him? We are the ones of whom He should be ashamed because we are the ones who have done shameful deeds:

> On a hill far away, stood an old rugged cross
> The emblem of suffering and shame;
> And I love that old cross where the dearest
>   and best
> For a world of lost sinners was slain.

Jesus said "whoever" confesses Him before men will be confessed by Him to God. That means anyone can be saved because He is able to save anyone who humbles himself and calls upon His name.

SOUL SEARCH

Do I appreciate that "whoever" includes me? What would my life look like now if I had not come to Christ?

Father, thank you for the universal nature of salvation.

Rebellious Children

And anyone who speaks a word against the Son of Man, it will be forgiven him; but to him who blasphemes against the Holy Spirit, it will not be forgiven.

LUKE 12:10

God is willing to forgive words spoken against Jesus, but He is not willing to forgive blasphemy against the Holy Spirit. That's a frightening thought.

It was saddening years ago when a group of atheists banded together and did what they called "The Blasphemy Challenge." They made video clips of themselves blaspheming the Holy Spirit, using this verse as a basis. They were like rebellious little children who were drinking arsenic just because their parents warned them not to drink it.

God only knows if any of them did actually blaspheme the Holy Spirit, but I sure wouldn't want to be in their shoes when they stand before God.

An atheist once stood by me when I was preaching the gospel and called out to God to strike him dead. Then he said, "Nothing happened!"

I replied, "Yes it did. You just stored up more wrath that will be revealed on judgment day."

SOUL SEARCH

Is my heart broken by this rebellious generation? Am I willing to start praying for them daily?

Father, I cry out for blind and lost sinners.

november

What We Ought to Say

Now when they bring you to the synagogues and magistrates and authorities, do not worry about how or what you should answer, or what you should say. For the Holy Spirit will teach you in that very hour what you ought to say.

LUKE 12:11-12

Jesus said when they bring you to the synagogues and magistrates and authorities, don't worry. It's consoling to know that God knows the future, even if it isn't rosy.

Jesus said that there was no cause for worry about how or what to say because He would teach them the very hour they needed to know.

The apostle Paul used "ought" several times when he spoke of his own evangelistic responsibility. He asked for prayer that he would speak as he ought to speak.

We ought to speak also. Sinners are dying and going to hell. How can we not warn them? Jesus was warning His disciples of coming persecution and saying that we must warn even those who hate us.

We know what we ought to say because we have the Holy Spirit, which the disciples didn't have. We also have the complete New Testament, which tells us to preach the gospel in season and out of season . . . as we ought to do.

SOUL SEARCH

Am I ever at a loss as to what I ought to tell lost sinners? Am I willing to study the subject to become proficient?

Father, teach me how to share the gospel with this dying world.

The Will of God

Man, who made Me a judge or an arbitrator over you?
LUKE 12:14

Human history shows us that mankind has consistently used God for its own end. We are free to speak our minds because our Creator gave each of us a free will. This is why some see themselves as spokespeople for God. They don't necessarily love His Word or have a fear of Him in their hearts, but they speak anyway . . . from their darkened imagination.

It's common for political protestors to hold signs with Bible verses on them, completely out of context, to try and justify their cause. Politicians will often quote a Bible verse and make references to God to get votes. Nations go to war and say, "God be with us," as did the Nazis or other harmful people groups.

In this verse, someone in the crowd wanted Jesus to side with him in his cause, but Jesus would have none of it. If we fear God we should never use God's Word to justify our actions. Rather, we will always be guided to His will by His Word.

SOUL SEARCH

Have I ever been guilty of trying to manipulate God for my own ends?

Father, may I always side with you rather than try and have you side with me.

Real Treasure

Take heed and beware of covetousness, for one's life does not consist in the abundance of the things he possesses.
LUKE 12:15

Perhaps one of the most well-known Bible verses is from Psalm 23: "The LORD is my shepherd, I shall not want." When God is our source of joy, when He is our exceedingly great treasure, all the material goods of this world heaped together are nothing but trash compared to what we have in Christ. This is what Paul affirmed: "Yet indeed I also count all things loss for the excellence of the knowledge of Christ Jesus my Lord, for whom I have suffered the loss of all things, and count them as rubbish, that I may gain Christ" (Philippians 3:8).

How much money would we like to have in the bank? What figure would give us perfect peace to face an uncertain future? One million? Ten million? Jesus said to beware of greed—it is important! Somehow violation of the tenth commandment seems less serious than theft or adultery, yet it is often the catalyst that sparks theft and adultery.

While the godless rich seem to have everything in life, they are desperately poor without the Savior. Financial riches are worthless on the day of wrath, but righteousness delivers from death.

SOUL SEARCH

Am I ever envious of the rich? Are there things that I covet?

Father, help me to be content in Christ.

Trampled Underfoot

The ground of a certain rich man yielded plentifully.
LUKE 12:16

If there's one thing that most of us take for granted, it is the ground. We call it "dirt," and we trample it underfoot as though it's good for nothing. But it was the ground that God used to make man: "And the LORD God formed man of the dust of the ground, and breathed into his nostrils the breath of life; and man became a living being" (Genesis 2:7).

It's interesting, but not surprising, to learn that science agrees with the Bible on this one. The elements that make up the soil are the same elements that make up the human body. Scientists say that we came from stardust! They at least got the dust part right. We say at funerals "from dust to dust."

The ground gives us our food. All of it. Even the animals we eat are sustained by food that was grown in the soil.

So next time you run your hands through rich soil, pause and think about what you have your hands on. Think about how incredible our God is to hide so much potential life in the soil.

SOUL SEARCH

If there is a conflict between the Word of God and the word of man (science), do I always side with the Bible?

Father, help me to always trust your Word.

On Loan

And he thought within himself, saying, "What shall I do, since I have no room to store my crops?" So he said, "I will do this: I will pull down my barns and build greater, and there I will store all my crops and my goods."

LUKE 12:17–18

A popular children's movie perfectly characterized greedy seagulls by having them continually squawk, "Mine! Mine!"

That also characterizes human beings. "Mine" is one of the first words a toddler says. The world revolves around him, and if he doesn't come to the foot of the cross when he's older, he will think that he is the master and center of the universe. Obviously, none of us are. In fact, we don't even own anything in life—it's all on loan from God.

In these two verses, Jesus shows us the result of covetousness. The greedy rich man said "I" five times and "my" four times. He had built his life around himself rather than God. He was rich with this world's goods but left them all behind when he died.

SOUL SEARCH

Are there things in my life I cling to selfishly? Do I hoard possessions others need more than I do?

Father, may I see all things as being on loan from you.

The Soul

And I will say to my soul, "Soul, you have many goods laid up for many years; take your ease; eat, drink, and be merry." But God said to him, "Fool! This night your soul will be required of you; then whose will those things be which you have provided?" So is he who lays up treasure for himself, and is not rich toward God.

LUKE 12:19–21

Some skeptics don't believe in the existence of the human soul. They really believe that the invisible doesn't exist, even though wind, love, electricity, and gravity are all unseen. And so is the soul.

The soul is simply our life, and it's our life that will leave our body when we die.

The man in the parable told himself that all was well with his soul when it wasn't. He went ahead and made his godless plans for the future, but it was not to be. Death doesn't wait for any man.

How tragic that there are multitudes just like him. They plan only for the future of this short life while laying up their treasures on earth and foolishly ignoring eternity. May God awaken them to their fate.

SOUL SEARCH

What kind of treasures am I accumulating? Are they in heaven or on earth?

Father, help me to be rich toward you.

Worry and Trust

Therefore I say to you, do not worry about your life, what you will eat; nor about the body, what you will put on. Life is more than food, and the body is more than clothing.

LUKE 12:22–23

This wonderful Bible verse is not just about clothes and food. It's about worry. Someone once said that worry doesn't do anything for tomorrow; it just saps today of its strength.

Worry and fear of the future saps each day of our joy—the joy that's from the Lord and is our strength. Most of the time, our fears are never realized. An old proverb says, "Worry often gives a small thing a big shadow."

Jesus is saying that we need not be stressed about our needs, even though they are legitimate. Of course, we need money for gas, food, and clothing, but if we do not look to God as the supplier of our needs, life can become overwhelming.

The issue rests on trust. Where is it, and what is it in? If it is in our Father in Heaven, we will keep our joy and peace.

SOUL SEARCH

Do the burdens of daily living overwhelm me at times? Do I worry or do I trust the Lord with my burdens?

Father, today I determine not to worry. Faith won't allow it.

Check the Birds

Consider the ravens, for they neither sow nor reap, which have neither storehouse nor barn; and God feeds them. Of how much more value are you than the birds?

LUKE 12:24

Think about birds for a minute. They have feathers, wings, amazing eyes, a heart, a liver, lungs, and an appetite. They have instincts to procreate, build nests, raise their young, and watch for predators. How is it that they greet each day with a song? Our God is incredibly creative!

The Wright Brothers also considered birds. That's how they learned the principle of flight.

By considering them, we can learn important principles of daily living. Birds aren't like us. They don't sow seed into the soil and reap the fruit of their labor, nor do they save up food or preserve it in refrigerators and cans like we do. Jesus said that they are directly taken care of by God Himself. He feeds them.

It's not random chance that they have a desire to eat certain foods and that those foods exist. God made them and He supplies their every need. He, therefore, values them enough to take care of them. And Jesus says we are of more value than many birds—so how much more will He take care of us?

SOUL SEARCH

Do I think of my incredible value to God? How will that affect my day?

Father, thank you for the wonderful words of Jesus.

Consider the Lilies

And which of you by worrying can add one cubit to his stature? If you then are not able to do the least, why are you anxious for the rest? Consider the lilies, how they grow: they neither toil nor spin; and yet I say to you, even Solomon in all his glory was not arrayed like one of these. If then God so clothes the grass, which today is in the field and tomorrow is thrown into the oven, how much more will He clothe you, O you of little faith?

LUKE 12:25–28

The Queen of Sheba was taken aback (beyond words) at the incredible glory of Solomon. However, the common and transient flowers outshine him. Flowers are here today and gone tomorrow; they blossom then wither and die.

Peter said that all flesh is just like transient grass: "All flesh is as grass, and all the glory of man as the flower of the grass. The grass withers, and its flower falls away" (1 Peter 1:24–25).

We are born, blossom, wither, and die. But there is a massive difference between us and flowers. We are eternal, and we are more than a lovely, fragrant plant. We are made in the image of God, so how much more will He take care of us?

SOUL SEARCH

Do I think about the wonder of being made in the image of God? How does that truth affect my sense of value?

Father, thank you that although I fade as a leaf, you will preserve my soul forever.

Total Surrender

*And seek not what you shall eat, or what you shall drink,
neither be of doubtful mind. For all these things do the
nations of the world seek after: and your Father knows that
you have need of these things. But rather seek the kingdom of
God; and all these things shall be added unto you.*

Luke 12:29-31

The great principle of the Christian life is to put God first in our affections. It is to love Him with all of our heart, mind, soul, and strength. It is to do what Paul beseeched the Romans to do—to present their bodies as living sacrifices, "holy, acceptable to God, which is your reasonable service" (Romans 12:1). It's to do what David said to do—to delight yourself in the Lord (Psalm 37:4).

It's by our obedience that we prove our love for God (John 14:21). In our obedience we seek first His kingdom, that is, His will above our own. It is the fruit of our own personal Gethsemane experience.

Those who don't surrender to God will never know perfect liberty (John 8:31–32).

SOUL SEARCH

Have I once and for all cried, "Not my will but yours be done"?

Father, this day I yield my all to you.

God's Good Pleasure

Fear not, little flock; for it is your Father's good pleasure to give you the kingdom.

LUKE 12:32

Here the Good Shepherd speaks to His beloved flock. He is the One who gave His life for the sheep, and we hear His wonderful voice telling us the most comforting words of our Father's great love. It is His good pleasure to give us everlasting life and pleasure forevermore.

"God loves us" isn't just some empty cliché. He proved His great love for us on the cross (Romans 5:8). Like any loving father, He gets great joy out of giving to His children. Think of it. Almighty God has prepared a glorious and everlasting kingdom of pleasure for those who love Him!

All pleasure in this life is temporal. The pleasure of the kingdom of God will be eternal. Believe it with all of your heart, and let your joy be full.

SOUL SEARCH

Do I have joy right now because I believe?

Father, thank you for my glorious future—a light that will shine more and more until that perfect day.

The Root of All Evil

Sell what you have and give alms; provide yourselves money bags which do not grow old, a treasure in the heavens that does not fail, where no thief approaches nor moth destroys. For where your treasure is, there your heart will be also.

LUKE 12:33-34

Only God, you, and your accountant know the location of your treasure, which reveals what you love in life.

The love of money should scare us because it is the root of all evil (1 Timothy 6:10). People are murdered, marriages destroyed, drugs sold, banks robbed, pockets picked, purses snatched, identities stolen, wars started, and much more—all for the love of money. The Bible warns that those who are given to greed pierce themselves through with many sorrows (v. 10).

So guard yourself from such a subtle evil. Have a loose hand on your money. Give to your local church, to missionaries, and Christ-centered ministries who are reaching the lost. Give also to those who are in need, and you will store up treasure where inflation, depression, thieves, moth, and rust can never touch it.

SOUL SEARCH

Do I love money? Do I give generously with joy?

Father, let me be a continual and cheerful giver.

The Lord of the Earth

Let your waist be girded and your lamps burning; and you yourselves be like men who wait for their master, when he will return from the wedding, that when he comes and knocks they may open to him immediately.

LUKE 12:35–36

The Bible often uses the words "The Lord, your God." Our Creator is the Master. He is the Lord. No one and nothing can change that. He is the ultimate authority—the Judge of the earth. Each of us will give an account to Him, and His final decree will say if we live or die, whether we will be eternally damned or eternally blessed.

He is the Creator of all humanity—atheist and religious. Every human being. However, He is not everyone's Lord until they personally yield to His Lordship through faith in Jesus.

It is when we are born into the family of God that we can then say with Thomas, "My Lord, and my God." That's when we are made whole.

SOUL SEARCH

Is every area of my life yielded to God's lordship? How will that translate today in my life?

Father, you are my Lord and my God.

Servants of Christ

Blessed are those servants whom the master, when he comes, will find watching. Assuredly, I say to you that he will gird himself and have them sit down to eat, and will come and serve them.

LUKE 12:37

It feels good to know our place in the universe. We are servants of God—the wonderful purpose for which we were created. We wait on Him, longing to do His perfect will.

The Bible uses the words servant and slaves interchangeably. Before we came to Christ, we were slaves to sin, but like the Prodigal Son, we have come to the Father with the desire to only be humble servants. Paul often referred to himself as a servant of Jesus Christ (Philippians 1:1–2).

As servants who have been bought with a price, we look to the Father to discern His will, and we are quick to do it.

Scripture tells us that we are more than servants. We are beloved sons and daughters of the living God.

SOUL SEARCH

Would I consider myself a servant of Jesus Christ? How could I best serve Him today?

Father, I am truly blessed to serve you.

Be Ready

But know this, that if the master of the house had known what hour the thief would come, he would have watched and not allowed his house to be broken into. Therefore you also be ready, for the Son of Man is coming at an hour you do not expect.

LUKE 12:39-40

If someone steals your car or breaks into your house when your back is turned, your first thought would probably be, *If I'd known what was going to happen, I would have done something to prevent it.* But you didn't know and so you didn't take any precautions.

In this passage, we are forewarned that Satan is a thief who wants to steal our souls by tempting us to serve him by sinning. Don't let him get his ugly foot in the door. Sin is a deadly evil, but its terrifying consequences won't be understood by most until the moment the sky rips apart and the wrath of God falls like lightning upon all who serve it. Be ready for that terrible day by always keeping your heart free from sin.

SOUL SEARCH

Is my heart free from sin today? Am I ready to resist its power?

Father, help me to keep the day of wrath before my eyes.

Our Unanswered Questions

Who then is that faithful and wise steward, whom his master will make ruler over his household, to give them their portion of food in due season? Blessed is that servant whom his master will find so doing when he comes. Truly, I say to you that he will make him ruler over all that he has.

LUKE 12:42–44

Peter had asked Jesus, "Lord, do You speak this parable only to us, or to all people?" (v. 41). It would seem that Jesus didn't answer his question. Who was His audience when He shared the parable about the homeowner being unprepared for a burglary? Peter actually did get an answer, but possibly not the one he expected. Jesus said that those who are faithful and wise stewards—those who do the will of God—will be rewarded.

We have questions about many things. Perhaps at the top of the list is "Why does God allow suffering?" We have some answers, but nothing really satisfies when we walk through the children's oncology ward in a hospital. Still, our trust in God's integrity helps us to settle our finite minds and to lay a hand on our often unwise mouths.

SOUL SEARCH

What unanswered questions do I have? Does my trust in God pacify my urgent questions?

Father, I trust you despite not being able to understand.

The Fertile Mind

But if that servant says in his heart, "My master is delaying his coming," and begins to beat the male and female servants, and to eat and drink and be drunk . . .

LUKE 12:45

Notice that the servant didn't openly say that his master was delaying his coming. It was a mere thought, and that thought governed his actions. It can never be overstated how important it is to diligently guard our thought life. It is in the secret caverns of the mind that we find the greatest place of battle, and we have a very subtle and relentless enemy who knows that. It is in the mind that we find bitterness, fear, greed, sexual lust, jealousy, and a host of other secret sins take root.

Once sin comes in, compromise and hypocrisy come with it, whispering that God doesn't see or that He doesn't mind a little sin here and there.

Look at how closely aligned idolatry is to sexual sin: "Now the works of the flesh are evident, which are: adultery, fornication, uncleanness, lewdness, idolatry . . ." (Galatians 5:19–20).

Lock the door of your heart. Pluck out the eye, cut off the hand, and run from the temptations in this evil world like you'd run from the plague.

SOUL SEARCH

Do I search my heart for any leprous spots of sin? Does the fear of God govern my days?

Father, help me to live in holiness and to be diligent about guarding my heart.

Self-Examination

The master of that servant will come on a day when he is not looking for him, and at an hour when he is not aware, and will cut him in two and appoint him his portion with the unbelievers.

LUKE 12:46

We should walk so that if the heavens should roll back and Jesus came today, we would have nothing to hide. There is no gossip on our lips, no unforgiveness, no love for this evil world—only great joy that the Second Coming has come: "Finally, there is laid up for me the crown of righteousness, which the Lord, the righteous Judge, will give to me on that Day, and not to me only but also to all who have loved His appearing" (2 Timothy 4:8).

It is, therefore, wise to obey the admonition to examine ourselves to see if our faith is genuine: "Examine yourselves as to whether you are in the faith. Test yourselves. Do you not know yourselves, that Jesus Christ is in you?—unless indeed you are disqualified" (2 Corinthians 13:5).

How terrifying will that day be for those who are serving sin instead of serving God?

SOUL SEARCH

Let me look daily for the coming of Jesus Christ. Am I ready?

Father, this day I reaffirm my commitment to humbly serve you.

Our Responsibility

And that servant who knew his master's will, and did not prepare himself or do according to his will, shall be beaten with many stripes. But he who did not know, yet committed things deserving of stripes, shall be beaten with few. For everyone to whom much is given, from him much will be required; and to whom much has been committed, of him they will ask the more.

LUKE 12:47–48

It has always been a mystery to me that even though the contemporary church is fully aware of what Jesus did on the cross and knows of the Great Commission to preach the gospel to every creature, they still remain indifferent. They are aware of the passion of the church in the book of Acts to preach the gospel, yet they do everything but the Master's will.

If somebody is drowning and I have a rope in my hand but do nothing to save them, I'm guilty of the crime of what criminal law calls "depraved indifference."

We have been given the message of everlasting life and have been commanded to take it to every creature (Mark 16:15). It is like a rope that can save dying humanity, and if we are indifferent about the salvation of the lost and don't throw them the rope we are holding onto, then we are guilty of a terrible crime.

SOUL SEARCH

Am I guilty of coldly ignoring this dying world?

Father, please take my stony heart and give me a heart of flesh.

The Revelation

I came to send fire on the earth, and how I wish it were already kindled! But I have a baptism to be baptized with, and how distressed I am till it is accomplished!

LUKE 12:49–50

We don't know what it must have been like for Jesus to come to the revelation that He was to suffer for the sin of the world. We do know, however, that the culmination of that revelation came as He kneeled before His Father in the garden of Gethsemane and sweat great drops of blood (Luke 22:44). Most of us shudder at the thought of a mere dentist's drill. We pull back from any sort of pain, yet Jesus had to endure unspeakable agony as He suffered for the sin of the world.

He could have turned His back on the pain of the cross, but instead, He gave His back to those who hated Him. He could have used His hands to resist and His feet to run. Rather, He gave His hands and His feet to be nailed to that wooden frame.

For this purpose He was born. It was a baptism of unspeakable suffering, and He endured it so that we could live.

SOUL SEARCH

Do I meditate much on the cross and what it meant for Jesus?

Father, may I shudder as I think of what I would have had to suffer for eternity had it not been for the suffering of the Savior.

The Division

Do you suppose that I came to give peace on earth? I tell you, not at all, but rather division. For from now on five in one house will be divided: three against two, and two against three. Father will be divided against son and son against father, mother against daughter and daughter against mother, mother-in-law against her daughter-in-law and daughter-in-law against her mother-in-law.

LUKE 12:51–53

In the beginning, God said, "Let there be light. . . . and God divided the light from the darkness" (Genesis 1:3–4). The same thing happens when gospel light comes in the form of salvation to a sinner. He or she is divided from the darkness—separated from this sinful world: "He has delivered us from the power of darkness and conveyed us into the kingdom of the Son of His love" (Colossians 1:13).

Tragically, families who are still in darkness are divided because they love darkness rather than light.

If we find ourselves shunned by loved ones, the wisest thing to do is show them our faith by our works. Showing the love of Christ in sincere ways—like gifts for no reason and kind words— can sometimes speak louder than a thousand sermons.

SOUL SEARCH

Have I been wise with those that I love? Do I let my light shine through my good works?

Father, help me to show my faith in you by my love to others.

The Future

Whenever you see a cloud rising out of the west,
immediately you say, "A shower is coming"; and so it is.
LUKE 12:54

No one but God knows the future. If we could rightly predict just ten seconds into the future, we could go to Las Vegas and become billionaires overnight. Instead, the best we can do is guess or make an estimate. Many a parade had been rained upon for those who had faith in weather forecasters who miscalculated. Political commentators are also put to shame when their predictions turn out to be wrong.

God is never put to shame because He never gets it wrong. He knows the end from the beginning because He isn't held captive by time; the day will come when time will be a thing of the past.

In the light of the future, the psalmist prays a prayer that should come from all godly lips:

> Who knows the power of Your anger?
> For as the fear of You, so is Your wrath.
> So teach us to number our days,
> That we may gain a heart of wisdom.
> (Psalm 90:11–12)

SOUL SEARCH

What are the things I do that steal my time?

Father, may I trust you always because you know every moment of my future.

We are Near

Hypocrites! You can discern the face of the sky and of the earth; but how is it you do not discern this time?

LUKE 12:56

This verse should make us interested in discerning the times in which we live. Bible scholars agree that all the signs of the times are lining up. We are nearing the midnight hour of the Second Coming.

Had the religious leaders searched and believed the Word of God, they would have known that Jesus was the promised Lamb of God. From the early chapters of Genesis through the Psalms and into the prophets, the Old Testament identified the nature and even the place of His birth, His life, and His cruel death. Yet it was hidden from these hypocrites' eyes because of their unbelief.

At the same time, we see religious leaders like Simeon and Nicodemus coming to the Savior because they patiently waited for the truth to be revealed. They wanted the truth. May we be like them, living with one eye on the headlines and the other on the heavens.

SOUL SEARCH

Am I ready for His coming? How will this affect my daily life?

Father, please help me to discern the signs of the times.

Stay Clear of Trouble

Yes, and why, even of yourselves, do you not judge what is right? When you go with your adversary to the magistrate, make every effort along the way to settle with him, lest he drag you to the judge, the judge deliver you to the officer, and the officer throw you into prison. I tell you, you shall not depart from there till you have paid the very last mite.

LUKE 12:57–59

Life has consequences. Like a rushing river, it can pull you in a direction in which you don't want to go. So ponder the path of your feet. Be careful what you step into because it may pull you under.

Think of the many men and women throughout the Bible who made terrible decisions—from Adam to Ahab, Jonah, Samson, Jezebel, and Judas.

It is good for us to stay away from the waters of strife. Bite your tongue. Don't cross people. Ask questions rather than make accusations. "Whoever guards his mouth and tongue keeps his soul from troubles" (Proverbs 21:23).

Forgive and forget. As much as depends on you, be at peace with all men, and you will save yourself a lot of pain (Romans 12:18).

SOUL SEARCH

Have I surrounded myself with the protective virtue of mercy toward others? Am I too quick with my tongue?

Father, help me to have love, mercy, and grace toward those who can potentially offend me.

The Problem of Evil

Do you suppose that these Galileans were worse sinners than all other Galileans, because they suffered such things?

LUKE 13:2

This was the big headline of the day. It seems that Roman soldiers, under orders from Pontius Pilate, had horribly slaughtered the Galileans as they were sacrificing to God at the Temple. The thought was that God had allowed Pilate to do such an evil thing because the Galileans were really bad sinners. Some have similar thoughts about terrible incidents that happen today. Is God sending judgments? Is He punishing particular people because of their sins?

The answer is to defer our judgment because we don't know the mind of the Lord. It is wise to lay our hands on our mouths and leave these questions to God. He allows evil for a reason, and real faith is satisfied without an immediate answer.

SOUL SEARCH

Could I trust in God even if I was in a lion's den? Am I able to trust God with unanswered questions?

Father, I trust you.

Amazing Grace

*I tell you, no; but unless you repent
you will all likewise perish.*

LUKE 13:3

Some say that repentance isn't necessary for salvation. They maintain that all a sinner needs to do is believe, and they have Bible verses to back up their error. The Bible makes it clear that neither repentance nor faith save us. It is grace and grace alone that saves a sinner from wrath: "For by grace you have been saved through faith, and that not of yourselves; it is the gift of God, not of works, lest anyone should boast" (Ephesians 2:8–9).

Repentance and faith are the means by which we partake of the grace of God. John Newton, the evangelistic clergyman best known for abolitionism and hymn writing, didn't write, "Amazing faith how sweet the sound that saved a wretch like me." It was "grace that taught his heart to fear and grace his fears relieved."

Jesus warned that unless sinners repent, they shall perish. God's Word also says, "He who covers his sins will not prosper, but whoever confesses and forsakes them will have mercy" (Proverbs 28:13).

SOUL SEARCH

Have I truly repented and trusted alone in Jesus for my eternal salvation?

Father, help me to examine myself and see if I have fruit worthy of repentance (Matthew 3:8).

This Issue of Tragedies

> *Or those eighteen on whom the tower in Siloam fell and killed them, do you think that they were worse sinners than all other men who dwelt in Jerusalem? I tell you, no; but unless you repent you will all likewise perish.*
>
> LUKE 13:4–5

Much of the world thinks that when something good happens to us, we have the favor of God, but when tragedy strikes, we have somehow lost His favor. They call it "karma." While the Bible speaks of reaping what we sow, life's tragedies don't always come in response to what we have done (or not done). Tragedy happens because we live in a fallen creation as fallen creatures.

The idea that Jesus was addressing was that these eighteen men were bad. Because they were bad people, the tower fell on them and killed them. Was God punishing them because they were the worst of sinners? Jesus said no. The point isn't who is the worst evil-doer. Rather, it's that all of us deserve to perish, and the only way from avoiding this fate is for us to repent.

When nonbelievers ask about such challenging issues, we should give them the gospel and help them examine their own hearts. We should open up the divine Law, show them the nature of sin, and tell them to repent or they will perish. That should be our number one concern.

SOUL SEARCH

Do I minimize the role of repentance in salvation? Do I prioritize the salvation of the lost?

Father, help me to be like Jesus and have a passion for the lost.

Check Your Parachute

*A certain man had a fig tree planted in his vineyard,
and he came seeking fruit on it and found none.*

LUKE 13:6

If you and I have passed from death to life, there should be certain fruits that are evidence of a work of grace in our lives. The Bible says to examine ourselves and see if we are in the faith. Think how carefully you would examine your parachute to make sure it was put on properly if you knew that there was a possibility you had to jump out of the plane at any moment.

The fruit we should be looking for in our own lives is the fruit of repentance, the fruit of praise, thanksgiving, good works, and the fruits of the Spirit—love, joy, peace, faith, self-control, goodness, gentleness, and meekness.

If there's no evidence of salvation, we need to get on our knees and plead with God to help us to make our calling and election sure (2 Peter 1:10).

If we are not sure, making Psalm 51 (a prayer of repentance) our own prayer is a good place to start. Then when God looks for fruit in our lives, the crop will be abundant!

SOUL SEARCH

Do I identify with Psalm 51? Can I make it my prayer today?

Father, let me see the contrast between your holiness and my sin.

Delusional Sinners

Then he said to the keeper of his vineyard, "Look, for three years I have come seeking fruit on this fig tree and find none. Cut it down; why does it use up the ground?" But he answered and said to him, "Sir, let it alone this year also, until I dig around it and fertilize it. And if it bears fruit, well. But if not, after that you can cut it down."

LUKE 13:7–9

The Bible says that God is not willing that any perish but that all come to repentance (2 Peter 3:9). That is why His wrath doesn't fall upon evil men. Many become emboldened in their sin because of heaven's silence. Sinners say in their hearts that God doesn't see. This is what David must have done when he sinned with Bathsheba. When we have an extreme admiration or love for something or someone else, we are blinded.

The hypocrite also mistakes divine silence for divine ignorance. His or her life lacks godly fruit and calls for judgment, but it doesn't come simply because God is merciful. However, He is looking for fruit, and if there is none, He will eventually cut sinners down in wrath.

SOUL SEARCH

May I never mistake God's mercy for His permission to sin.

Father, keep me from the self-deception of hypocrisy.

We are Loosed

Woman, you are loosed from your infirmity.
LUKE 13:12

Sin caused us to stoop. We were bowed down to the earth, unable to see heaven, hopeless and helpless, without God, without understanding, and without salvation. Look at how the ungodly are described in Ephesians 4: "Having their understanding darkened, being alienated from the life of God, because of the ignorance that is in them, because of the blindness of their heart" (v. 18).

However, in the next verses, we are reminded of what Jesus made possible for us:

> That you put off, concerning your former conduct, the old man which grows corrupt according to the deceitful lusts, and be renewed in the spirit of your mind, and that you put on the new man which was created according to God, in true righteousness and holiness. (vv. 22–24)

Jesus spoke to us in our hopelessness. He loosed us from the infirmity of sin and death, taking us from darkness to light, from the kingdom of this world into the kingdom of God.

SOUL SEARCH

May we always look to Jesus, thanking Him for the cross where He demonstrated His great love for us.

Father, keep me looking to Jesus, the author and finisher of our faith.

December

The Most Feared Word

Hypocrite!
LUKE 13:15

Like the woman with the spirit of infirmity, we too are immediately made straight in Christ. We now walk a straight and narrow path of righteousness. We were instantly forgiven, washed, and justified in the sight of our holy Creator. We no longer entertain the thought of sin because of the cost of our redemption. How could we? While lust, selfishness, greed, and many other sins pull at our flesh, we reckon them all dead in Christ and their power over us defused.

Therefore, the accusation of "hypocrite" should never be leveled at us as Jesus leveled it at the religious leaders. It is a stinging rebuke we never want to receive from God. Imagine having it aimed at you by the One who bore the agony of sin because you were secretly serving its pleasure. Hypocrisy is to despise Calvary's sacrifice. Such a thought should bring with it instant and terrible shame.

While the world may justly accuse us of being narrow-minded and foolish for believing the Bible, may they never be able to justly accuse us of hypocrisy.

SOUL SEARCH

Sin no longer has dominion over me. I will declare I am no longer a slave of sin, and I am free from its bondage.

Father, keep me on the straight and narrow.

Crooked Rulers

Does not each one of you on the Sabbath loose his ox or donkey from the stall, and lead it away to water it?

LUKE 13:15

The synagogue ruler almost sounded sensible. Yes, there are six days in which men ought to work. It's on those days that sick people should come and be healed. But after a little thought, you will see there's a big problem. The ruler didn't care about worshipping God and was not concerned about the sick people. He was a whining, accusing, camel-swallowing religious hypocrite. Jesus cut through the smoke screen and told him so.

His contemporaries complain that the poor savages in distant countries don't get to hear the gospel. This isn't because they care about the salvation of the lost. They just love their sins and will grasp at straws, trying to find excuses to keep sinning.

Neither are skeptics who complain about hypocrites being in the church concerned that those who profess faith are insincere. This is just one more smoke screen.

SOUL SEARCH

In what ways could I be tempted to lie to myself about certain sins that still attract me?

Father, protect me from myself.

Eighteen Long Years

*So ought not this woman, being a daughter of Abraham,
whom Satan has bound—think of it—for eighteen years,
be loosed from this bond on the Sabbath?*

LUKE 13:16

In a day when many believe that human beings have no more
worth than mere animals, Jesus sets us straight. If an ox was to be
taken and watered on the Sabbath day, how much more should a
human being, made in the image of God, be cared for?

Jesus gave this poor woman value. After all, she was a daughter of Abraham. Still, some of the world's major religions treat
women like cattle, giving them less honor than a cow.

Jesus, on the other hand, exalted women, and in Luke 13:16
He opened our understanding further by saying that Satan had
bound the woman for eighteen long years. This not only gives us
insight into the spiritual realm, but it also helps us to approach
God with more confidence for His healing touch.

The Bible says that the prayer of faith shall save the sick, so if
we are afflicted by sickness, we can have confidence that God will
hear us (James 5:15).

SOUL SEARCH

How can I best strengthen my faith so that I can have more
confidence in God when I pray?

*Father, touch the lives of those millions who are lost in hopeless
religions.*

The Third Eye

*What is the kingdom of God like? And to what shall
I compare it? It is like a mustard seed, which a man took
and put in his garden; and it grew and became a large tree,
and the birds of the air nested in its branches.*

LUKE 13:18–19

I once spoke to a man who believed that the kingdom of God was
determined by the sun. He said that it's the sun that gives us life
and that the kingdom of God is within us. He knew just enough
Scripture to hang himself.

Two days earlier, I met a young man who said that he came to
know God through his third eye while using LSD. He was confident, outspoken, and suicidal.

Jesus said that the kingdom of God is like a huge tree, and
that tree is filled with birds. Birds are often a "type" of the
demonic realm. This interpretation is in line with many verses
that speak of true and false converts—tares among the wheat,
goats among the sheep—with so much deception in the spiritual
realm. We need to be well-versed in God's Word to know the true
from the false.

SOUL SEARCH

What doctrines do I know to be false? Am I searching the
Scriptures for truth and discernment?

Father, keep me close. Lead me and guide me into all truth.

The Heart of a Child

To what shall I liken the kingdom of God?
It is like leaven, which a woman took and hid
in three measures of meal till it was all leavened.
LUKE 13:20–21

Notice that the kingdom of God is hidden. As Christians, we know that the true church is made up of genuine believers—those who have the Son and, therefore, have life (1 John 5:11–13). There should be no confusion even though there are thousands of denominations. The Lord knows those who are His. They are the children of the kingdom.

Jesus thanked God that He had hidden these things from the wise and the prudent and revealed them to babes. He warned that unless we become as little children, we will not inherit the kingdom of God. The proud are offended at the thought of being childlike. After all, they have their intellectual dignity.

As we have previously seen, the predominant property of leaven is that it puffs up. God resists those who are puffed up with their own self-importance. He not only resists the proud, but He even hates a proud look (Proverbs 6:16–17).

SOUL SEARCH

What are some of the things in my life that could puff me up in my own conceit—intellect, wealth, looks, possessions, knowledge, or my humility?

Father, keep me simple in my faith.

The Agonizing Birth

Strive to enter through the narrow gate, for many,
I say to you, will seek to enter and will not be able.

LUKE 13:24

This is one of the most frightening verses in the Bible! Jesus had just been asked if only a few would be saved and this was His answer. Modern evangelism tells us that it is easy to be saved— you simply give your heart to Jesus. However, the Bible says the opposite.

Jesus said to strive to enter in at the straight gate. That word *strive* is made up of the same Greek word from which we derive our word "agonize." Jesus warned that we should agonize to enter into the kingdom of God. Most of us were born into this world through our mother's agony. No doubt if we could remember the experience, we would know it wasn't an easy process for us either.

We can enter the kingdom of God because of the pain of the cross, but in order to, we must have the experience of which James speaks when addressing sinners: "Let your laughter be turned to mourning and your joy to gloom" (James 4:9). In other words, our repentance should be mixed with contrition, a sorrow for our sins, and for the cost of our redemption.

SOUL SEARCH

Am I a stranger to contrition? Have I truly experienced sorrow for my sin?

Father, help me to be sorry for my sins.

Knock, Knock

When once the Master of the house has risen up and shut the door, and you begin to stand outside and knock at the door, saying, "Lord, Lord, open for us," and He will answer and say to you, "I do not know you, where you are from . . ."

LUKE 13:25

An important question we must ask ourselves is, *Do I know the Lord?* What does that mean? It is more than a belief that He exists as Lord or that He existed as a historical figure. Knowing the Lord in a true sense is an intimate relationship with our Creator based on a childlike trust. We trust Him with our eternal salvation. We trust that He hears our prayers, will supply our needs, and that He will work all things out for our good. Knowing the Lord is yielding our will to His. We delight to do His will: "Now by this we know that we know Him, if we keep His commandments" (1 John 2:3).

Think of the terror of Noah's unrepentant generation when they found that the door to the ark was closed when the rain began to fall. The generation to whom Jesus spoke, and all generations following, know the terror of a closed door. For when they cried out to the One, they called "Lord" but didn't obey. He said, "I never knew you!"

SOUL SEARCH

If I'm committed to doing God's will, how will that affect what I do today?

Father, help me to be completely yielded to you.

Followers of Jesus

Then you will begin to say, "We ate and drank in Your presence, and You taught in our streets." But He will say, "I tell you I do not know you, where you are from. Depart from Me, all you workers of iniquity."

LUKE 13:26–27

The identity of this great multitude of people is not a mystery. It was a group of "believers" who followed Jesus. Unsaved believers. Jesus also spoke of unsaved believers in the parable of the sower: "But the ones on the rock are those who, when they hear, receive the word with joy; and these have no root, who believe for a while and in time of temptation fall away" (Luke 8:13).

The false convert believes for a time. Judas was a believer, but he was never saved. In referring to him, Jesus said, "One of you is a devil." These verses are speaking about those who follow the example of Judas. He followed Jesus but stole from the collection bag (John 12:4–6). He was a "worker of iniquity."

James said that demons who believe "tremble." Possibly, the missing virtue of this great multitude was their lack of the fear of God because it's the fear of the Lord that keeps us from evil (Proverbs 16:6).

SOUL SEARCH

Is there an "evil" that I haven't identified but still cling to because I don't fear God?

Father, may I daily see evidence of my faith.

To the Jew First

There will be weeping and gnashing of teeth, when you see Abraham and Isaac and Jacob and all the prophets in the kingdom of God, and yourselves thrust out.

LUKE 13:28

In an effort to make Christians look like bigots, skeptics will often ask if Jewish people will end up in hell because they don't embrace Jesus. However, here we have the fathers of the Jewish nation included in the kingdom of God. Jesus said that Abraham, Isaac, Jacob, and all of the prophets will be in the kingdom of God. None of these godly men were saved because they were holy but because they trusted God's mercy. Jesus said, "Abraham rejoiced to see my day," and Hebrews chapter 11 lists those Jews who were saved by grace through justification by faith.

Christianity rests on a Jewish Messiah, who was promised in the Jewish Scripture. All of the disciples were Jewish. The first five thousand who were saved were Jewish. The gospel was birthed in the land of the Jews and taken to the Jew first before it went to the Gentiles.

SOUL SEARCH

If I share the gospel with a Jewish person, am I nervous to mention Jesus? Why?

Father, help me to be bold and loving.

East from West

They will come from the east and the west, from the north and the south, and sit down in the kingdom of God.

LUKE 13:29

The next time the accuser of the brethren comes to you and tries to make you feel condemned and guilty in spite of your faith in Jesus, think about the compass. It always points to the north. Be like the compass. Always look to Jesus—the author and finisher of our faith. He completed the work on the cross when He cried out, "It is finished!" Your salvation has nothing to do with how you feel but with what Jesus accomplished. You will sit down in the kingdom because it's your Father's good pleasure to see you there (Luke 12:32).

Next, consider the four points of the compass—north, south, east, and west. God didn't remove our sins only as far as the north is from the south. That's a finite distance and can be measured because the North Pole and the South Pole are two definite locations. But you'll never find east and west. They are an infinite distance from each other. That's how far God has removed our sins from us (Psalm 103:12).

SOUL SEARCH

What reoccurring sins plague me? Is the battle against them making me strong or weak? Humble or proud?

Father, when I am weak in myself, I'm strong in you.

More Than a Conqueror

*And indeed there are last who will be first,
and there are first who will be last.*
LUKE 13:30

A sure winner at the box office is a true story about someone who was running in last place but came in first. The runner falls during the race, picks himself up, and moves to first place. Or the weak kid who is bullied by the big kid, trains himself to become strong, and one day gives the bully a big black eye. Stories such as these win over audiences and bring them to their feet with applause.

Christianity is for those who may see themselves as losers. It is for the bruised nobodies. It makes the sinners better than they once were. It makes losers winners, the lost found, the cursed blessed, the condemned accepted . . . and takes the dead and makes them alive!

Jesus of Nazareth, who became a curse in our place, made this possible. It happened because our God is kind to the evil, loving to the unlovely, rich in mercy to guilty criminals, and wonderfully tenderhearted toward lost sinners. He is able to save all of those who come to Him through Christ. The last will be first.

SOUL SEARCH

In what ways am I going to live as a conqueror today?

Father, your kindness overwhelms me.

He has the Power

Go, tell that fox . . .
LUKE 13:31

They weren't kidding. Herod was an evil and sly fox. He had John the Baptist killed on a whim. We don't know if these "certain Pharisees" who warned Jesus about Herod were concerned about Jesus' welfare or if they wanted to get rid of Him and this was a surefire way of doing it.

But Jesus didn't fear the king. Ten thousand kings' armies couldn't stop Him from accomplishing His purpose. His time had not yet come. He came to suffer and die, but that wouldn't be at the hand of a mere fox. It would be Pontius Pilate who would hand Him over to die. That would happen not because of the will of man but because of the purposes of God. Jesus said that no man would take His life from Him. He was the One who had the power of life and of death: "No one takes it from Me, but I lay it down of Myself. I have power to lay it down, and I have power to take it again. This command I have received from My Father" (John 10:18).

SOUL SEARCH

How is my knowledge of God's incredible power going to affect my attitude this day?

Father, open up my mind to your power.

Stubborn Agenda

*Behold, I cast out demons and perform cures today
and tomorrow, and the third day I shall be perfected.*
LUKE 13:32

This was the message Jesus wanted the Pharisees to relay to King Herod. The sly fox had divorced his first wife because he wanted Herodias, who had formerly been married to his half-brother, Herod II. Charles Spurgeon said of him: "He was a man of dissolute habits and frivolous mind. He was very much under the sway of a wicked woman, who destroyed any little good there might have been in him. He was a lover of pleasure, a lover of himself, depraved, weak, and trifling to the last degree. I almost object to call him a man, therefore let him only be called a tetrarch."[14]

Instead of running from Herod, Jesus sent him a mission statement: Nothing was going to stop Him. He was trampling over the enemy, healing the sick, and defeating death.

We need to adopt a similar attitude. We have a gospel that must be preached to dying sinners, and neither demon nor king should be able to stop us from fulfilling the Great Commission.

SOUL SEARCH

What are you doing today to fulfill that mission?

Father, set my face to do your will.

He Shall Not Fail

*Nevertheless I must journey today, tomorrow,
and the day following; for it cannot be that
a prophet should perish outside of Jerusalem.*

LUKE 13:33

Jesus lived with an imperative. He said that He must walk today, tomorrow, and the day after that. In John 4, the Bible says that He must pass through Samaria. He came down to this earth to do His Father's will, and nothing else mattered.

"The Son of Man must suffer many things, and be rejected by the elders and chief priests and scribes, and be killed, and be raised the third day" (Luke 9:22). There's the word *must* once again. The cross had to happen.

He had a terrible baptism of suffering ahead of him and was under a heavy burden until it was accomplished (Luke 12:50). He also knew of the surety of His mission. No one and nothing can resist the perfect will of God. The prophet said of Him and His redemptive mission to seek and save the lost, "He will not fail nor be discouraged" (Isaiah 42:4).

SOUL SEARCH

What is it that sometimes discourages me? How can I make sure I am always living in the light of God's promises?

Father, help me never to be discouraged—to never have my courage removed.

The Farmer and the Hen

O Jerusalem, Jerusalem, the one who kills the prophets and stones those who are sent to her! How often I wanted to gather your children together, as a hen gathers her brood under her wings, but you were not willing!

LUKE 13:34

A farmer was once walking through a burned-out barn, and His eyes fell on the sorry sight of a dead hen that had been caught in the blaze. When he pushed the smoldering bird over with his foot, he found a number of live chicks beneath its dead body. She had gathered her brood under her wings to protect them from the fire. Meanwhile, she sacrificed her own life.

That was what God desired to do with Jerusalem. Unfortunately, they refused His love and, instead, came under the fire of His wrath. Had they been willing, this would have been their portion:

> He shall cover you with His feathers,
> And under His wings you shall take refuge;
> His truth shall be shield and buckler.
> (Psalm 91:4)

We have the same message for this sinful world. In Christ, God made a way for us to be sheltered from the wrath to come.

SOUL SEARCH

When and how did I learn of God's love for me? How did it change my life?

Father, thank you for gathering me under the shelter of your wings.

Desolate House

See! Your house is left to you desolate; and assuredly, I say to you, you shall not see Me until the time comes when you say, "Blessed is He who comes in the name of the Lord!"

LUKE 13:35

The words of Jesus are without parallel. Here He is speaking of a future event—of the devastating judgment that will fall upon the city of Jerusalem.

Matthew Henry said of this portion of Scripture:

> Jerusalem and her children had a large share of guilt, and their punishment has been a signal. But ere long, deserved vengeance will fall on every church, which is Christian in name only. In the meantime, the Savior stands ready to receive all who come to him. There is nothing between sinners and eternal happiness, but their proud and unbelieving unwillingness.[15]

We live in dark days when many a professing Christian church is desolate of biblical truth, where the authority of Scripture is denied, salvation by grace is not preached, and that which is considered an abomination to the Lord is embraced.

SOUL SEARCH

What am I doing today to "hold fast what is good" (1 Thessalonians 5:21)?

Father, may I always love what you love and hate what you hate.

Pride and Prejudice

Is it lawful to heal on the Sabbath?
LUKE 14:3

Jesus asked if it was lawful to heal on the Sabbath. That was a big issue to the lawyers and Pharisees. The lawyers should have been able to answer quickly because they were professing experts in the Law. However, they held their peace.

Perhaps they bit their tongues because Jesus had been invited to have a meal in the house of a chief Pharisee on the Sabbath. If it was permissible to feed the body on the Sabbath, it should be permissible for the body to be healed on the Sabbath.

Instead of conceding, they watched Him. They eyed Him like a hungry hawk. Actually, their reasoning made no sense. If Jesus did miracles, it was because God was doing miracles through Him. If God was with Him, they should believe His words—but they didn't.

Instead, they strained the plankton and swallowed the whale because they were proud and prejudiced. They couldn't see the forest for the trees.

SOUL SEARCH

Do I prejudge people by their appearance? When do I do this?

Father, help me see past the externals and into the souls of people.

Stay Low

Which of you, having a donkey . . .

LUKE 14:4

After Jesus healed a man with dropsy on the Sabbath, He contrasted the humility of a donkey to the pride of the Pharisees. When He noticed how the guests at the dinner were choosing to sit in the places of honor, He told them a parable to illustrate His point. "For whoever exalts himself will be humbled, and he who humbles himself will be exalted" (Luke 14:11).

Jesus chose a humble beast of burden to carry Him to the multitudes in Jerusalem. If you and I want God to use us to carry the Savior to this dying world, then we must take this lesson in humility to heart. Stay low in your own eyes, and God will lift you high.

Andrew Murray said, "Humility is perfect quietness of heart. It is to expect nothing, to wonder at nothing that is done to me, to feel nothing done against me. It is to be at rest when nobody praises me, and when I am blamed or despised. It is to have a blessed home in the Lord, where I can go in and shut the door, and kneel to my Father in secret, and am at peace as in a deep sea of calmness, when all around and above is trouble."[16]

SOUL SEARCH

Do I truly see others as being more important than myself? How will a humble attitude affect my day?

Father, remind me of who I am.

Animal Rescue

Which of you, having a donkey or an ox that has fallen into a pit, will not immediately pull him out on the Sabbath day?
Luke 14:5

Think of what Jesus was saying. He's talking about a beast of burden, and yet He uses the word "immediately." If an animal is in trouble, the owner who sees his beast in such a state would have an urgency to rescue it.

We often see people unify (with a sense of urgency) to rescue an animal—a horse stuck in the mud, a dog that has fallen through the ice, or a beached whale.

It seems, at times, that people have more concern for animals than they have for human beings. Even in the church, there seems to be little concern that sinners are dying and going to hell.

May God give us half the concern that we have for our animals so that we immediately run to the lost and pull them out of the pit of death and an impending hell.

SOUL SEARCH

Do I have more compassion for animals than for those made in the image of God?

Father, help me get my priorities sorted to match yours.

The Bride

When you are invited by anyone to a wedding feast . . .
LUKE 14:8

We have been invited to a wedding—the ultimate wedding when the Groom comes for His spotless Bride, the church:

> And I heard, as it were, the voice of a great multitude, as the sound of many waters and as the sound of mighty thunderings, saying, "Alleluia! For the Lord God Omnipotent reigns! Let us be glad and rejoice and give Him glory, for the marriage of the Lamb has come, and His wife has made herself ready." And to her it was granted to be arrayed in fine linen, clean and bright, for the fine linen is the righteous acts of the saints. Then he said to me, "Write: 'Blessed are those who are called to the marriage supper of the Lamb!'" And he said to me, "These are the true sayings of God." (Revelation 19:6–9)

The marriage supper of the Lamb will be the glorious culmination of our faith in Jesus! Make sure you have on a wedding garment.

SOUL SEARCH

Am I making myself ready? What does it mean to do that?

Father, my heart yearns for that day.

My Way

Lest one more honorable than you . . .
LUKE 14:9

We are honored when we are invited to a celebration, but more than likely, other attendees at the celebration are given higher places of honor.

If there is one thing that marks human nature, it is egocentric selfishness. The Scripture says that from the moment we are born, we go astray: "The wicked are estranged from the womb; they go astray as soon as they are born, speaking lies" (Psalm 58:3).

The terrible twos aren't confined to two-year-olds. If a child is left to himself, he will become a rascal, grow into an insolent rebellious teenager, and become an adult who still acts like a two-year-old.

In our unregenerate state, we want to be honored. We want the best rooms; it's my way or the highway; nobody matters but me. The new birth changes everything. We now esteem others better than ourselves. Your way is the highway, and my way takes a lowly back seat.

SOUL SEARCH

Do I see myself as I am? Or am I conceited and believe I'm something I'm not?

Father, may I see myself as you see me.

Humiliation

*And he who invited you and him come and say to you,
"Give place to this man," and then you begin with shame
to take the lowest place.*

LUKE 14:9

Humiliation doesn't feel good. The Merriam-Webster dictionary
says that to humiliate someone is "to reduce (someone) to a lower
position in one's own eyes or others' eyes." We need only experience it once to want to avoid it. It leaves a bitter taste.

Many years ago, I showed up at a church to speak at a mid-
week meeting. I set up a book table and, as I had done many
times before, stood at the pulpit waiting for the congregation to
be seated. I was then approached by someone with an unenviable
task. The person informed me that there had been a mix-up, and
I wasn't their speaker that night. The speaker was sitting in the
front row wondering what I was doing. Needless to say, it was
embarrassing and humbling to have to pick up my books and
leave. It brought personal meaning to these words of Jesus: "'Give
place to this man,' and then you begin with shame to take the
lowest place."

SOUL SEARCH

Have I had experiences that personalize any words Jesus
spoke? Did I learn a lesson?

Father, thank you for the wisdom of Scripture.

The Low Room

But when you are invited, go and sit down in the lowest place, so that when he who invited you comes he may say to you, "Friend, go up higher." Then you will have glory in the presence of those who sit at the table with you.

LUKE 14:10–11

It is because God has invited us that we take the lowest place. We follow in the steps of Jesus who served the ungodly. He was God in human form, and yet He washed His disciples' feet, healed the sick, touched lepers, raised the dead, fed hungry crowds, and forgave sinners their sins.

If you want a low place, step into the call of evangelism. There you will find a life where you continually battle your fears, carry the weight of a dying world, and cry out to God for the salvation of the lost. Your compassionate heart aches, and you will be driven to plead with the lost to give their lives to Christ. It is often a thankless task. Luckily, the day will come when God Himself says, "Friend, go up higher," and we will hear those wonderful words, "Well done, good and faithful servant" (Matthew 25:21).

John Newton, the 1700s slave trader turned abolitionist, said, "I am persuaded that love and humility are the highest attainments in the school of Christ and the brightest evidences that He is indeed our Master."

SOUL SEARCH

Is the highest goal in my life to be a good and faithful servant of God?

Father, thank you for the honor of being your servant.

Giving to get Nothing

*When you give a dinner or a supper, do not ask your friends,
your brothers, your relatives, nor rich neighbors, lest they
also invite you back, and you be repaid.*

LUKE 14:12–13

We tend to only want to give in order to get. It isn't easy for us to give with no strings attached, but we must. Jesus said to give with no ulterior motives, hoping for nothing in return (Luke 6:35).

There is something warming about dining with friends and family—and rich neighbors. Perhaps they may return the favor by asking us to join them on their yacht. But to host a dinner for strangers who are homeless, poor, or sick isn't so appealing.

Love dismisses these things because it cares about human beings. They have worth because they are made in God's image. Therefore, they deserve to be respected and treated with love. We care first about their eternal salvation.

SOUL SEARCH

Do I give to get?

Father, may I always check my motives for giving.

How to be Blessed

And you will be blessed, because they cannot repay you;
for you shall be repaid at the resurrection of the just.

LUKE 14:14

Strive to be blessed. I'm not talking about being blessed with prosperity but to be blessed with God's smile. In Christ we can please Him. As committed Christians, we stand on the high mountain of the righteousness of Jesus Christ, so we have our Father's full attention and His wonderful smile.

When we serve the poor, we have His blessing. When we reach out to the lost with His glorious gospel, we have His blessing:

> Blessed is the man
> Who walks not in the counsel of the ungodly,
> Nor stands in the path of sinners,
> Nor sits in the seat of the scornful;
> But his delight is in the law of the LORD,
> And in His law he meditates day and night…
> And whatever he does shall prosper.
> (Psalm 1:1–3)

SOUL SEARCH

Do I meditate on the Bible daily? If not, why not?

Father, my greatest desire is to have your blessing.

A Certain Man

A certain man gave a great supper and invited many . . .
LUKE 14:16

Jesus often began His parables with "a certain man." This certain man was a reference to God—He planned a great supper and invited many. The invitation of the gospel is to all of humanity. Oh, how our hearts break when sinners show interest in everything except their own eternal salvation. How grievous it is when sinners mock the offer of eternal life. It is nothing short of tragic.

I remember as I shared the unspeakably good news of salvation with a young man, he looked at his watch as I pleaded with him. It was as though I was trying to guide him into hell rather than heaven. If he dies in his sins, how terrible it will be for him to have the memory of showing nothing but contempt for salvation from death and hell.

We must never give up on the hardest of sinners or be so shallow in character to even think *You will be sorry* without a tear in our eye.

SOUL SEARCH

Do I sometimes give up too easily on the lost?

Father, may I never give up on the hardest of the unsaved.

The Work has Been Done

Come, for all things are now ready.
LUKE 14:17

Perhaps the three greatest words ever spoken on this earth were "It is finished!" Jesus cried them out just before He died, signifying that His suffering on the cross had paid the great debt against God's Law. Now the perfect Judge of the universe can dismiss our crimes. He can let us live.

Yet there are billions of human beings who are sitting in the shadow of death not knowing that the gift of God is eternal life through Jesus Christ our Lord. God bids them to come to the marriage supper of the Lamb: "Come, for all things are now ready."

Herein lies the essence of the gospel. All the work has been done; all things are ready. There's no need to get religious. Whosoever will may come. That means Jews, Muslims, Buddhists, Hindus, atheists, and agnostics alike. The gospel is a universal call to all of humanity. Come.

SOUL SEARCH

Am I prepared to bump into an atheist today and know what to say? Have I studied their arguments? Do I care about their eternity?

Father, give me wisdom when it comes to speaking with the unsaved.

The Excuses

. . . one accord . . .
LUKE 14:18

"But they all with one accord began to make excuses. The first said to him, 'I have bought a piece of ground, and I must go and see it. I ask you to have me excused'"(Luke 14:18).

There is no reasonable excuse or any legitimate reason for sinners to reject the gospel. The only justification that could ever be on the table would be willful delusion, and that is the case with those who offer their excuses. God, in His great mercy, offers forgiveness of sins—a way out of the terrors of a just hell. Instead of sending them to hell, He offers heaven. He holds out everlasting life as a free gift with pleasure forever!

Often, sinners are too busy, too intelligent, or too proud. One day it will be too late. Death will seize them, and they will be dragged before the Judge of the universe. Then how comforting will their excuses be? They will forget evolution, atheism, hypocrisy in the church, and the "mistakes" they found in the Bible. The all-consuming thought that will come to them is *I've played the fool!*

And fools we are until, like the prodigal son, we come to our senses.

SOUL SEARCH

What excuses did I entertain before surrendering to God?

Father, give me the wisdom I need to contend for the faith.

No Excuses

And another said, "I have bought five yoke of oxen, and I am going to test them. I ask you to have me excused." Still another said, "I have married a wife, and therefore I cannot come."
LUKE 14:19–20

The ungodly offer excuses as to why they reject salvation, but they are not reasons. They aren't even justifiable excuses:

> For the wrath of God is revealed from heaven against all ungodliness and unrighteousness of men, who suppress the truth in unrighteousness, because what may be known of God is manifest in them, for God has shown it to them. For since the creation of the world His invisible attributes are clearly seen, being understood by the things that are made, even His eternal power and Godhead, so that they are without excuse. (Romans 1:18–20)

The massive heavens declare His glory (Psalm 19:1). Every tiny atom testifies to His genius. To this God, the ungodly say they cannot come. In reality, it's not that they cannot come but that they *will* not come.

SOUL SEARCH

Is my heart broken for the lost? Do I want it to be broken, or do I have excuses as to why I don't care?

Father, I don't offer excuses today. I offer myself as a servant to reach the unsaved.

Go Quickly

So that servant came and reported these things to his master.
Then the master of the house, being angry, said to his servant,
"Go out quickly into the streets and lanes of the city, and bring
in here the poor and the maimed and the lame and the blind."

LUKE 14:21

He told his servant to go "quickly." Would it please God if the church would quickly reach out to the unsaved?

Do we have a sense of urgency when it comes to reaching the lost, or is there a comfortable complacency? Does the fear of man cause us to set aside the will of God and, instead, have us busying ourselves with other things?

We are told to redeem the time because the days are evil (Ephesians 5:16). If you are wasting your time with other things while sinners are going to hell, please get on your knees before the Lord and ask God to give you a love that will swallow your fears. I battle fear and complacency daily, but I have learned not to think of myself. Instead, I think of the terrible fate awaiting the lost, and those thoughts dwarf my fear of rejection.

Here's the key to getting out of the prison of fear: simply greet strangers; find out their names and ask if they think there is an afterlife. That question has been a huge key for me when it comes to overcoming my fears and gives me a good place to start.

SOUL SEARCH

Today, I determine to forget about my selfish fears.

Father, use me today for your eternal purposes.

Today, if You Hear His Voice

Then the master said to the servant, "Go out into the highways and hedges, and compel them to come in, that my house may be filled."
Luke 14:23

People who are on highways are busy going places. It is our job to tell them to stop and consider their eternal salvation because nothing is more important than the issue of where they will spend eternity. After one second in hell, they will scream with agonizing remorse. Oh, such thoughts should horrify us and motivate us to run to the rescue.

Hedges are places where people hide from God—like Adam after he sinned. We must take the time to expose their sin with the rod of God's Law and tell them that nothing is hidden from the eyes of Him with whom they have to give an account.

We must compel them to come in. Love will not be passive about the terrifying and sobering issue of their eternal salvation. We must plead, exhort, and encourage them with a sense of overwhelming urgency to get right with God by repenting and trusting in Jesus. We must do it today for they may not have tomorrow. Neither may we.

SOUL SEARCH

Do I hear His voice saying to go into all the world and preach the gospel to every creature? Have I been ignoring this mandate?

Father, I need your help to do this, and I will trust you as I go.

About the Author

Ray Comfort is the best-selling author of more than ninety books. He is the co-host of an award-winning TV program that airs in 190 countries and the producer of award-winning movies that have been seen by millions (see www.FullyFreeFilms.com). He lives in Southern California with his wife, Sue, and has three grown children. For further information, see LivingWaters.com.

About the Author

Ray Comfort is the best-selling author of more than ninety books. He is the co-host of an award-winning TV program that airs in 190 countries and the producer of award-winning movies that have been seen by millions (see www.FullyFreeFilms.com). He lives in Southern California with his wife, Sue, and has three grown children. For further information, see LivingWaters.com.

1   Charles Haddon Spurgeon, "The Fourth Beatitude," *Spurgeon's Sermons*, vol. 55 (1909), Christian Classics Ethereal Library, sermon delivered December 14, 1873, https://www.ccel.org/ccel/spurgeon/sermons55.xxxiii.html.

2   John Wesley, as quoted by Robert Southey, *The Life of Wesley: And the Rise and Progress of Methodism*, vol. 1 (1820), https://books.google.com/books?id=mgpOAQAAMAAJ&pg=PA127&lpg=PA127&dq="I+have+-seen+(as+far+as+it+can+be+seen)+many+persons+changed+in+a+moment+from+the+spirit+of+hor-ror,+fear,+and+despair%22&source=bl&ots=XZI0CsBamz&sig=ACfU3U2_5Q16zGI_X5_W4LV1A7FGxVJX-aw&hl=en&sa=X&ved=2ahUKEwiv3-fnlpfhAhWFw4MKHdokAjYQ6AEwBXoECAkQAQ#v=onepage&q="I%20have%20seen%20(as%20far%20as%20it%20can%20be%20seen)%20many%20persons%20changed%20in%20a%20moment%20from%20the%20spirit%20of%20horror%2C%20fear%2C%20and%20despair%22&f=false.

3   Spurgeon, "Stumbling at the Word," *Spurgeon's Sermons*, vol. 57 (1911), sermon delivered March 6, 1864, https://www.ccel.org/ccel/spurgeon/sermons57.

4   JOSEPH MEDLICOTT SCRIVEN, "WHAT A FRIEND WE HAVE IN JESUS," 1855.

5   Spurgeon, "A New Year's Wish," *Spurgeon's Sermons*, vol. 57, sermon delivered January 5, 1911, http://www.ccel.org/ccel/spurgeon/sermons57.txt.

6   Charles Haddon Spurgeon, "The Best Bread," The Complete Works of C. H. Spurgeon, vol. 33, sermon delivered January 16, 1887, https://books.google.com/books?id=pOCoBwAAQBAJ&pg=PT41&lpg=PT41&dq=%22It+is+of+the+utmost+importance+to+those+of+you+who+have+spiritual+life+that+you+should+feed+upon+the+Lord+Jesus%22&source=bl&ots=HtjEsLG7aH&sig=ACfU3U24whPHbwngjZzFkd7gEqM7suHSRw&hl=en&sa=X&ved=2ahUKEwi0vZ2I15PhAhWD8oMKHZQ_C60Q6AEwAHoECAMQAQ#v=onepage&q=%22It%20is%20of%20the%20utmost%20importance%20to%20those%20of%20you%20who%20have%20spiritual%20life%20that%20you%20should%20feed%20upon%20the%20Lord%20Jesus%22&f=false.

7   See Ray Comfort, *The Way of the Master* (Orlando: Bridge-Logos, 2006).

8   Charles Haddon Spurgeon, *The Gospel of the Kingdom: A Popular Exposition of the Gospel According to Matthew*, 132, https://books.google.com/books?id=TVI7AQAAMAAJ&pg=PA132&lpg=PA132&dq=He+used+a+parabolic+expression,+which+they+would+readily+have+understood,+had+not+their+minds+been+already+absorbed+by+their+lack+of+bread&source=bl&ots=gDZSKY7ei6&sig=ACfU3U0YXY2rhWi6tpivmmc9oJSs6Ca9PA&hl=en&sa=X&ved=2ahUKEwjnsavJopbhAhXsrIMKHTBtAs4Q6AEwAHoECAkQAQ#v=onepage&q=He%20used%20a%20parabolic%20expression%2C%20which%20they%20would%20readily%20have%20understood%2C%20had%20not%20their%20minds%20been%20already%20absorbed%20by%20their%20lack%20of%20bread&f=false.

9   Spurgeon, "Christ the Seeker and Saviour of the Lost," The Complete Works, vol. 58, sermon delivered July 4, 1912, https://books.google.com/books?id=DndhCgAAQBAJ&pg=PT401&dq=Better+a+whole+world+on+fire+than+a+soul+lost!&hl=en&sa=X&ved=0ahUKEwiumoj-35PhAhWGoYMKHZPtC00Q6AEIKjAA#v=onepage&q=Better%20a%20whole%20world%20on%20fire%20than%20a%20soul%20lost!&f=false.

10   Charles Haddon Spurgeon, "Abraham, a Pattern to Believers," sermon #2292, spurgeongems.org, sermon delivered January 22, 1893, https://www.spurgeongems.org/vols37-39/chs2292.pdf.

11   Charles Haddon Spurgeon, "Satan's Banquet," sermon #225, The Spurgeon Center, sermon delivered November 28, 1858, https://www.spurgeon.org/resource-library/sermons/satans-banquet#flipbook/.

12   Spurgeon, "The Master Key—Opening the Gate Of Heaven," sermon #1938, spurgeongems.org, sermon delivered May 23, 1886, https://www.spurgeongems.org/vols31-33/chs1938.pdf.

13   Pulpit Commentary, https://biblehub.com/luke/11-47.htm.

14   Spurgeon, "Our Lord before Herod," sermon #1645, spurgeongems.org, sermon delivered February 19, 1882, https://www.spurgeongems.org/vols28-30/chs1645.pdf.

15   Matthew Henry, Matthew Henry's Concise Commentary, https://biblehub.com/commentaries/matthew/23-36.htm.

16   Andrew Murray, https://www.goodreads.com/quotes/234475-humility-is-perfect-quietness-of-heart-it-is-to-expect.

1   Charles Haddon Spurgeon, "The Fourth Beatitude," *Spurgeon's Sermons*, vol. 55 (1909), Christian Classics Ethereal Library, sermon delivered December 14, 1873, https://www.ccel.org/ccel/spurgeon/sermons55.xxxiii.html.

2   John Wesley, as quoted by Robert Southey, *The Life of Wesley: And the Rise and Progress of Methodism*, vol. 1 (1820), https://books.google.com/books?id=mgpOAQAAMAAJ&pg=PA127&lpg=PA127&dq="I+have+-seen+(as+far+as+it+can+be+seen)+many+persons+changed+in+a+moment+from+the+spirit+of+hor-ror,+fear,+and+despair%22&source=bl&ots=XZI0CsBamz&sig=ACfU3U2_5Q16zGI_X5_W4LV1A7FGxVJX-aw&hl=en&sa=X&ved=2ahUKEwiv3-fnlpfhAhVFw4MKHdokAjYQ6AEwBXoECAkQAQ#v=onepage&q="I%20have%20seen%20(as%20far%20as%20it%20can%20be%20seen)%20many%20persons%20changed%20in%20a%20moment%20from%20the%20spirit%20of%20horror%2C%20fear%2C%20and%20despair%22&f=false.

3   Spurgeon, "Stumbling at the Word," *Spurgeon's Sermons*, vol. 57 (1911), sermon delivered March 6, 1864, https://www.ccel.org/ccel/spurgeon/sermons57.

4   JOSEPH MEDLICOTT SCRIVEN, "WHAT A FRIEND WE HAVE IN JESUS," 1855.

5   Spurgeon, "A New Year's Wish," *Spurgeon's Sermons*, vol. 57, sermon delivered January 5, 1911, http://www.ccel.org/ccel/spurgeon/sermons57.txt.

6   Charles Haddon Spurgeon, "The Best Bread," *The Complete Works of C. H. Spurgeon*, vol. 33, sermon delivered January 16, 1887, https://books.google.com/books?id=pOCoBwAAQBAJ&pg=PT41&lpg=PT41&dq=%22It+is+of+the+utmost+importance+to+those+of+you+who+have+spiritual+life+that+you+should+feed+upon+the+Lord+Jesus%22&source=bl&ots=HtjEsLG7aH&sig=ACfU3U24whPHbwngjZzFkd7gEqM7suHSRw&hl=en&sa=X&ved=2ahUKEwi0vZ2I15PhAhWD8oMKHZQ_C60Q6AEwAHoECAMQAQ#v=onepage&q=%22It%20is%20of%20the%20utmost%20importance%20to%20those%20of%20you%20who%20have%20spiritual%20life%20that%20you%20should%20feed%20upon%20the%20Lord%20Jesus%22&f=false.

7   See Ray Comfort, *The Way of the Master* (Orlando: Bridge-Logos, 2006).

8   Charles Haddon Spurgeon, *The Gospel of the Kingdom: A Popular Exposition of the Gospel According to Matthew*, 132, https://books.google.com/books?id=TVI7AQAAMAAJ&pg=PA132&lpg=PA132&dq=He+used+a+parabolic+expression,+which+they+would+readily+have+understood,+had+not+their+minds+been+already+absorbed+by+their+lack+of+bread&source=bl&ots=gDZSKY7ei6&sig=ACfU3U0YXY2rhWi6tpivmmc9oJSs6Ca9PA&hl=en&sa=X&ved=2ahUKEwjnsavJopbhAhXsrIMKHTBtAs4Q6AEwAHoECAkQAQ#v=onepage&q=He%20used%20a%20parabolic%20expression%2C%20which%20they%20would%20readily%20have%20understood%2C%20had%20not%20their%20minds%20been%20already%20absorbed%20by%20their%20lack%20of%20bread&f=false.

9   Spurgeon, "Christ the Seeker and Saviour of the Lost," *The Complete Works*, vol. 58, sermon delivered July 4, 1912, https://books.google.com/books?id=DndhCgAAQBAJ&pg=PT401&dq=Better+a+whole+world+on+fire+than+a+soul+lost!&hl=en&sa=X&ved=0ahUKEwiumoj-35PhAhWGoYMKHZPtC00Q6AEIKjAA#v=onepage&q=Better%20a%20whole%20world%20on%20fire%20than%20a%20soul%20lost!&f=false.

10   Charles Haddon Spurgeon, "Abraham, a Pattern to Believers," sermon #2292, spurgeongems.org, sermon delivered January 22, 1893, https://www.spurgeongems.org/vols37-39/chs2292.pdf.

11   Charles Haddon Spurgeon, "Satan's Banquet," sermon #225, The Spurgeon Center, sermon delivered November 28, 1858, https://www.spurgeon.org/resource-library/sermons/satans-banquet#flipbook/.

12   Spurgeon, "The Master Key—Opening the Gate Of Heaven," sermon #1938, spurgeongems.org, sermon delivered May 23, 1886, https://www.spurgeongems.org/vols31-33/chs1938.pdf.

13   *Pulpit Commentary*, https://biblehub.com/luke/11-47.htm.

14   Spurgeon, "Our Lord before Herod," sermon #1645, spurgeongems.org, sermon delivered February 19, 1882, https://www.spurgeongems.org/vols28-30/chs1645.pdf.

15   Matthew Henry, *Matthew Henry's Concise Commentary*, https://biblehub.com/commentaries/matthew/23-36.htm.

16   Andrew Murray, https://www.goodreads.com/quotes/234475-humility-is-perfect-quietness-of-heart-it-is-to-expect.